THE DEATH OF DAREDEVIL

JED MacKAY
WRITER

DANILO S. BEYRUTH (#1 & #5),
STEFANO LANDINI (#2),
IBAN COELLO (#3) &
PAOLO VILLANELLI (#4)
ARTISTS

ANDRES MOSSA
COLOR ARTIST

VC's CLAYTON COWLES
LETTERER

COVER ART **KYLE HOTZ & DAN BROWN**

ASSISTANT EDITOR **LAUREN AMARO**

EDITOR **DEVIN LEWIS**

EXECUTIVE EDITOR **NICK LOWE**

COLLECTION EDITOR **JENNIFER GRÜNWALD**
ASSISTANT EDITOR **CAITLIN O'CONNELL**
ASSOCIATE MANAGING EDITOR **KATERI WOODY**
EDITOR, SPECIAL PROJECTS **MARK D. BEAZLEY**
VP PRODUCTION & SPECIAL PROJECTS **JEFF YOUNGQUIST**
SVP PRINT, SALES & MARKETING **DAVID GABRIEL**
BOOK DESIGNER **JAY BOWEN**

EDITOR IN CHIEF **C.B. CEBULSKI**
CHIEF CREATIVE OFFICER **JOE QUESADA**
PRESIDENT **DAN BUCKLEY**
EXECUTIVE PRODUCER **ALAN FINE**

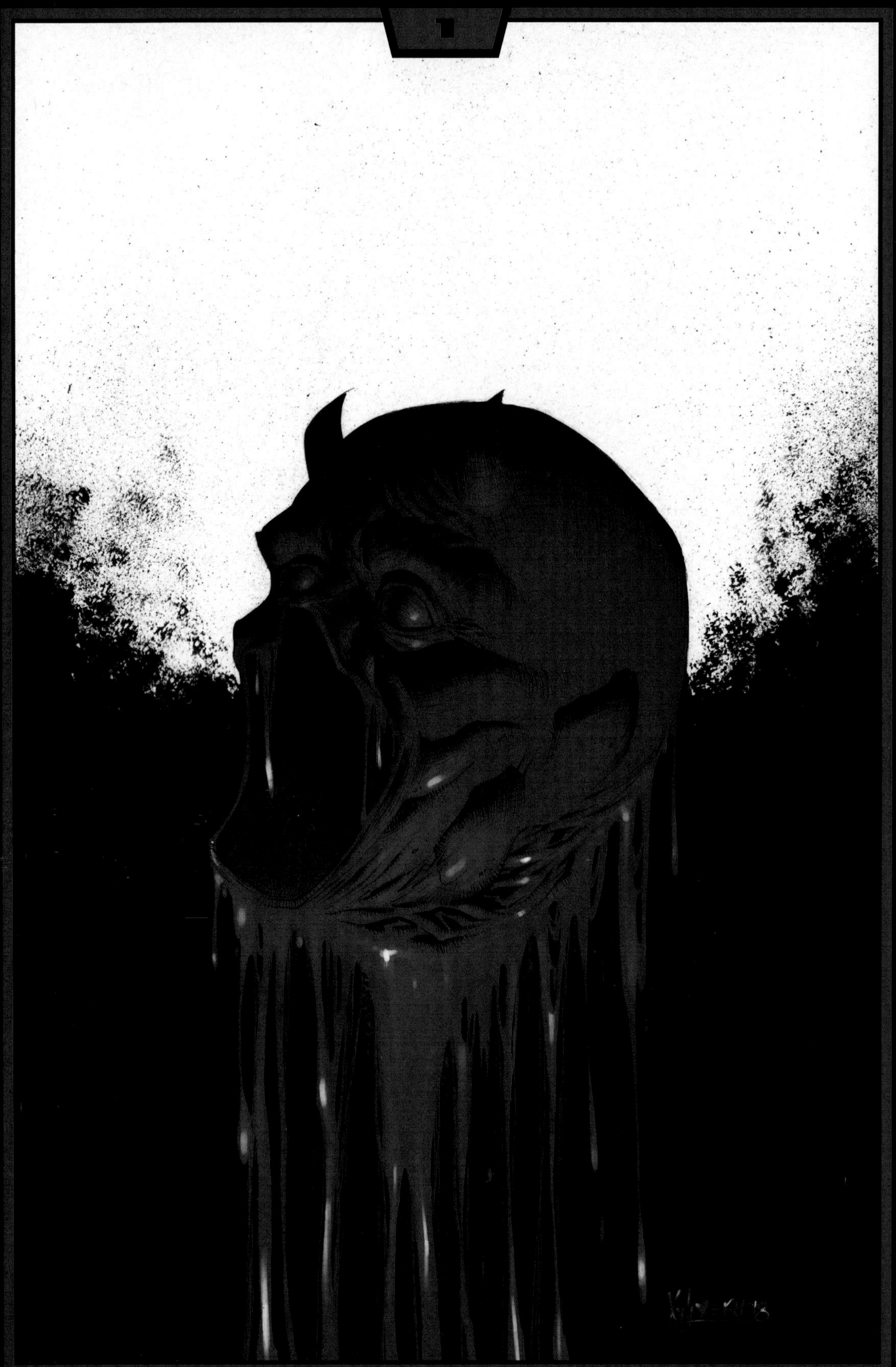

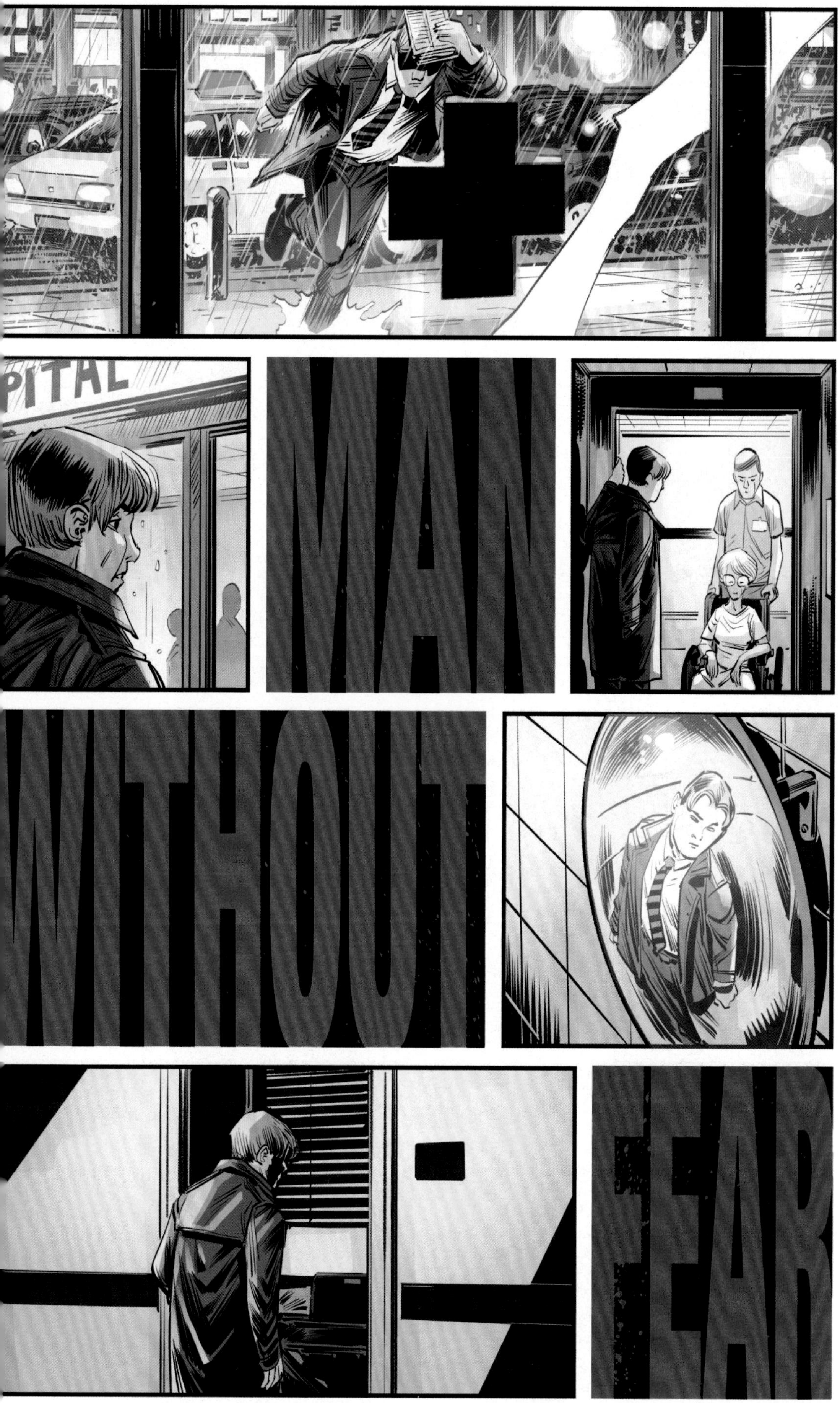

PITAL
MAN
WITHOUT
FEAR

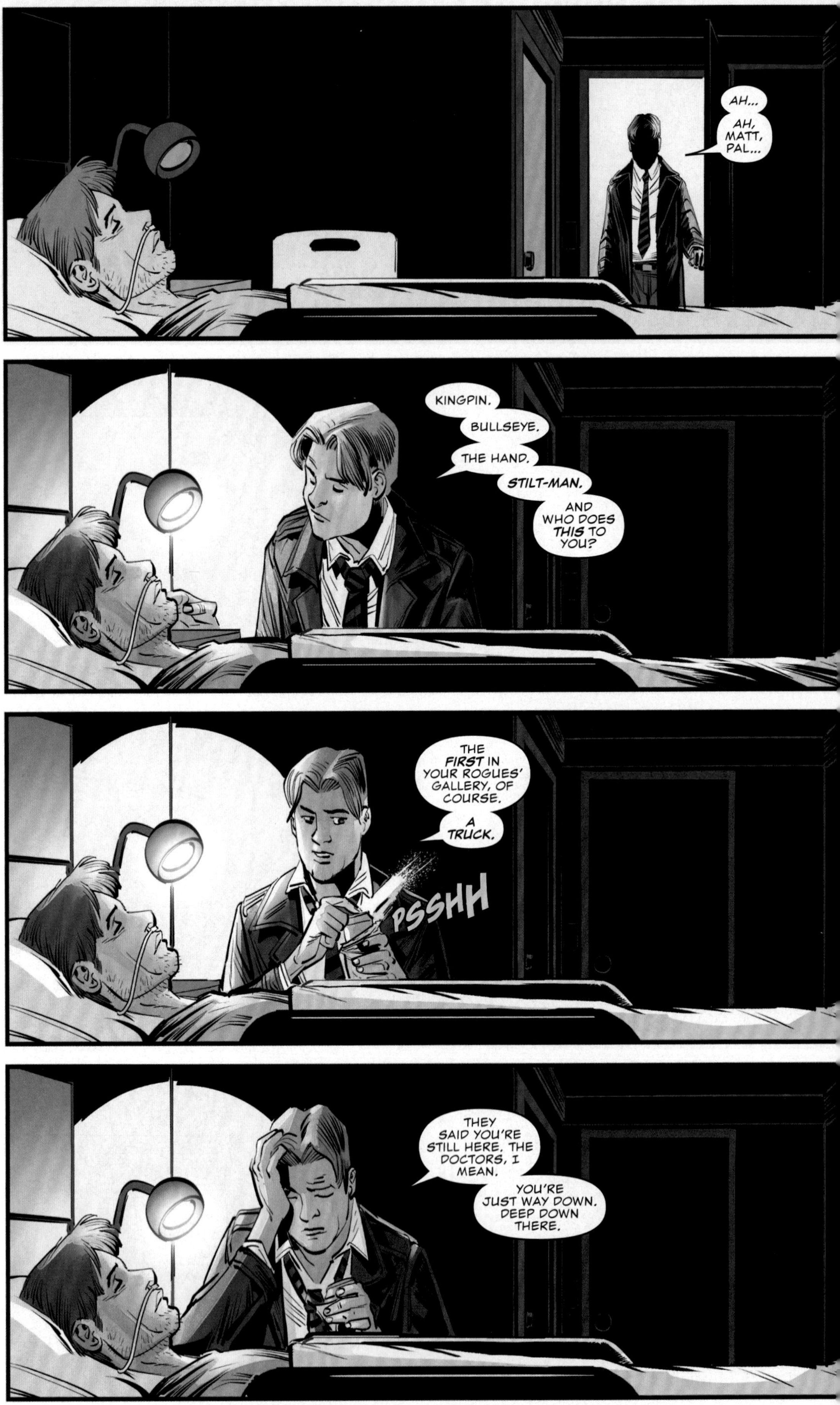
AH...
AH, MATT, PAL...
KINGPIN.
BULLSEYE.
THE HAND.
STILT-MAN.
AND WHO DOES THIS TO YOU?
THE FIRST IN YOUR ROGUES' GALLERY, OF COURSE.
A TRUCK.
PSSHH
THEY SAID YOU'RE STILL HERE. THE DOCTORS, I MEAN.
YOU'RE JUST WAY DOWN. DEEP DOWN THERE.

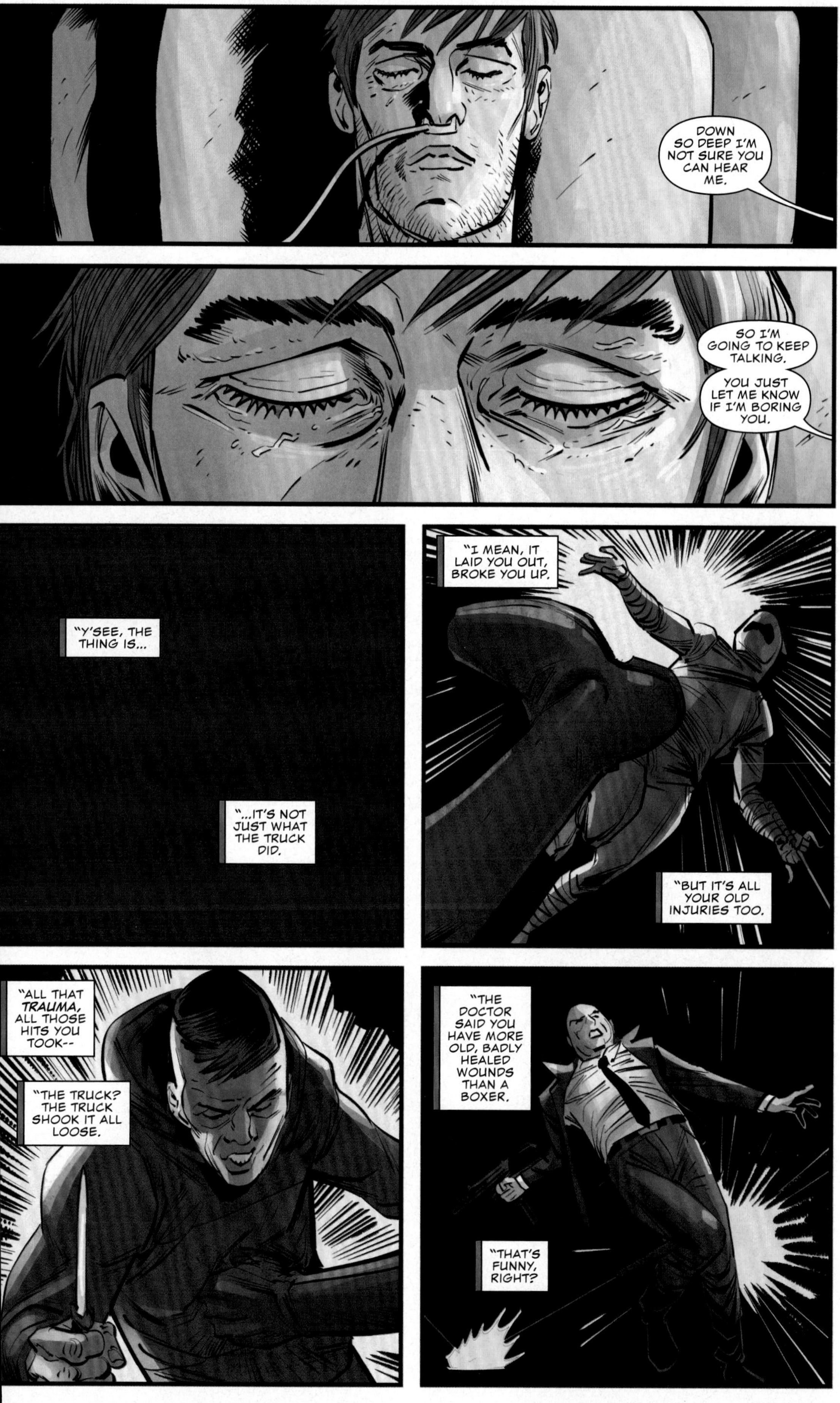
DOWN SO DEEP I'M NOT SURE YOU CAN HEAR ME.
SO I'M GOING TO KEEP TALKING.
YOU JUST LET ME KNOW IF I'M BORING YOU.
"Y'SEE, THE THING IS...
"...IT'S NOT JUST WHAT THE TRUCK DID.
"I MEAN, IT LAID YOU OUT, BROKE YOU UP.
"BUT IT'S ALL YOUR OLD INJURIES TOO.
"ALL THAT *TRAUMA,* ALL THOSE HITS YOU TOOK--
"THE TRUCK? THE TRUCK SHOOK IT ALL LOOSE.
"THE DOCTOR SAID YOU HAVE MORE OLD, BADLY HEALED WOUNDS THAN A BOXER.
"THAT'S FUNNY, RIGHT?

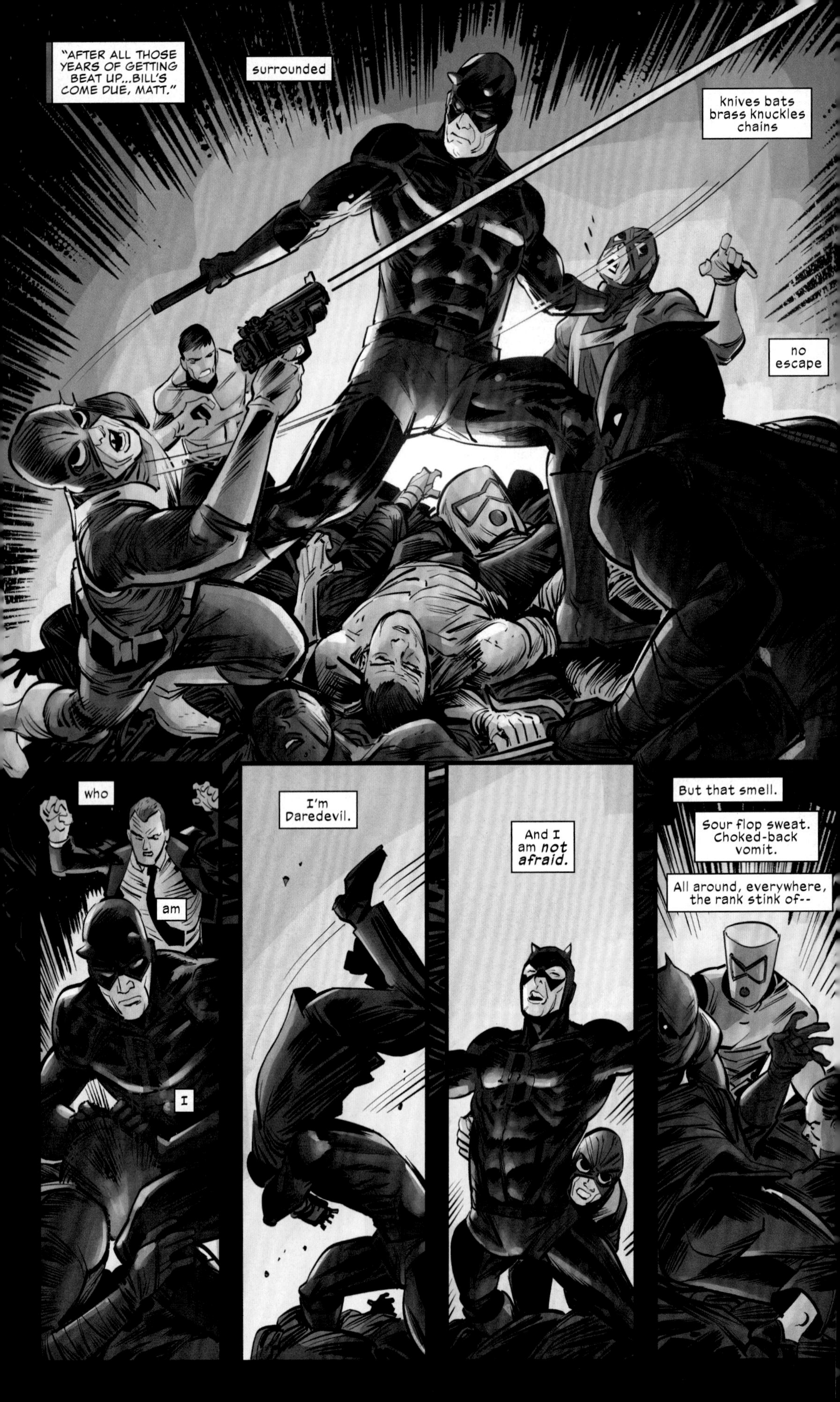
"AFTER ALL THOSE YEARS OF GETTING BEAT UP...BILL'S COME DUE, MATT."
surrounded
knives bats brass knuckles chains
no escape
who
am
I
I'm Daredevil.
And I am *not afraid.*
But that smell.
Sour flop sweat. Choked-back vomit.
All around, everywhere, the rank stink of--

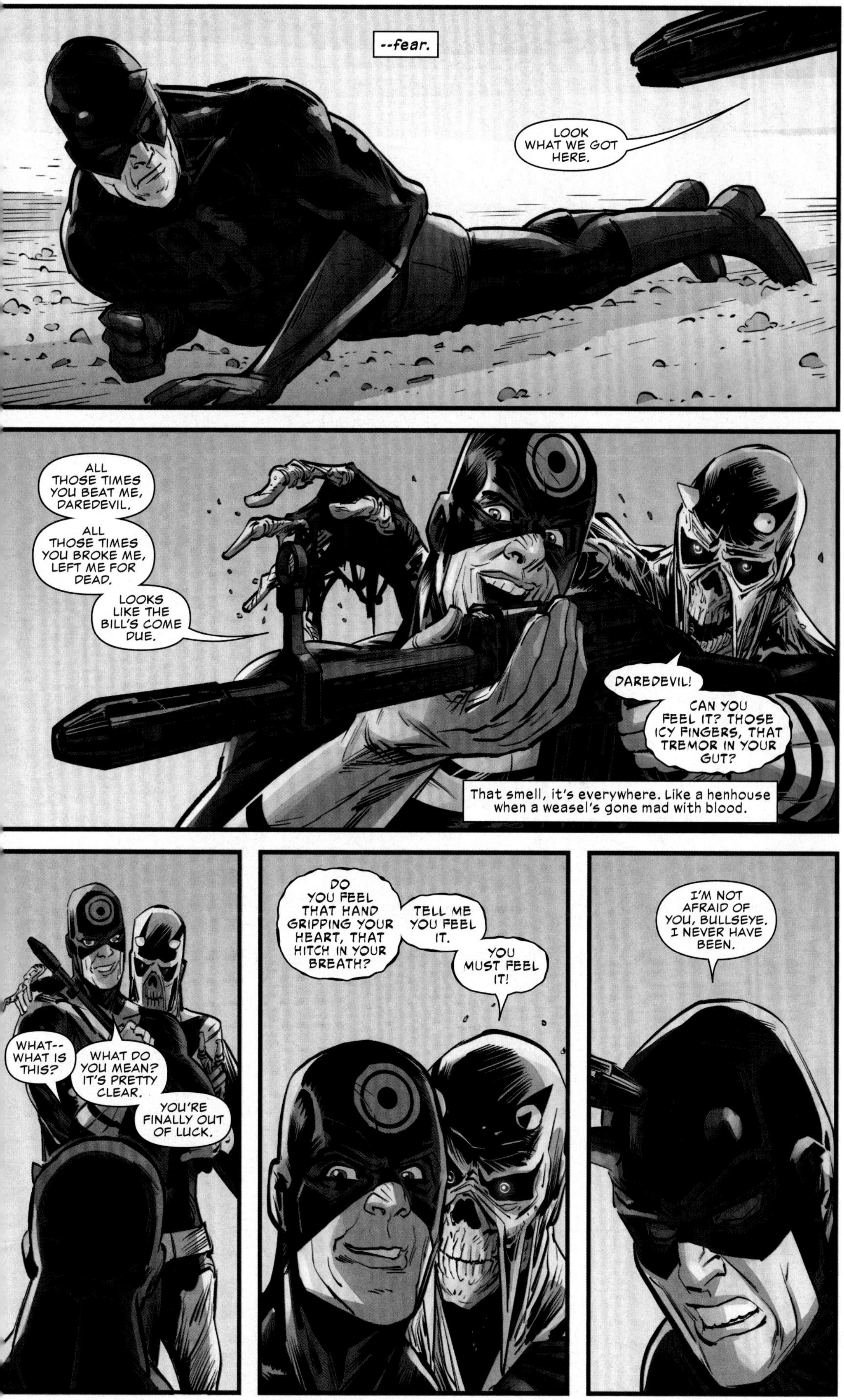
--fear.
LOOK WHAT WE GOT HERE.
ALL THOSE TIMES YOU BEAT ME, DAREDEVIL.
ALL THOSE TIMES YOU BROKE ME, LEFT ME FOR DEAD.
LOOKS LIKE THE BILL'S COME DUE.
DAREDEVIL!
CAN YOU FEEL IT? THOSE ICY FINGERS, THAT TREMOR IN YOUR GUT?
That smell, it's everywhere. Like a henhouse when a weasel's gone mad with blood.
WHAT-- WHAT IS THIS?
WHAT DO YOU MEAN? IT'S PRETTY CLEAR.
YOU'RE FINALLY OUT OF LUCK.
DO YOU FEEL THAT HAND GRIPPING YOUR HEART, THAT HITCH IN YOUR BREATH?
TELL ME YOU FEEL IT.
YOU MUST FEEL IT!
I'M NOT AFRAID OF YOU, BULLSEYE. I NEVER HAVE BEEN.

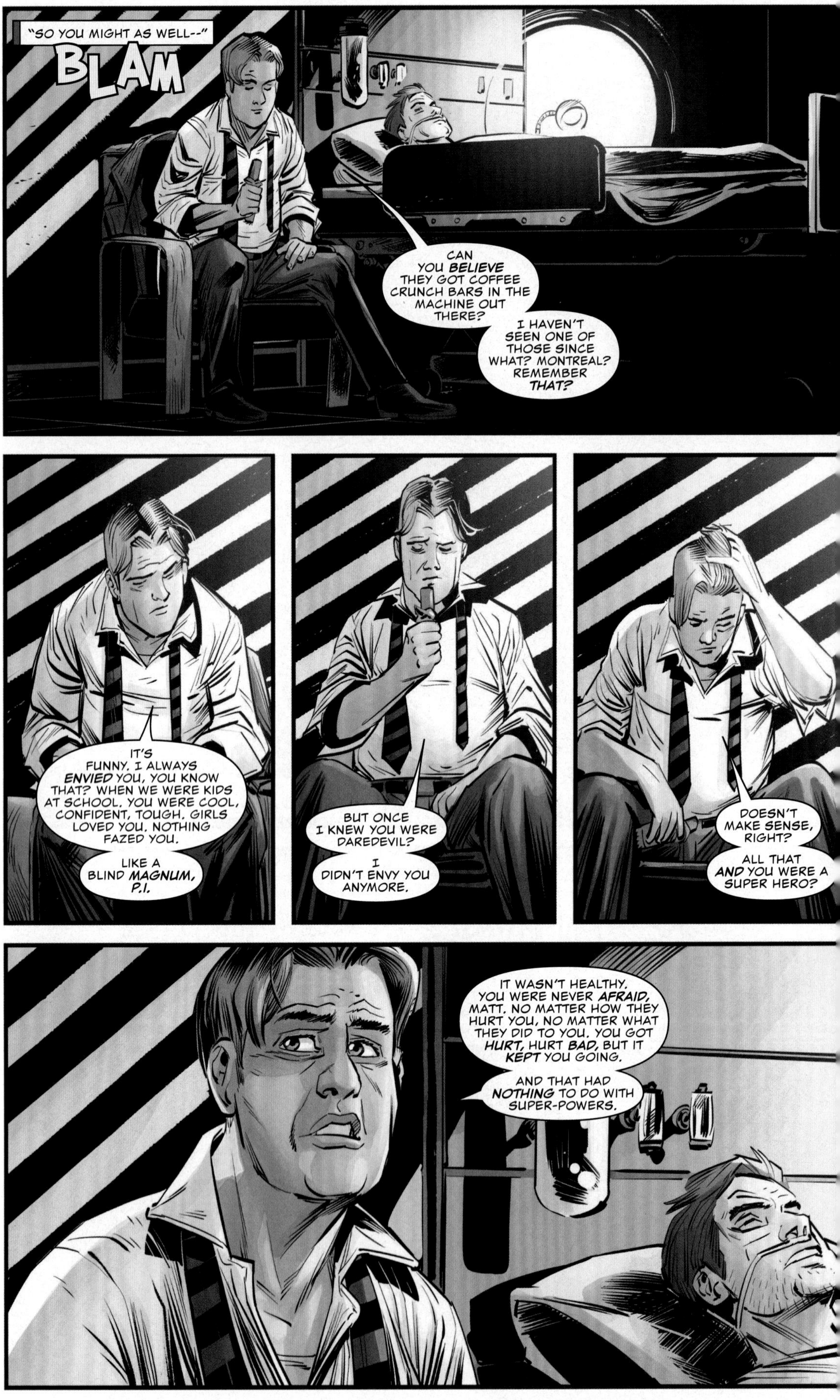
"SO YOU MIGHT AS WELL--"
BLAM
CAN YOU BELIEVE THEY GOT COFFEE CRUNCH BARS IN THE MACHINE OUT THERE?
I HAVEN'T SEEN ONE OF THOSE SINCE WHAT? MONTREAL? REMEMBER THAT?
IT'S FUNNY. I ALWAYS ENVIED YOU, YOU KNOW THAT? WHEN WE WERE KIDS AT SCHOOL. YOU WERE COOL, CONFIDENT, TOUGH. GIRLS LOVED YOU. NOTHING FAZED YOU.
LIKE A BLIND MAGNUM, P.I.
BUT ONCE I KNEW YOU WERE DAREDEVIL?
I DIDN'T ENVY YOU ANYMORE.
DOESN'T MAKE SENSE, RIGHT?
ALL THAT AND YOU WERE A SUPER HERO?
IT WASN'T HEALTHY. YOU WERE NEVER AFRAID, MATT. NO MATTER HOW THEY HURT YOU, NO MATTER WHAT THEY DID TO YOU. YOU GOT HURT, HURT BAD, BUT IT KEPT YOU GOING.
AND THAT HAD NOTHING TO DO WITH SUPER-POWERS.

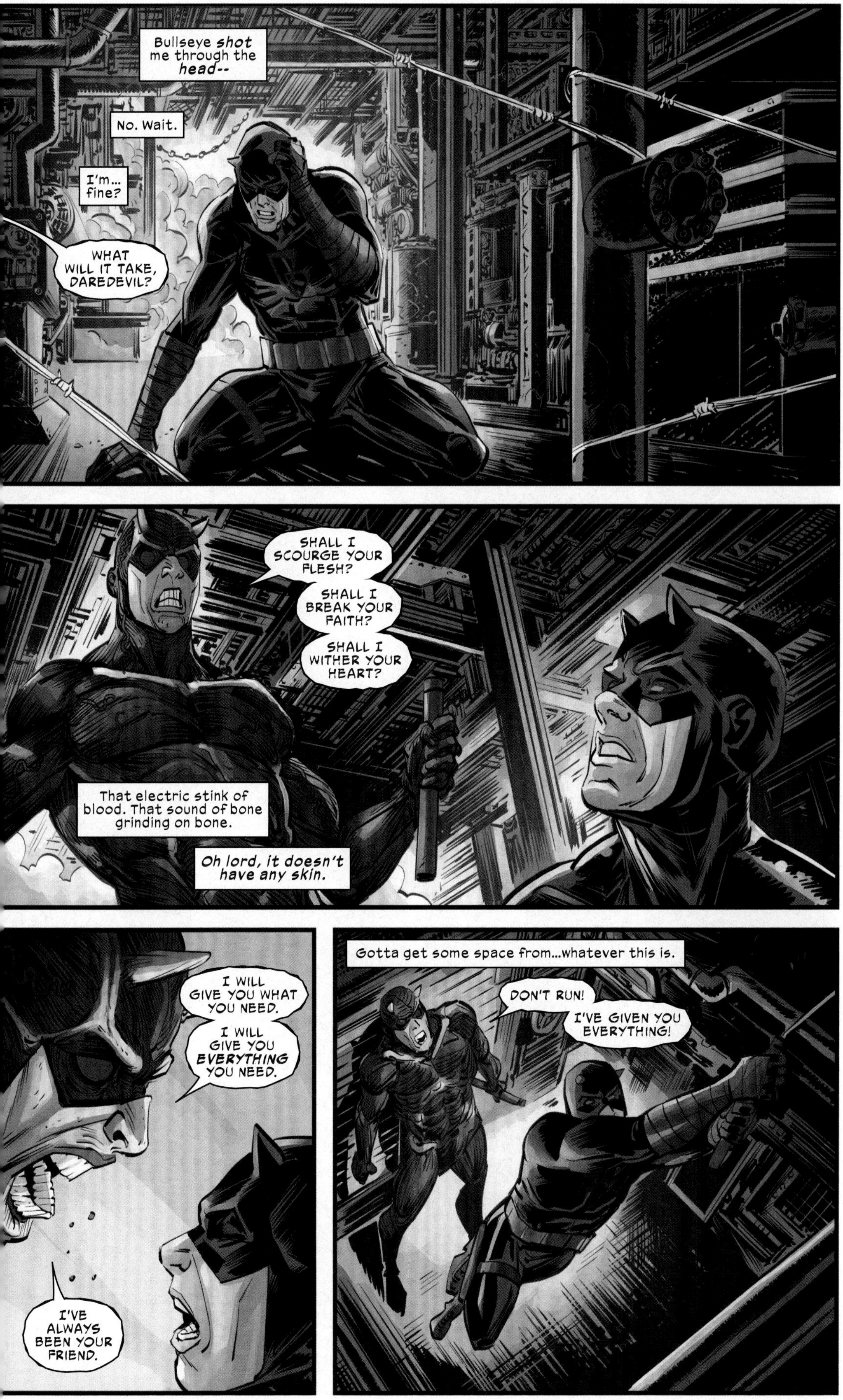

Bullseye shot me through the head--
No. Wait.
I'm... fine?
WHAT WILL IT TAKE, DAREDEVIL?
SHALL I SCOURGE YOUR FLESH?
SHALL I BREAK YOUR FAITH?
SHALL I WITHER YOUR HEART?
That electric stink of blood. That sound of bone grinding on bone.
Oh lord, it doesn't have any skin.
I WILL GIVE YOU WHAT YOU NEED.
I WILL GIVE YOU EVERYTHING YOU NEED.
I'VE ALWAYS BEEN YOUR FRIEND.
Gotta get some space from...whatever this is.
DON'T RUN!
I'VE GIVEN YOU EVERYTHING!

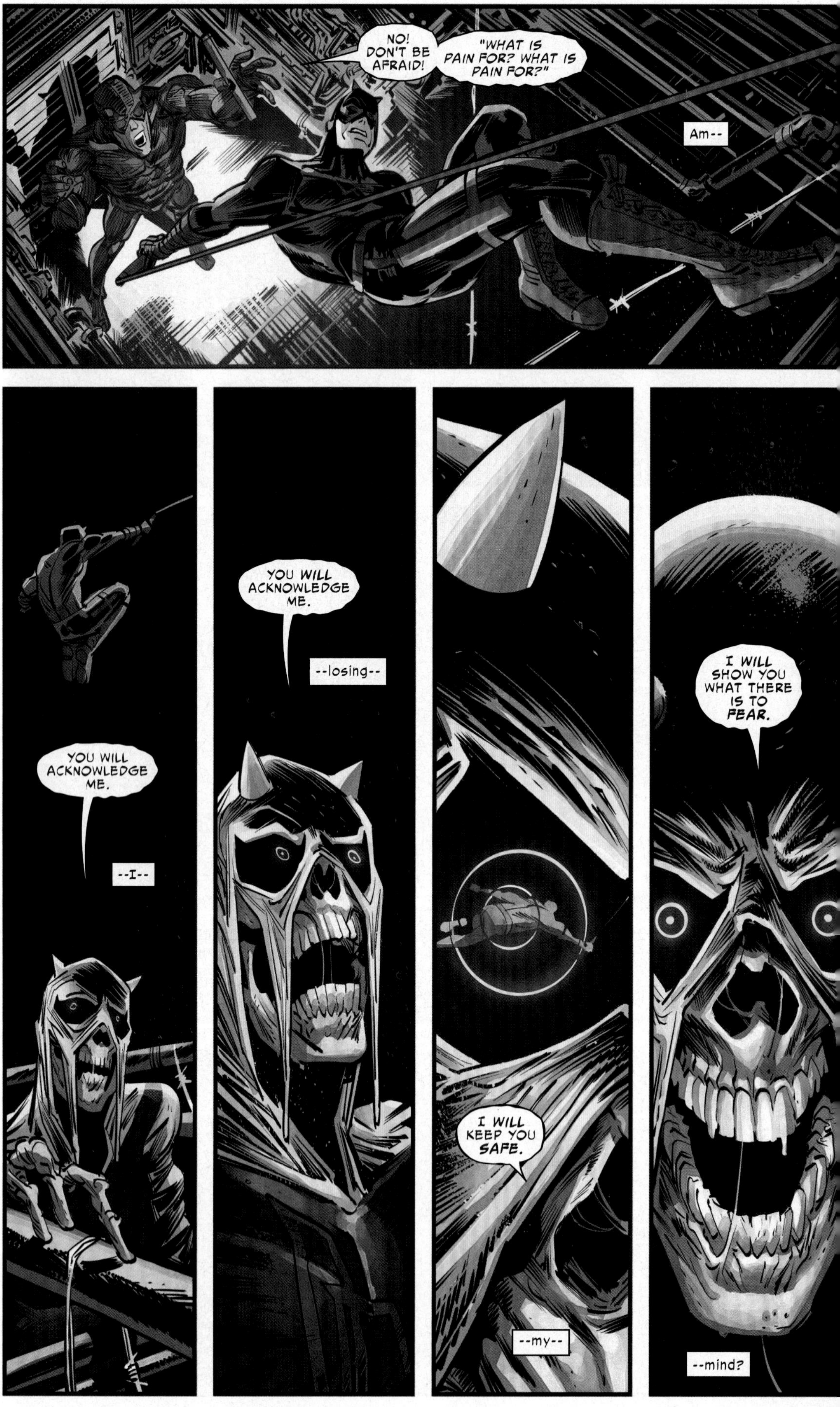
NO! DON'T BE AFRAID!
"WHAT IS PAIN FOR? WHAT IS PAIN FOR?"
Am--
YOU WILL ACKNOWLEDGE ME.
--I--
YOU WILL ACKNOWLEDGE ME.
--losing--
I WILL KEEP YOU SAFE.
--my--
I WILL SHOW YOU WHAT THERE IS TO FEAR.
--mind?

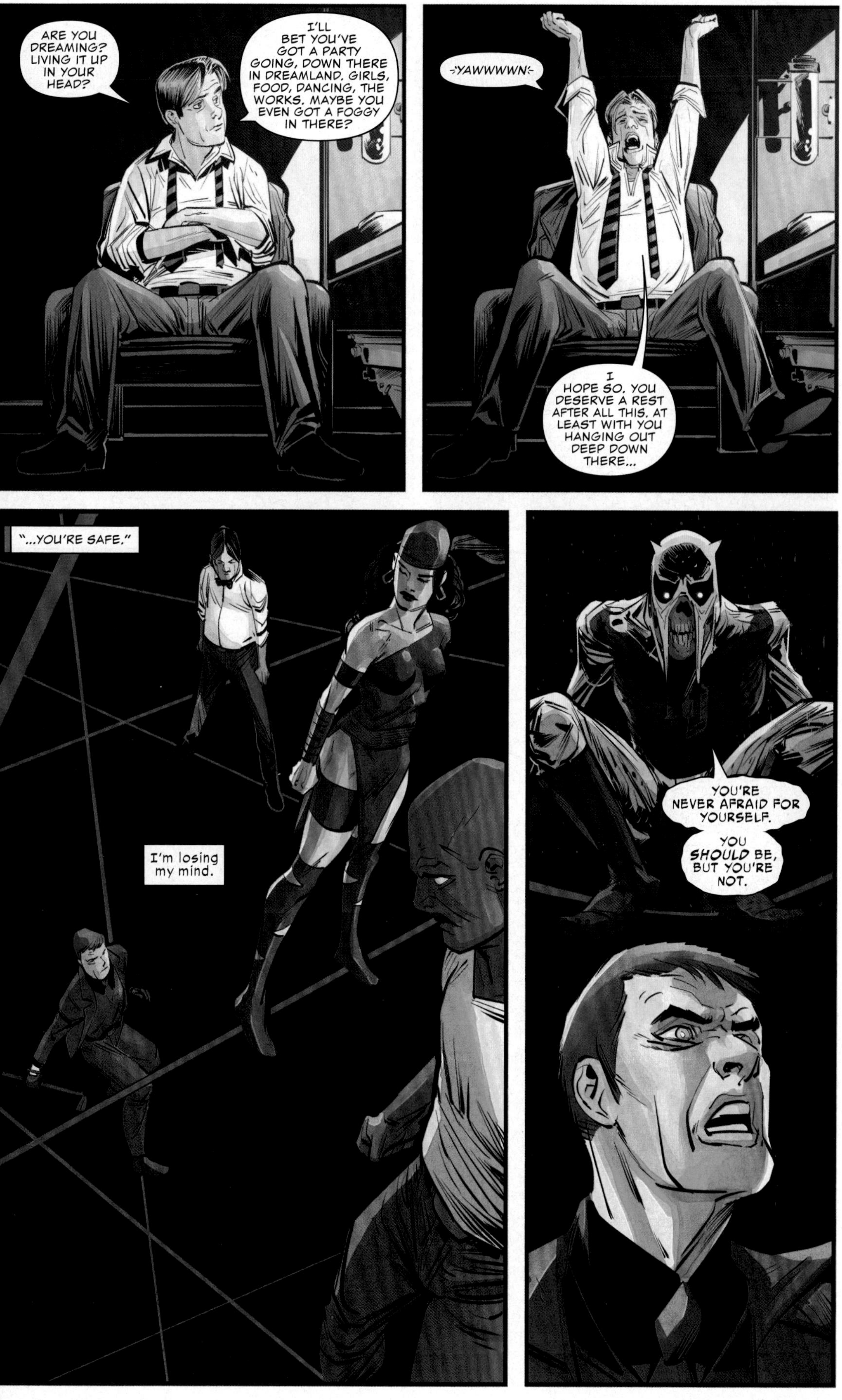
ARE YOU DREAMING? LIVING IT UP IN YOUR HEAD?
I'LL BET YOU'VE GOT A PARTY GOING, DOWN THERE IN DREAMLAND. GIRLS, FOOD, DANCING, THE WORKS. MAYBE YOU EVEN GOT A FOGGY IN THERE?
-YAWWWWN-
I HOPE SO. YOU DESERVE A REST AFTER ALL THIS. AT LEAST WITH YOU HANGING OUT DEEP DOWN THERE...
"...YOU'RE SAFE."
I'm losing my mind.
YOU'RE NEVER AFRAID FOR YOURSELF.
YOU *SHOULD* BE, BUT YOU'RE NOT.

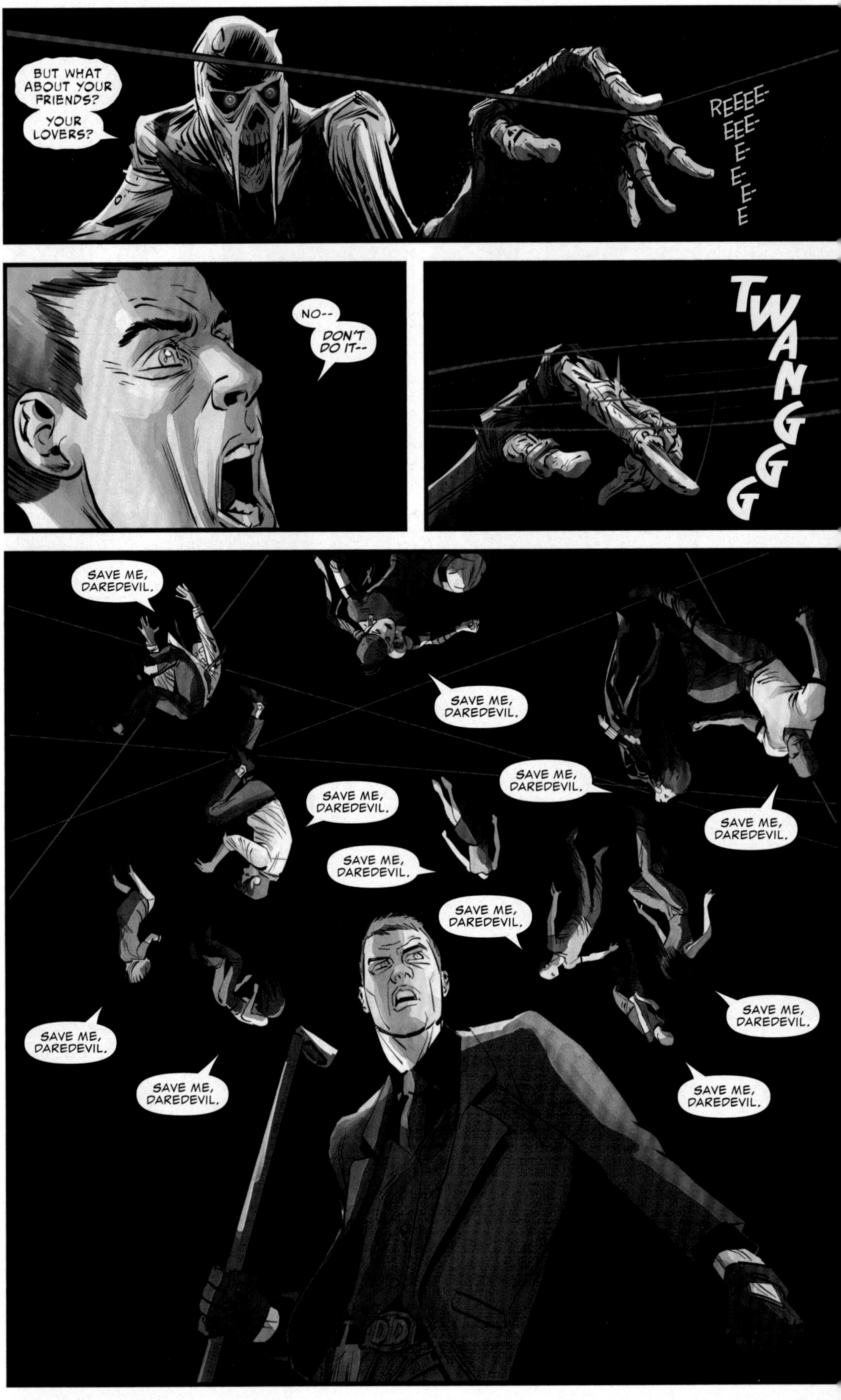
BUT WHAT ABOUT YOUR FRIENDS?
YOUR LOVERS?
REEEE-EEE-E-E-E-E
NO--
DON'T DO IT--
TWANGGG
SAVE ME, DAREDEVIL.
SAVE ME, DAREDEVIL.
SAVE ME, DAREDEVIL.
SAVE ME, DAREDEVIL.
SAVE ME, DAREDEVIL.
SAVE ME, DAREDEVIL.
SAVE ME, DAREDEVIL.
SAVE ME, DAREDEVIL.
SAVE ME, DAREDEVIL.
SAVE ME, DAREDEVIL.
SAVE ME, DAREDEVIL.

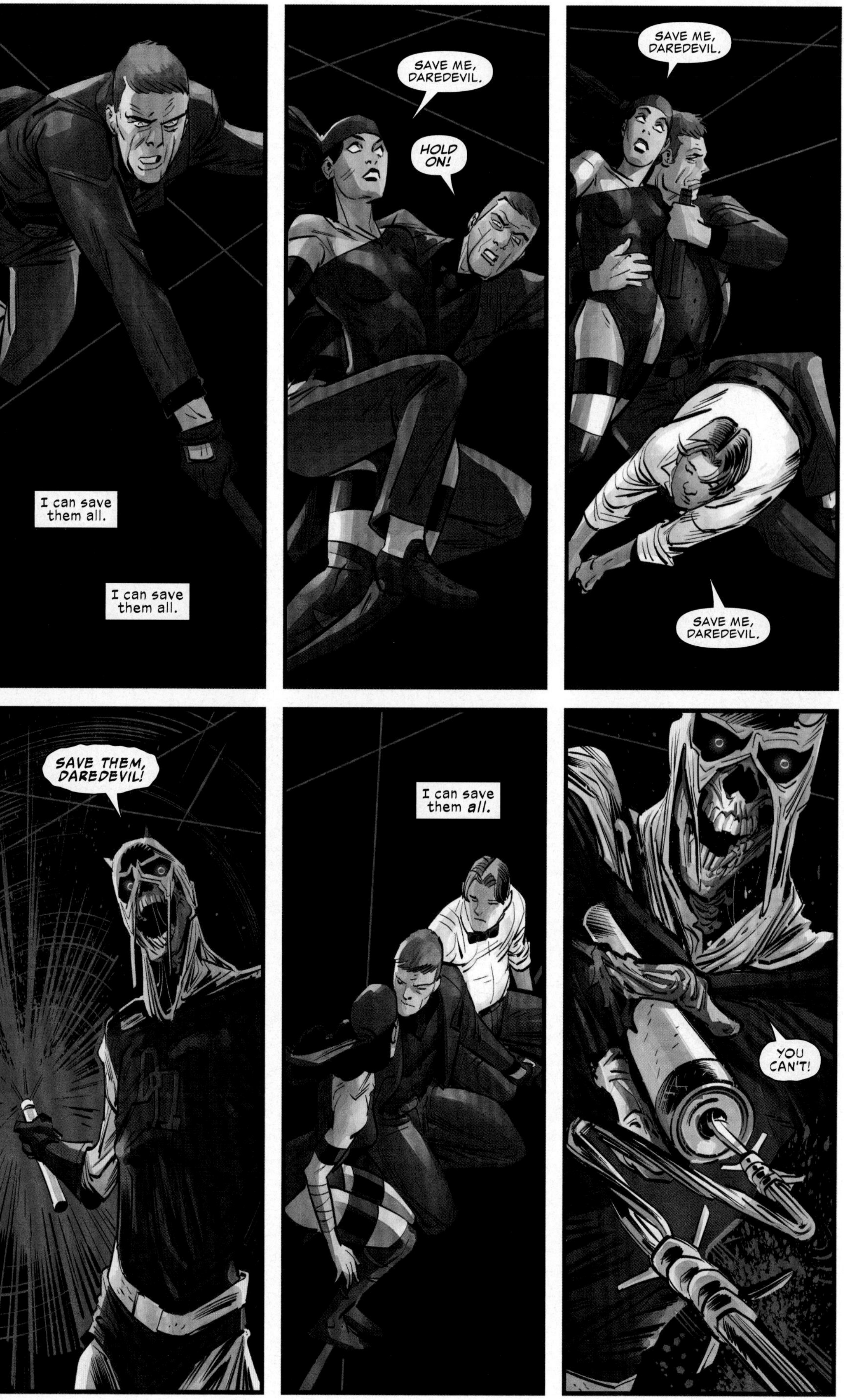
I can save them all.
I can save them all.
SAVE ME, DAREDEVIL.
HOLD ON!
SAVE ME, DAREDEVIL.
SAVE ME, DAREDEVIL.
SAVE THEM, DAREDEVIL!
I can save them all.
YOU CAN'T!

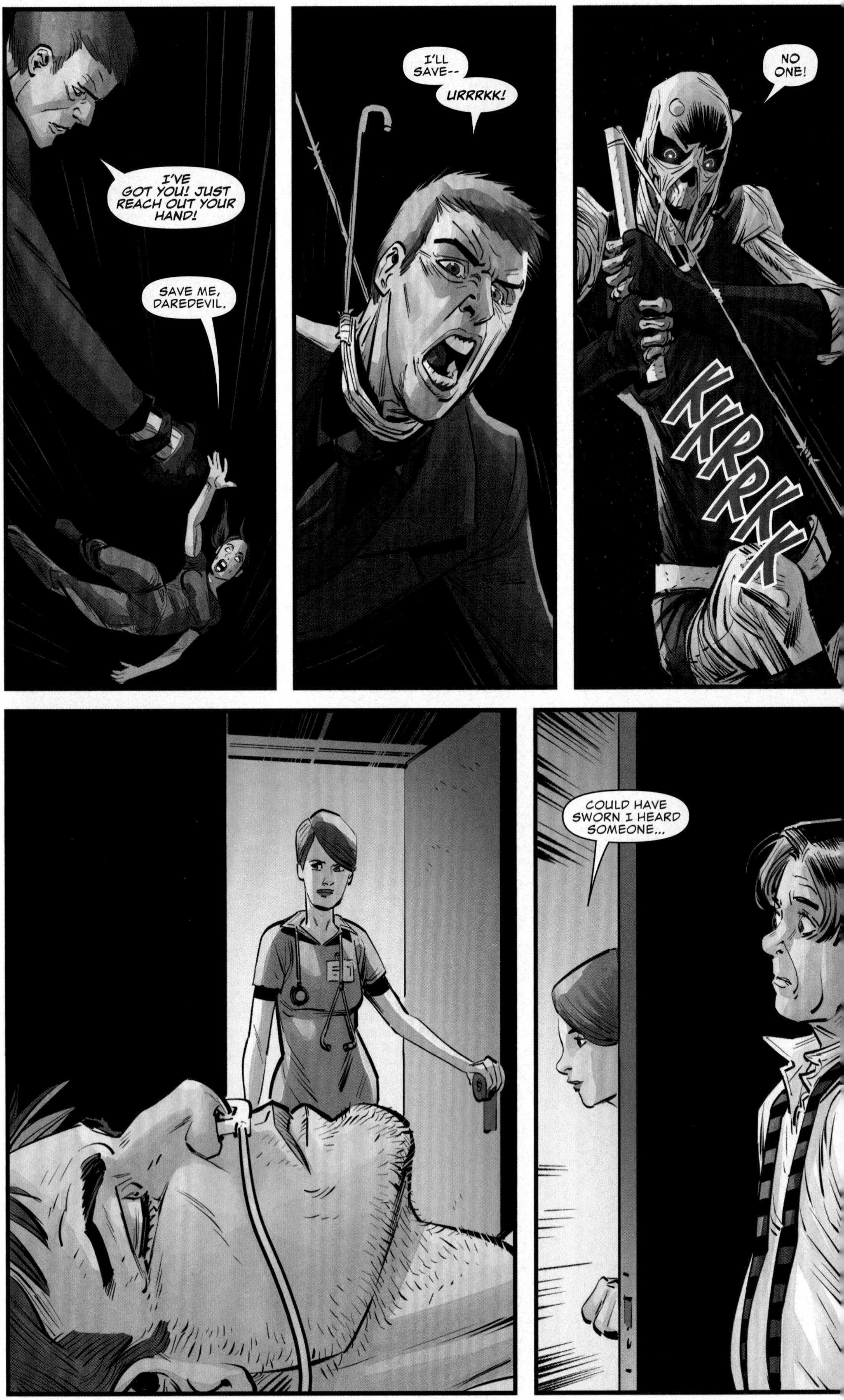
I'VE GOT YOU! JUST REACH OUT YOUR HAND!
SAVE ME, DAREDEVIL.
I'LL SAVE--
URRRKK!
NO ONE!
KKRRKK
COULD HAVE SWORN I HEARD SOMEONE...

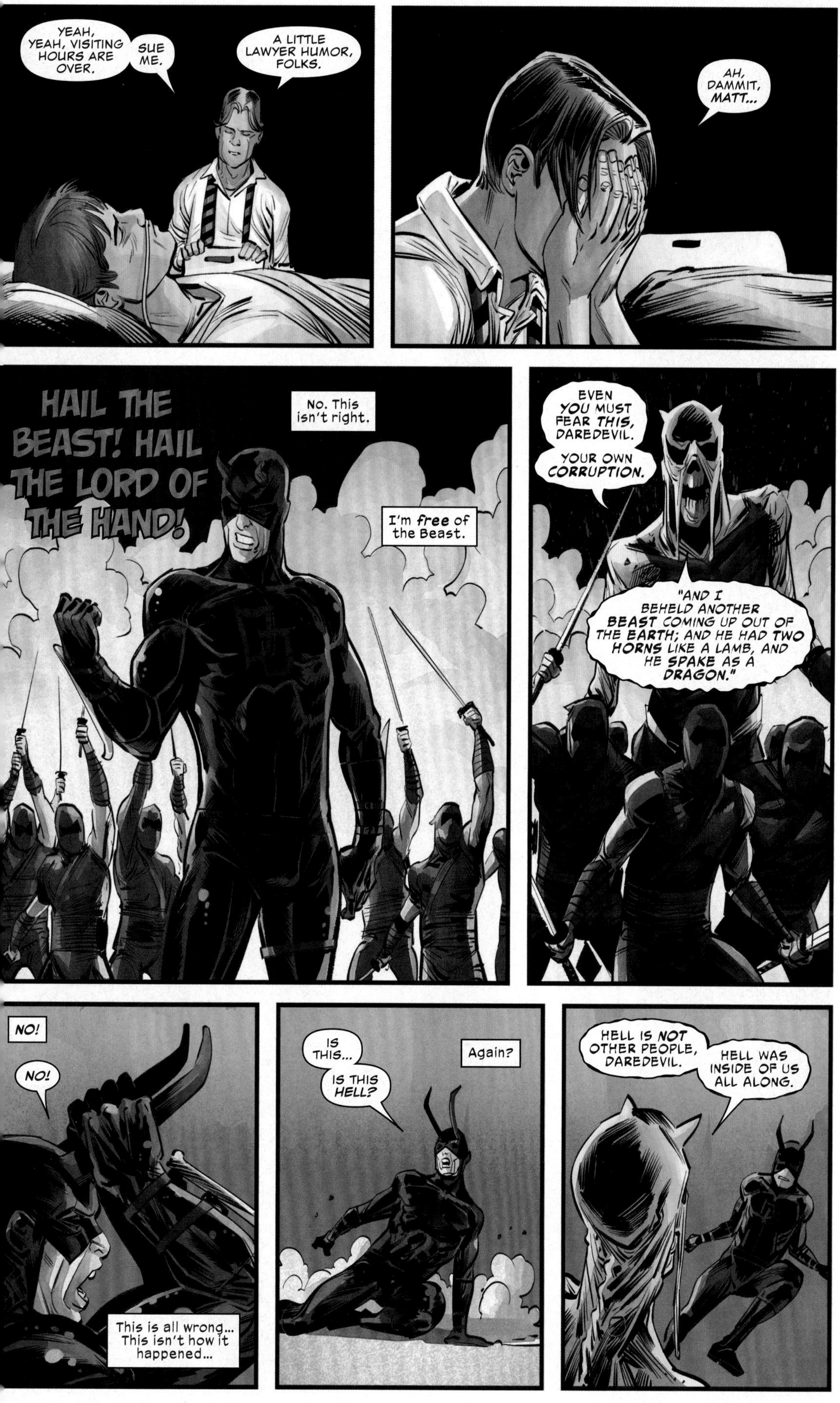

YEAH, YEAH, VISITING HOURS ARE OVER.
SUE ME.
A LITTLE LAWYER HUMOR, FOLKS.
AH, DAMMIT, MATT...
HAIL THE BEAST! HAIL THE LORD OF THE HAND!
No. This isn't right.
I'm free of the Beast.
EVEN YOU MUST FEAR THIS, DAREDEVIL.
YOUR OWN CORRUPTION.
"AND I BEHELD ANOTHER BEAST COMING UP OUT OF THE EARTH; AND HE HAD TWO HORNS LIKE A LAMB, AND HE SPAKE AS A DRAGON."
NO!
NO!
This is all wrong... This isn't how it happened...
IS THIS...
IS THIS HELL?
Again?
HELL IS NOT OTHER PEOPLE, DAREDEVIL.
HELL WAS INSIDE OF US ALL ALONG.

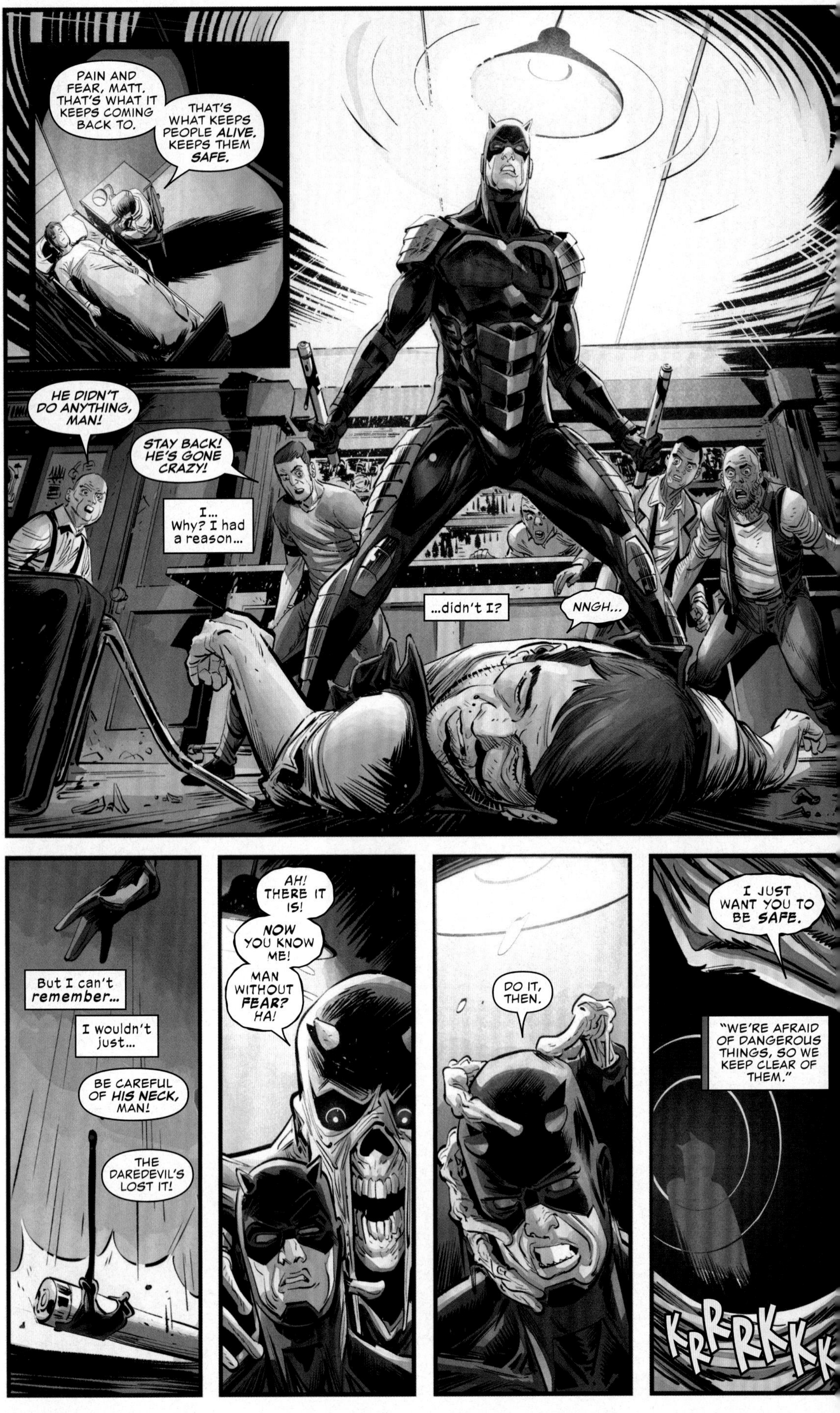
PAIN AND FEAR, MATT. THAT'S WHAT IT KEEPS COMING BACK TO.
THAT'S WHAT KEEPS PEOPLE ALIVE. KEEPS THEM SAFE.
HE DIDN'T DO ANYTHING, MAN!
STAY BACK! HE'S GONE CRAZY!
I... Why? I had a reason...
...didn't I?
NNGH...
But I can't remember...
I wouldn't just...
BE CAREFUL OF HIS NECK, MAN!
THE DAREDEVIL'S LOST IT!
AH! THERE IT IS!
NOW YOU KNOW ME!
MAN WITHOUT FEAR? HA!
DO IT, THEN.
I JUST WANT YOU TO BE SAFE.
"WE'RE AFRAID OF DANGEROUS THINGS, SO WE KEEP CLEAR OF THEM."
KRRRKKKK

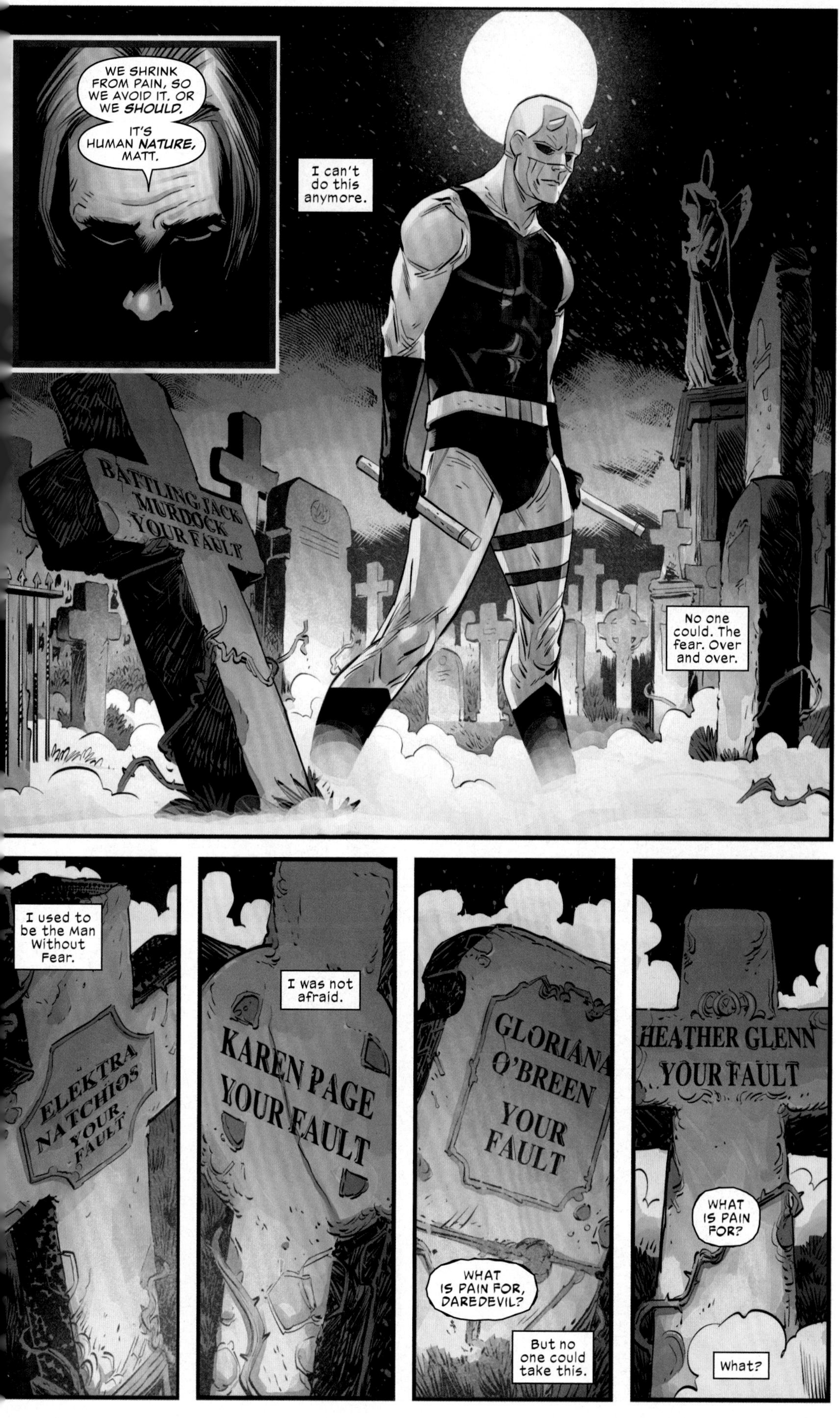

WE SHRINK FROM PAIN, SO WE AVOID IT. OR WE SHOULD.
IT'S HUMAN NATURE, MATT.
I can't do this anymore.
BATTLING JACK MURDOCK YOUR FAULT
No one could. The fear. Over and over.
I used to be the Man Without Fear.
ELEKTRA NATCHIOS YOUR FAULT
I was not afraid.
KAREN PAGE YOUR FAULT
GLORIANA O'BREEN YOUR FAULT
WHAT IS PAIN FOR, DAREDEVIL?
But no one could take this.
HEATHER GLENN YOUR FAULT
WHAT IS PAIN FOR?
What?

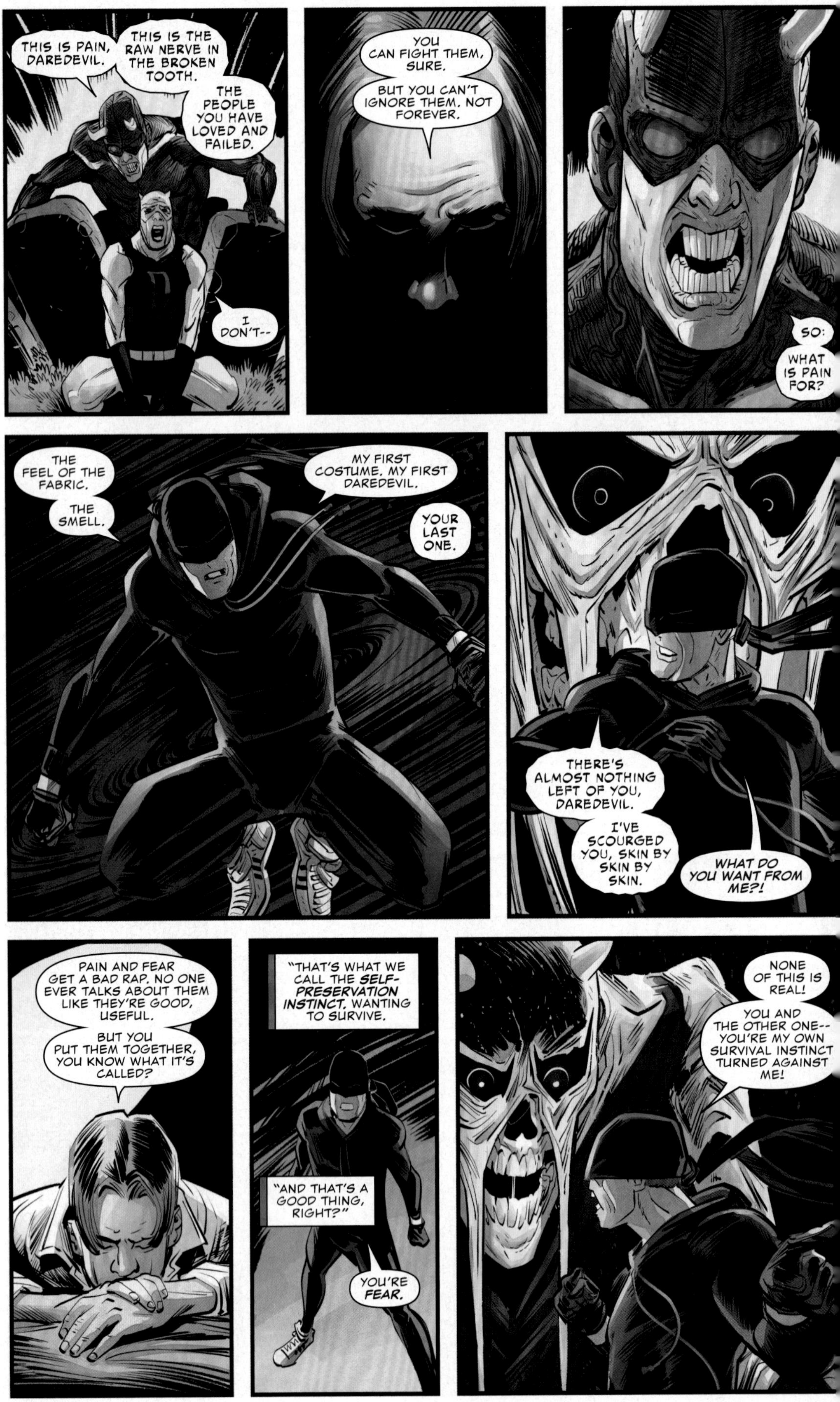
THIS IS PAIN, DAREDEVIL.
THIS IS THE RAW NERVE IN THE BROKEN TOOTH.
THE PEOPLE YOU HAVE LOVED AND FAILED.
I DON'T--
YOU CAN FIGHT THEM, SURE.
BUT YOU CAN'T IGNORE THEM. NOT FOREVER.
SO:
WHAT IS PAIN FOR?
THE FEEL OF THE FABRIC.
THE SMELL.
MY FIRST COSTUME. MY FIRST DAREDEVIL.
YOUR LAST ONE.
THERE'S ALMOST NOTHING LEFT OF YOU, DAREDEVIL.
I'VE SCOURGED YOU, SKIN BY SKIN BY SKIN.
WHAT DO YOU WANT FROM ME?!
PAIN AND FEAR GET A BAD RAP. NO ONE EVER TALKS ABOUT THEM LIKE THEY'RE GOOD, USEFUL.
BUT YOU PUT THEM TOGETHER, YOU KNOW WHAT IT'S CALLED?
"THAT'S WHAT WE CALL THE SELF-PRESERVATION INSTINCT. WANTING TO SURVIVE.
"AND THAT'S A GOOD THING, RIGHT?"
YOU'RE FEAR.
NONE OF THIS IS REAL!
YOU AND THE OTHER ONE--YOU'RE MY OWN SURVIVAL INSTINCT TURNED AGAINST ME!

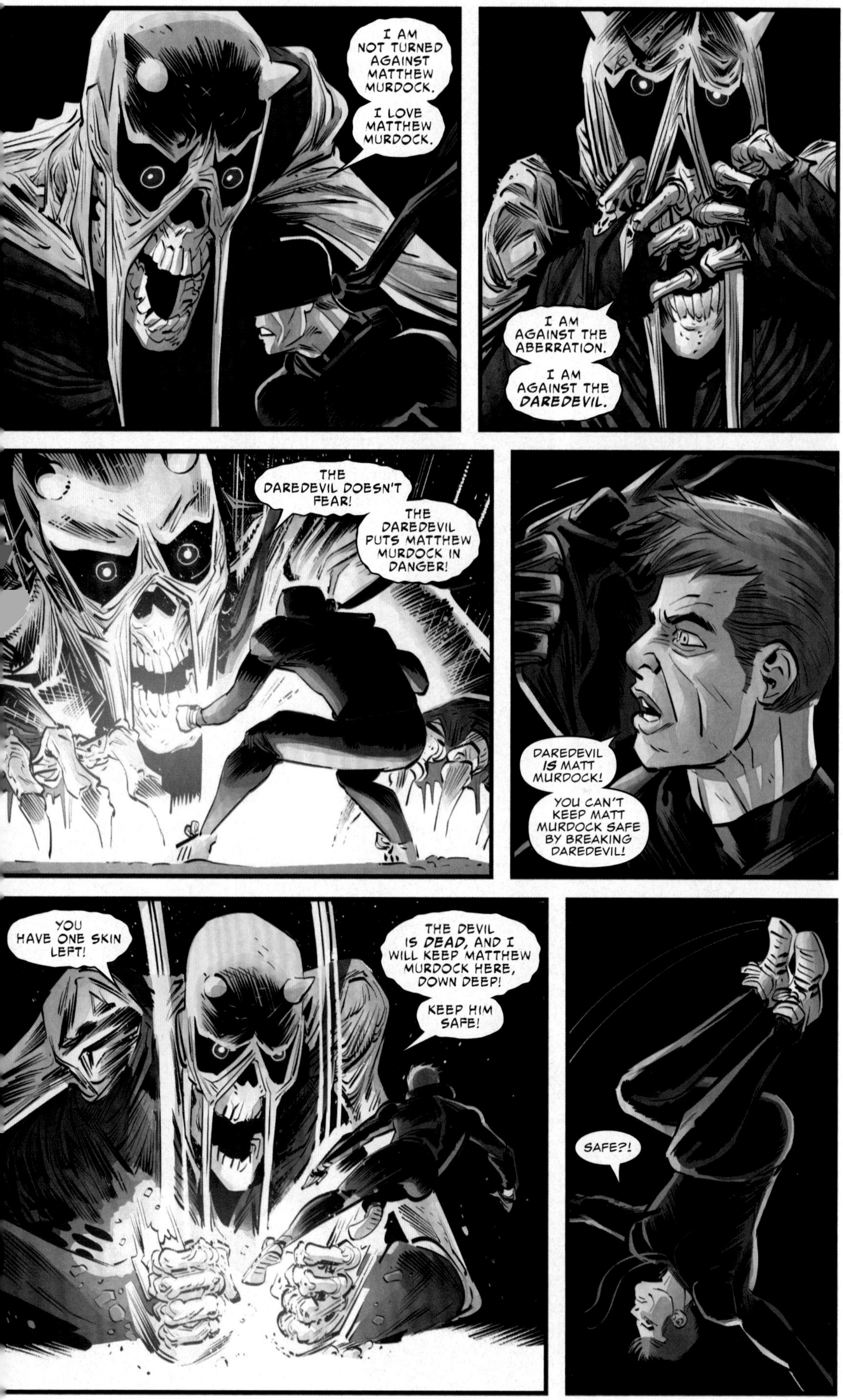

I AM NOT TURNED AGAINST MATTHEW MURDOCK.
I LOVE MATTHEW MURDOCK.
I AM AGAINST THE ABERRATION.
I AM AGAINST THE *DAREDEVIL.*
THE DAREDEVIL DOESN'T FEAR!
THE DAREDEVIL PUTS MATTHEW MURDOCK IN DANGER!
DAREDEVIL *IS* MATT MURDOCK!
YOU CAN'T KEEP MATT MURDOCK SAFE BY BREAKING DAREDEVIL!
YOU HAVE ONE SKIN LEFT!
THE DEVIL IS *DEAD*, AND I WILL KEEP MATTHEW MURDOCK HERE, DOWN DEEP!
KEEP HIM SAFE!
SAFE?!

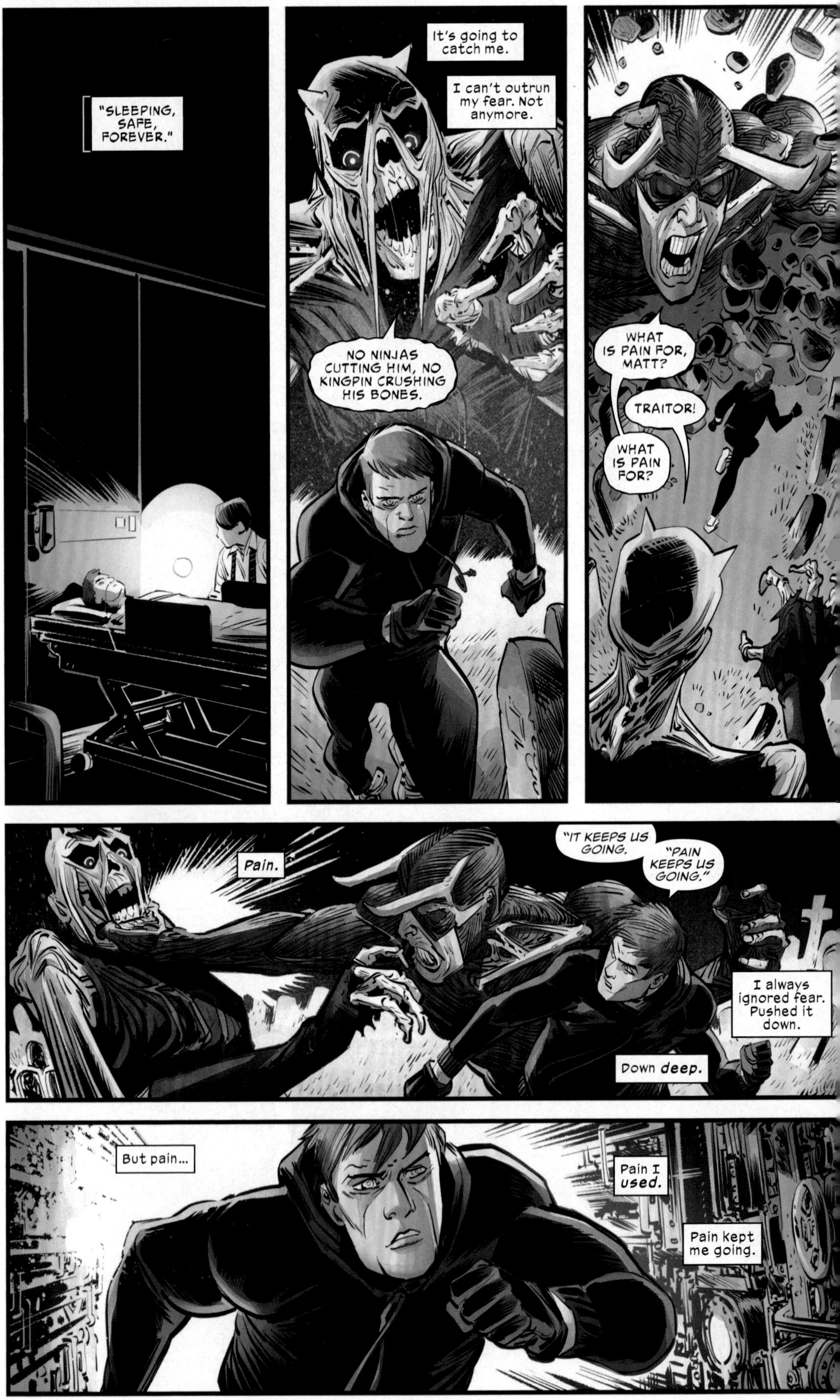
"SLEEPING, SAFE, FOREVER."
It's going to catch me.
I can't outrun my fear. Not anymore.
NO NINJAS CUTTING HIM, NO KINGPIN CRUSHING HIS BONES.
WHAT IS PAIN FOR, MATT?
TRAITOR!
WHAT IS PAIN FOR?
Pain.
"IT KEEPS US GOING.
"PAIN KEEPS US GOING."
I always ignored fear. Pushed it down.
Down deep.
But pain...
Pain I used.
Pain kept me going.

"LET DAREDEVIL STAY DEAD.

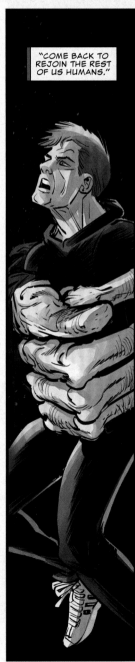

"COME BACK TO REJOIN THE REST OF US HUMANS."

YOU'LL *NEVER TRULY* ESCAPE!

YOU'LL *NEVER BE FREE OF ME!*

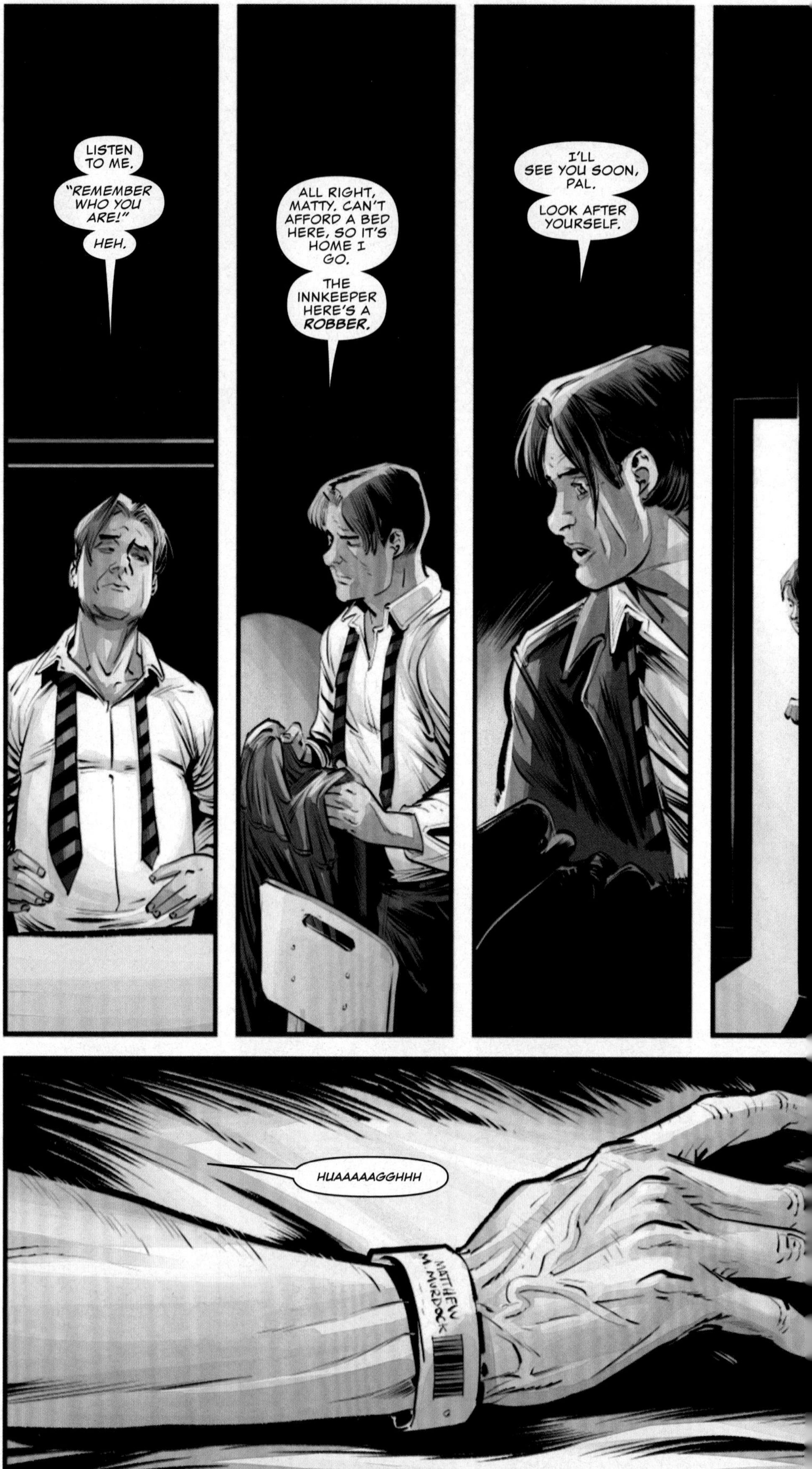
LISTEN TO ME.
"REMEMBER WHO YOU ARE!"
HEH.
ALL RIGHT, MATTY. CAN'T AFFORD A BED HERE, SO IT'S HOME I GO.
THE INNKEEPER HERE'S A ROBBER.
I'LL SEE YOU SOON, PAL.
LOOK AFTER YOURSELF.
HUAAAAAGGHHH
MATTHEW M. MURDOCK

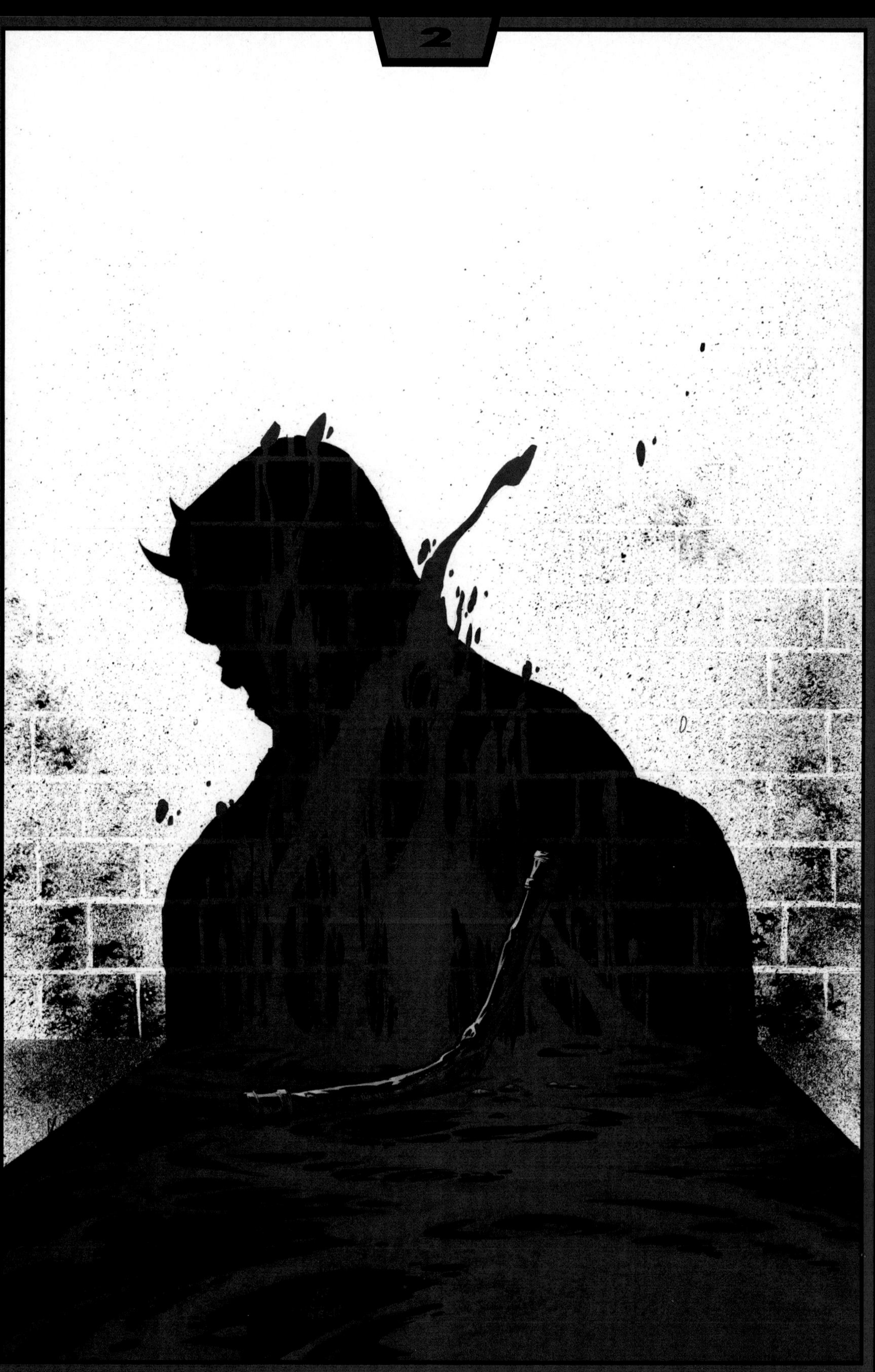
2

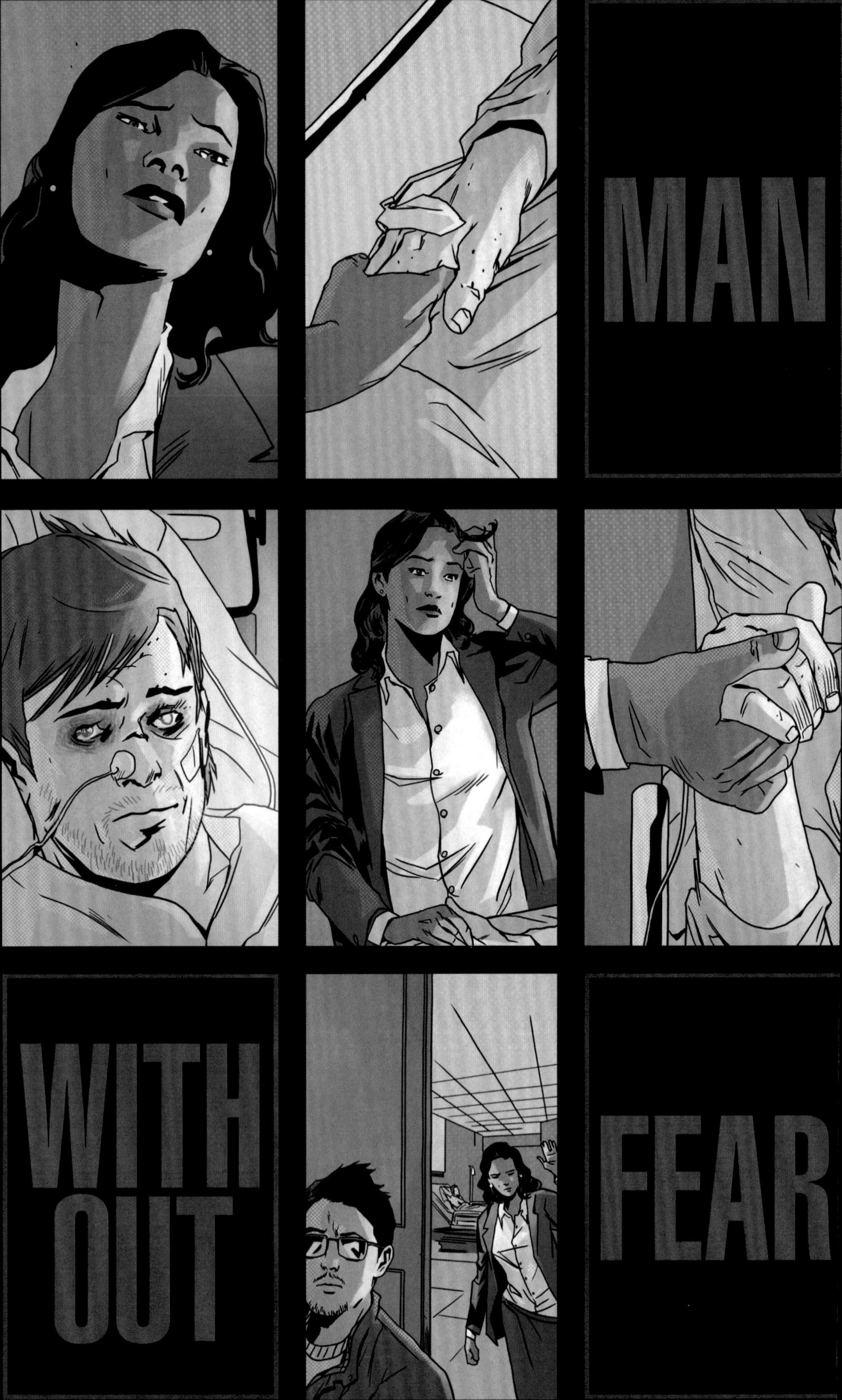
MAN
WITH OUT
FEAR

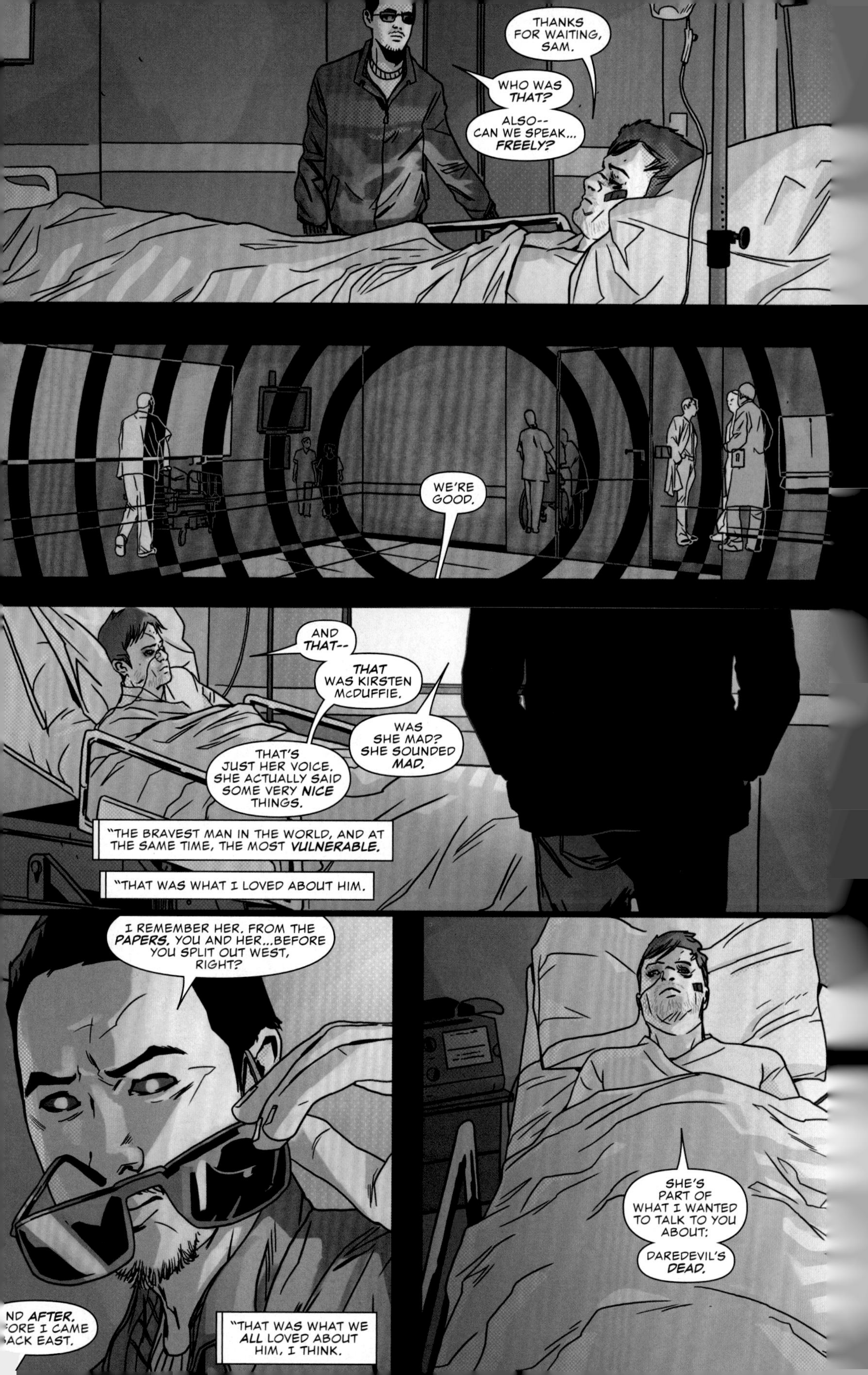

THANKS FOR WAITING, SAM.
WHO WAS THAT?
ALSO-- CAN WE SPEAK... FREELY?
WE'RE GOOD.
AND THAT--
THAT WAS KIRSTEN McDUFFIE.
WAS SHE MAD? SHE SOUNDED MAD.
THAT'S JUST HER VOICE. SHE ACTUALLY SAID SOME VERY NICE THINGS.
"THE BRAVEST MAN IN THE WORLD, AND AT THE SAME TIME, THE MOST VULNERABLE.
"THAT WAS WHAT I LOVED ABOUT HIM.
I REMEMBER HER. FROM THE PAPERS. YOU AND HER...BEFORE YOU SPLIT OUT WEST, RIGHT?
ND AFTER. FORE I CAME ACK EAST.
"THAT WAS WHAT WE ALL LOVED ABOUT HIM, I THINK.
SHE'S PART OF WHAT I WANTED TO TALK TO YOU ABOUT:
DAREDEVIL'S DEAD.

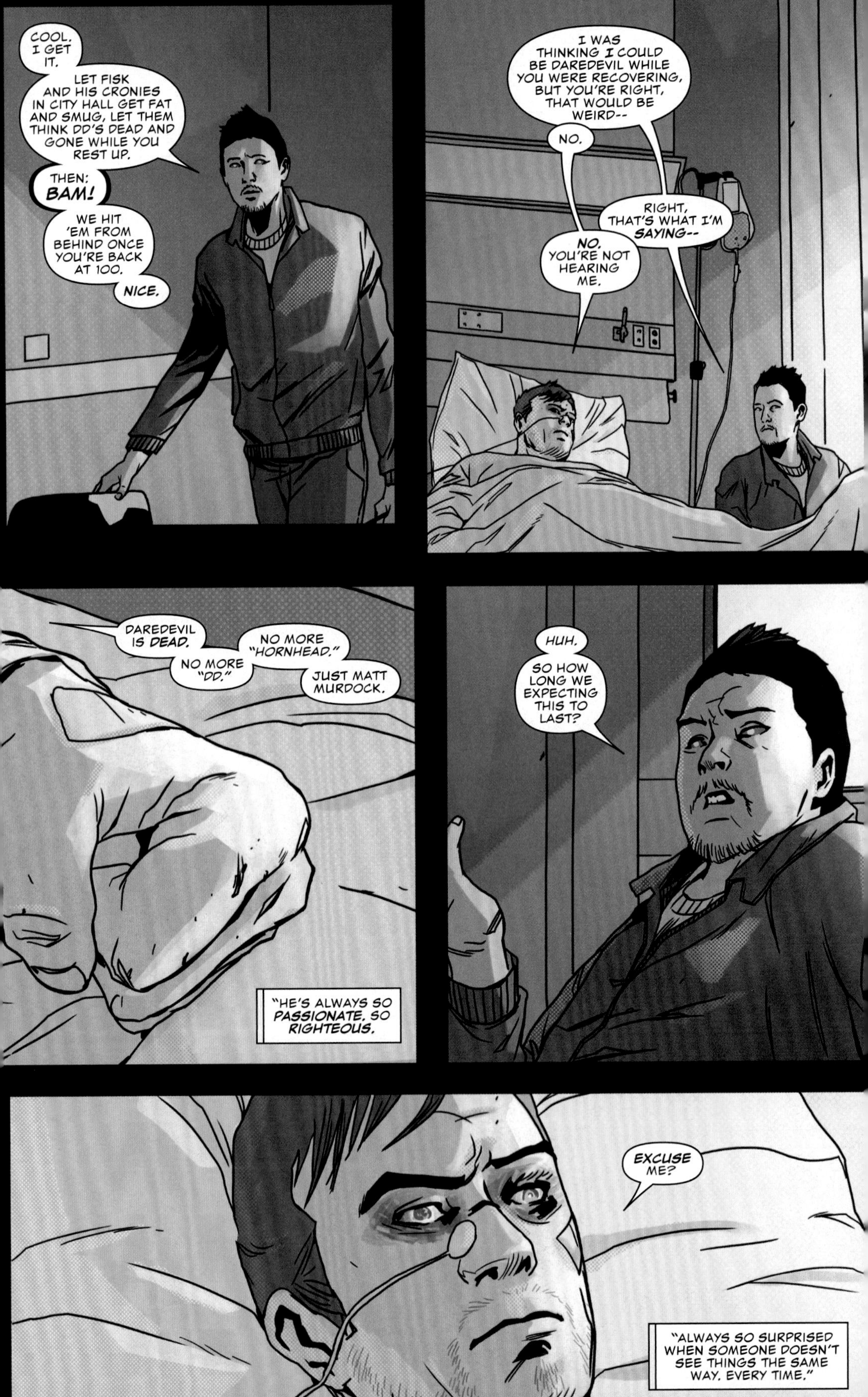
COOL, I GET IT.
LET FISK AND HIS CRONIES IN CITY HALL GET FAT AND SMUG, LET THEM THINK DD'S DEAD AND GONE WHILE YOU REST UP.
THEN: BAM!
WE HIT 'EM FROM BEHIND ONCE YOU'RE BACK AT 100.
NICE.
I WAS THINKING I COULD BE DAREDEVIL WHILE YOU WERE RECOVERING, BUT YOU'RE RIGHT, THAT WOULD BE WEIRD--
NO.
RIGHT, THAT'S WHAT I'M SAYING--
NO. YOU'RE NOT HEARING ME.
DAREDEVIL IS DEAD.
NO MORE "DD."
NO MORE "HORNHEAD."
JUST MATT MURDOCK.
"HE'S ALWAYS SO PASSIONATE, SO RIGHTEOUS.
HUH.
SO HOW LONG WE EXPECTING THIS TO LAST?
EXCUSE ME?
"ALWAYS SO SURPRISED WHEN SOMEONE DOESN'T SEE THINGS THE SAME WAY. EVERY TIME."

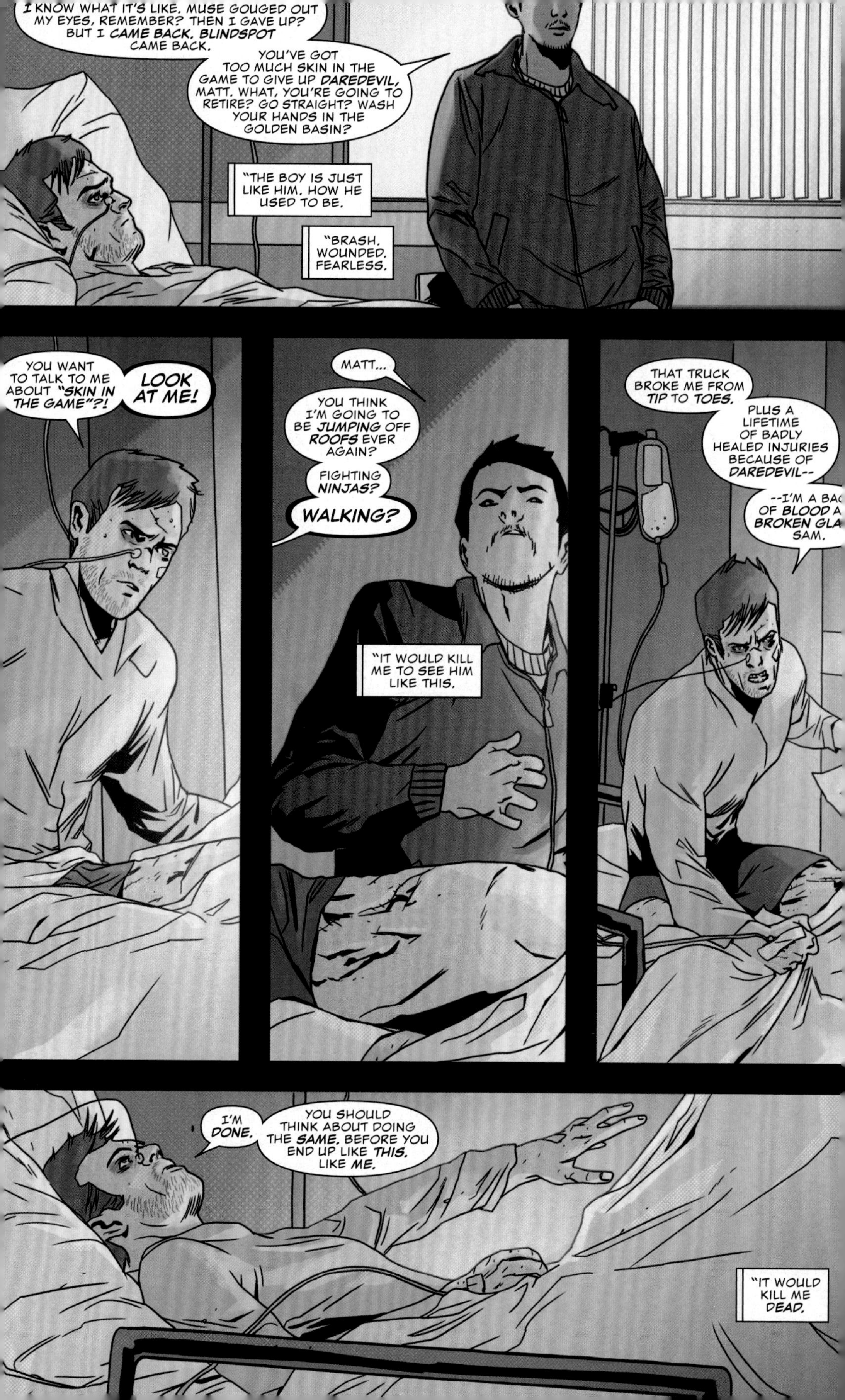

I KNOW WHAT IT'S LIKE. MUSE GOUGED OUT MY EYES, REMEMBER? THEN I GAVE UP? BUT I CAME BACK. BLINDSPOT CAME BACK.
YOU'VE GOT TOO MUCH SKIN IN THE GAME TO GIVE UP DAREDEVIL, MATT. WHAT, YOU'RE GOING TO RETIRE? GO STRAIGHT? WASH YOUR HANDS IN THE GOLDEN BASIN?
"THE BOY IS JUST LIKE HIM. HOW HE USED TO BE.
"BRASH. WOUNDED. FEARLESS.
YOU WANT TO TALK TO ME ABOUT "SKIN IN THE GAME"?!
LOOK AT ME!
MATT...
YOU THINK I'M GOING TO BE JUMPING OFF ROOFS EVER AGAIN?
FIGHTING NINJAS?
WALKING?
"IT WOULD KILL ME TO SEE HIM LIKE THIS.
THAT TRUCK BROKE ME FROM TIP TO TOES.
PLUS A LIFETIME OF BADLY HEALED INJURIES BECAUSE OF DAREDEVIL--
I'M DONE.
YOU SHOULD THINK ABOUT DOING THE SAME. BEFORE YOU END UP LIKE THIS. LIKE ME.
"IT WOULD KILL ME DEAD.

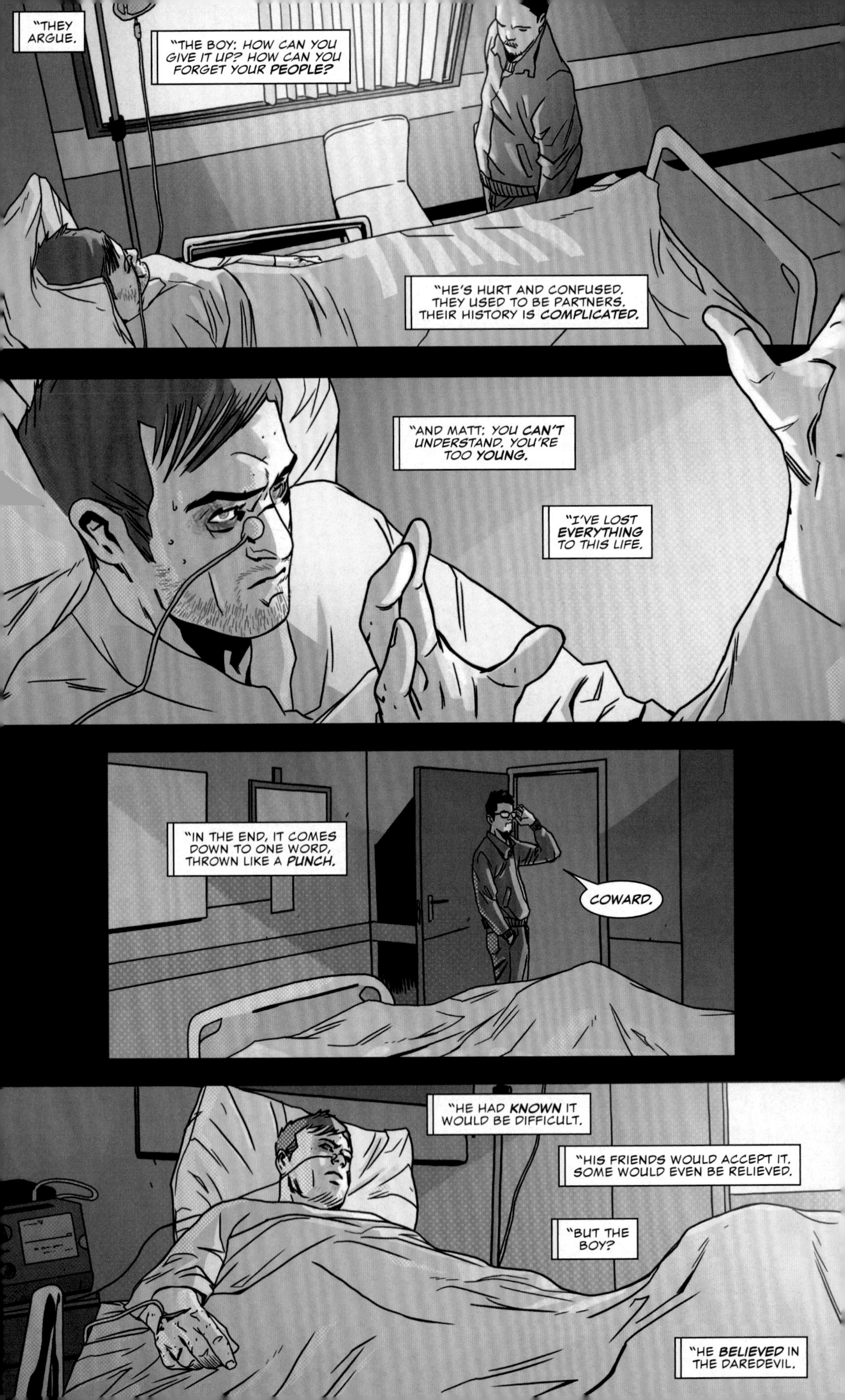
"THEY ARGUE.
"THE BOY: HOW CAN YOU GIVE IT UP? HOW CAN YOU FORGET YOUR PEOPLE?
"HE'S HURT AND CONFUSED. THEY USED TO BE PARTNERS. THEIR HISTORY IS COMPLICATED.
"AND MATT: YOU CAN'T UNDERSTAND. YOU'RE TOO YOUNG.
"I'VE LOST EVERYTHING TO THIS LIFE.
"IN THE END, IT COMES DOWN TO ONE WORD, THROWN LIKE A PUNCH.
COWARD.
"HE HAD KNOWN IT WOULD BE DIFFICULT.
"HIS FRIENDS WOULD ACCEPT IT. SOME WOULD EVEN BE RELIEVED.
"BUT THE BOY?
"HE BELIEVED IN THE DAREDEVIL.

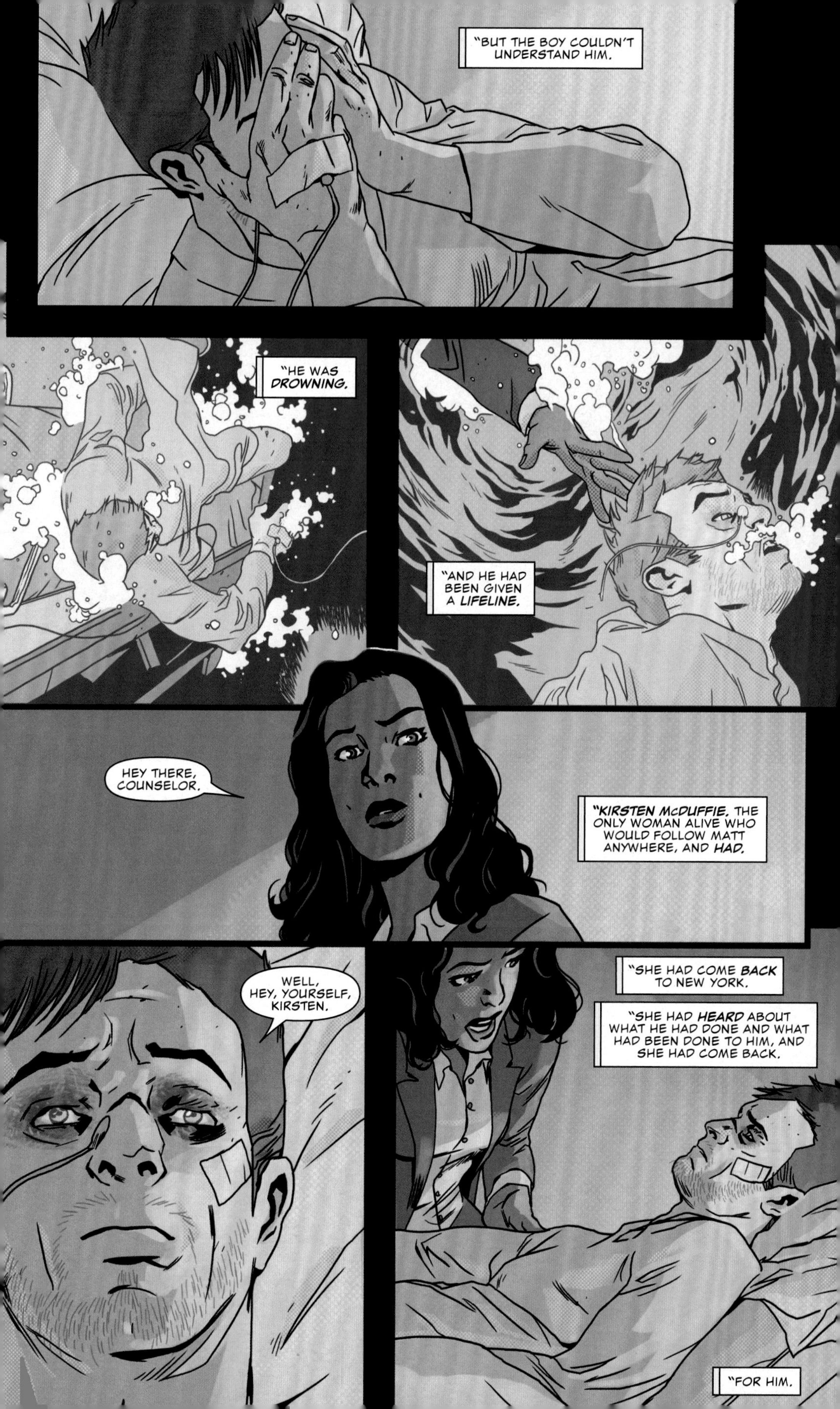
"BUT THE BOY COULDN'T UNDERSTAND HIM.
"HE WAS DROWNING.
"AND HE HAD BEEN GIVEN A LIFELINE.
HEY THERE, COUNSELOR.
"KIRSTEN McDUFFIE. THE ONLY WOMAN ALIVE WHO WOULD FOLLOW MATT ANYWHERE, AND HAD.
WELL, HEY, YOURSELF, KIRSTEN.
"SHE HAD COME BACK TO NEW YORK.
"SHE HAD HEARD ABOUT WHAT HE HAD DONE AND WHAT HAD BEEN DONE TO HIM, AND SHE HAD COME BACK.
"FOR HIM.

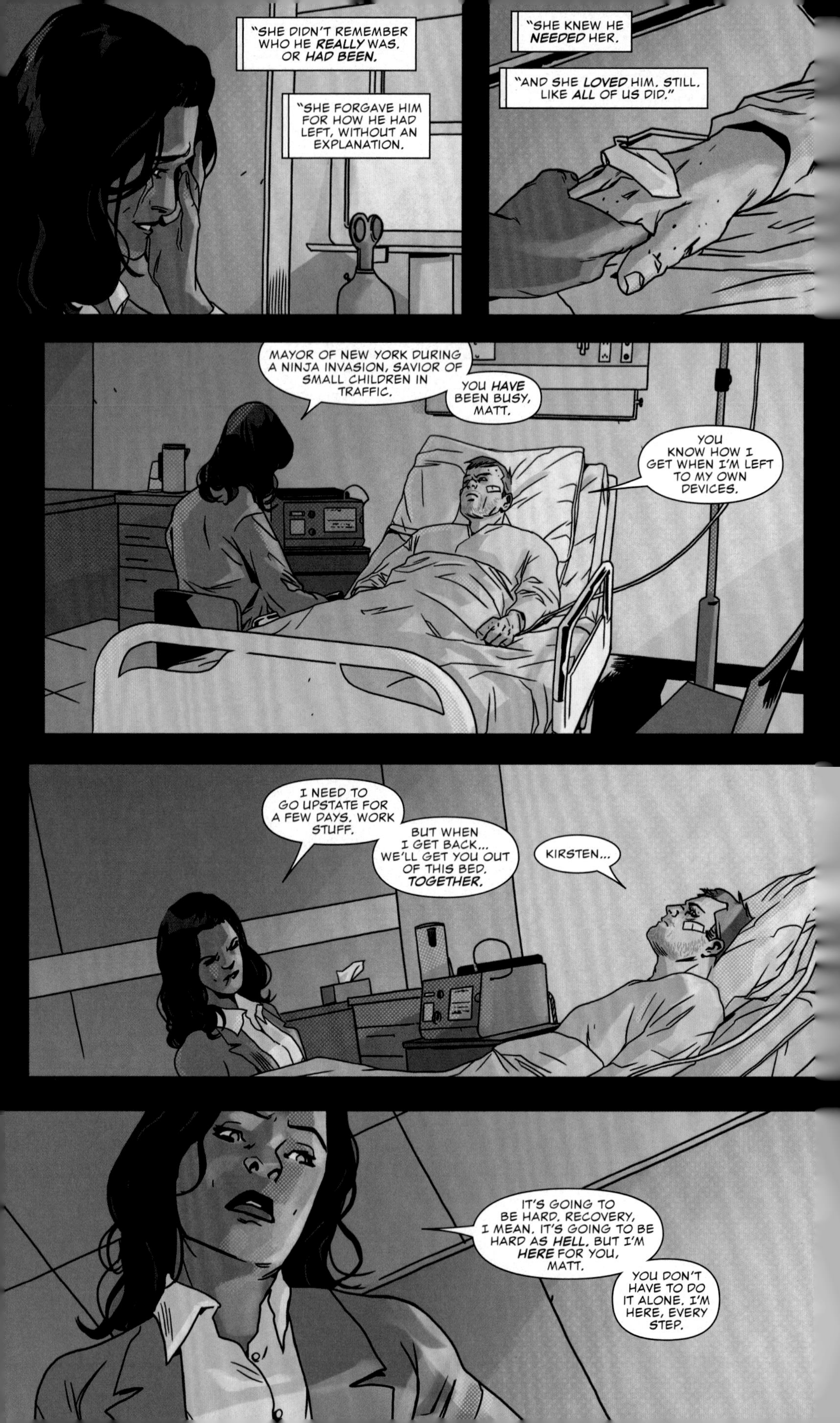
"SHE DIDN'T REMEMBER WHO HE REALLY WAS. OR HAD BEEN.
"SHE FORGAVE HIM FOR HOW HE HAD LEFT, WITHOUT AN EXPLANATION.
"SHE KNEW HE NEEDED HER.
"AND SHE LOVED HIM. STILL. LIKE ALL OF US DID."
MAYOR OF NEW YORK DURING A NINJA INVASION, SAVIOR OF SMALL CHILDREN IN TRAFFIC.
YOU HAVE BEEN BUSY, MATT.
YOU KNOW HOW I GET WHEN I'M LEFT TO MY OWN DEVICES.
I NEED TO GO UPSTATE FOR A FEW DAYS. WORK STUFF.
BUT WHEN I GET BACK... WE'LL GET YOU OUT OF THIS BED. TOGETHER.
KIRSTEN...
IT'S GOING TO BE HARD. RECOVERY, I MEAN. IT'S GOING TO BE HARD AS HELL. BUT I'M HERE FOR YOU, MATT.
YOU DON'T HAVE TO DO IT ALONE. I'M HERE, EVERY STEP.

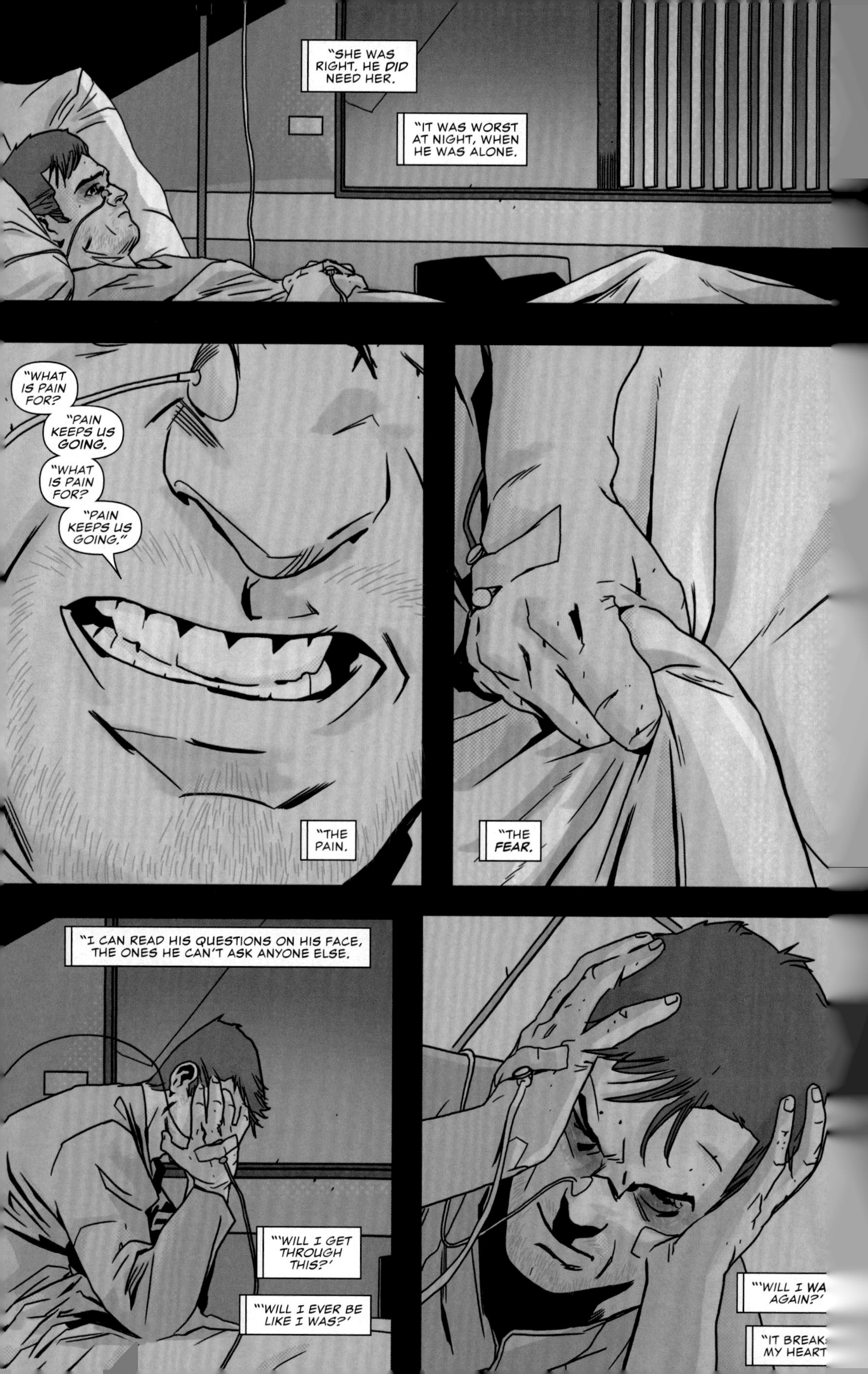

"SHE WAS RIGHT. HE *DID* NEED HER.
"IT WAS WORST AT NIGHT, WHEN HE WAS ALONE.
"WHAT IS PAIN FOR?
"PAIN KEEPS US **GOING.**
"WHAT IS PAIN FOR?
"PAIN KEEPS US GOING."
"THE PAIN.
"THE ***FEAR.***
"I CAN READ HIS QUESTIONS ON HIS FACE, THE ONES HE CAN'T ASK ANYONE ELSE.
"'WILL I GET THROUGH THIS?'
"'WILL I EVER BE LIKE I WAS?'
"'WILL I WA AGAIN?'
"IT BREAKS MY HEART

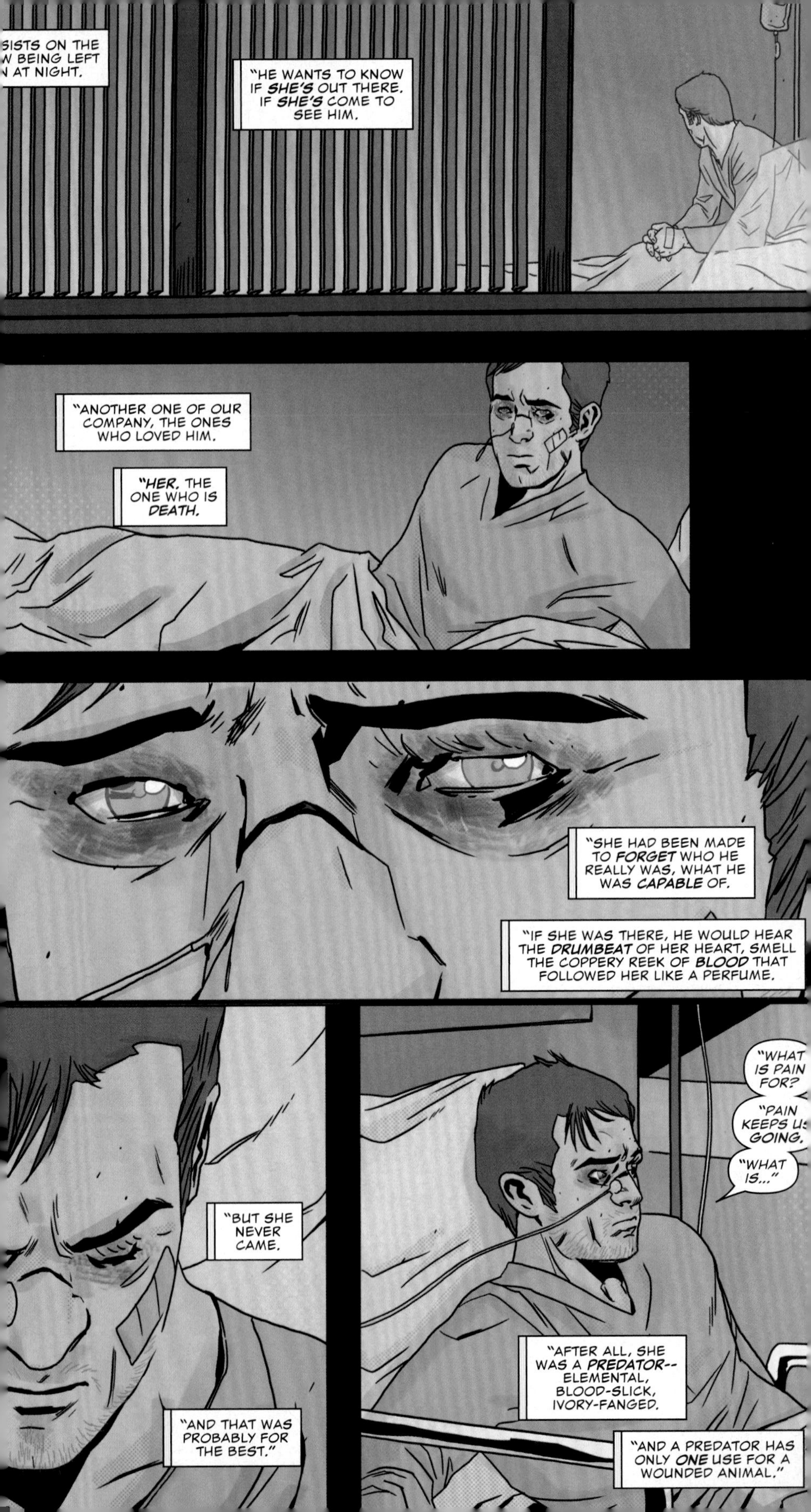

SISTS ON THE
W BEING LEFT
N AT NIGHT.
"HE WANTS TO KNOW IF SHE'S OUT THERE. IF SHE'S COME TO SEE HIM.
"ANOTHER ONE OF OUR COMPANY, THE ONES WHO LOVED HIM.
"HER. THE ONE WHO IS DEATH.
"SHE HAD BEEN MADE TO FORGET WHO HE REALLY WAS, WHAT HE WAS CAPABLE OF.
"IF SHE WAS THERE, HE WOULD HEAR THE DRUMBEAT OF HER HEART, SMELL THE COPPERY REEK OF BLOOD THAT FOLLOWED HER LIKE A PERFUME.
"BUT SHE NEVER CAME.
"AND THAT WAS PROBABLY FOR THE BEST."
"WHAT IS PAIN FOR?
"PAIN KEEPS US GOING.
"WHAT IS..."
"AFTER ALL, SHE WAS A PREDATOR-- ELEMENTAL, BLOOD-SLICK, IVORY-FANGED.
"AND A PREDATOR HAS ONLY ONE USE FOR A WOUNDED ANIMAL."

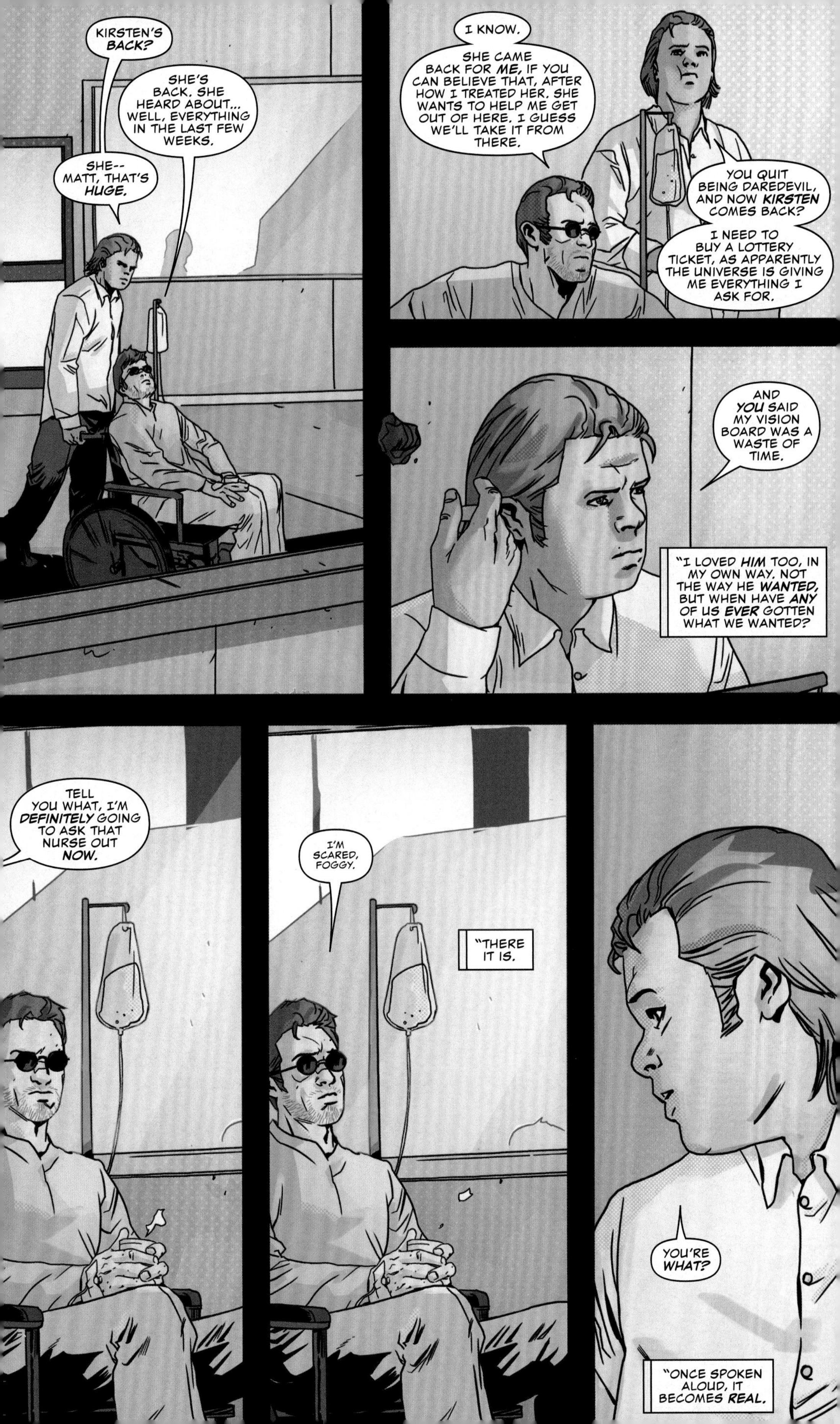
KIRSTEN'S BACK?
SHE'S BACK. SHE HEARD ABOUT... WELL, EVERYTHING IN THE LAST FEW WEEKS.
SHE-- MATT, THAT'S HUGE.
I KNOW.
SHE CAME BACK FOR ME, IF YOU CAN BELIEVE THAT, AFTER HOW I TREATED HER. SHE WANTS TO HELP ME GET OUT OF HERE. I GUESS WE'LL TAKE IT FROM THERE.
YOU QUIT BEING DAREDEVIL, AND NOW KIRSTEN COMES BACK?
I NEED TO BUY A LOTTERY TICKET, AS APPARENTLY THE UNIVERSE IS GIVING ME EVERYTHING I ASK FOR.
AND YOU SAID MY VISION BOARD WAS A WASTE OF TIME.
"I LOVED HIM TOO, IN MY OWN WAY. NOT THE WAY HE WANTED, BUT WHEN HAVE ANY OF US EVER GOTTEN WHAT WE WANTED?
TELL YOU WHAT, I'M DEFINITELY GOING TO ASK THAT NURSE OUT NOW.
I'M SCARED, FOGGY.
"THERE IT IS.
YOU'RE WHAT?
"ONCE SPOKEN ALOUD, IT BECOMES REAL.

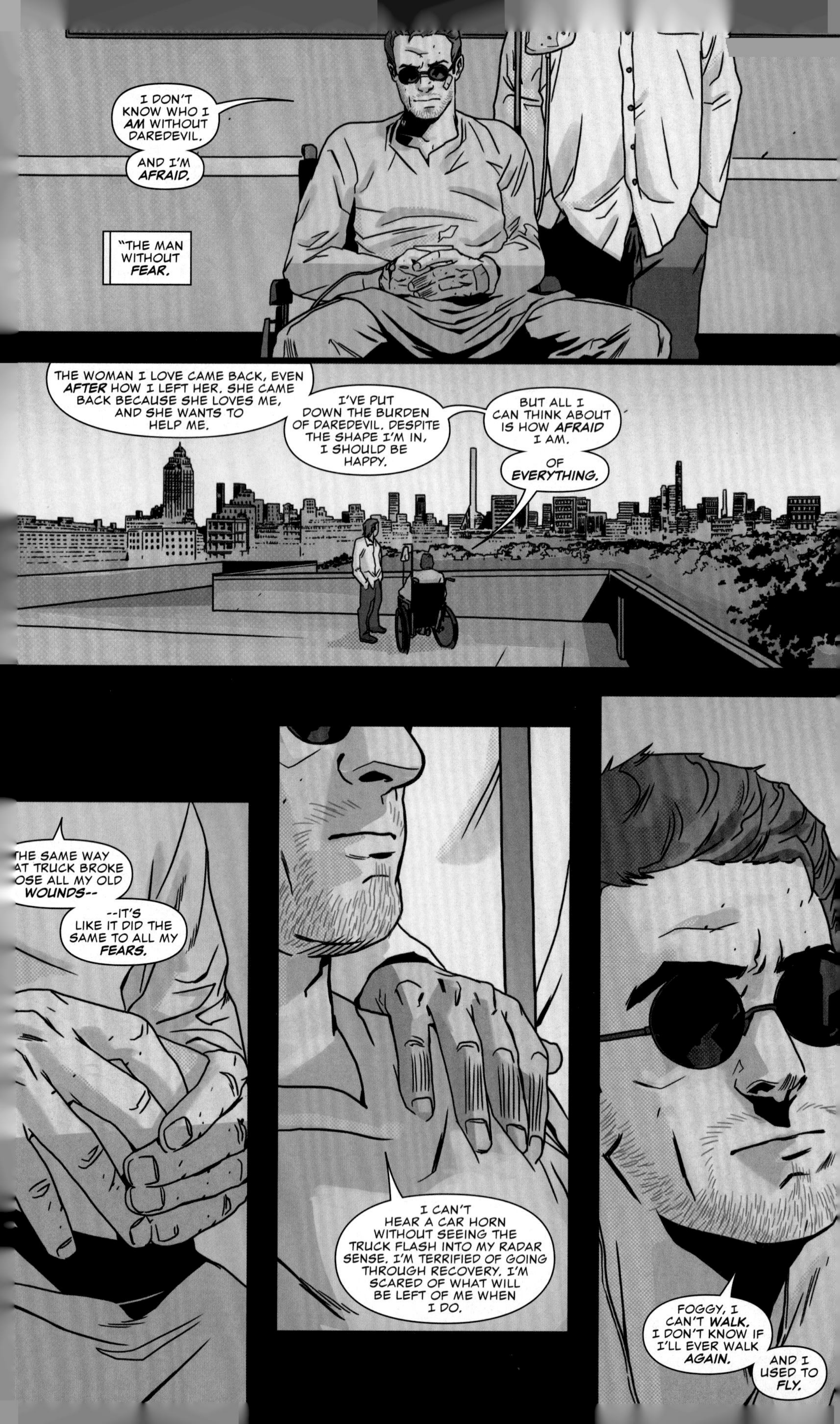
I DON'T KNOW WHO I AM WITHOUT DAREDEVIL.
AND I'M AFRAID.
"THE MAN WITHOUT FEAR.
THE WOMAN I LOVE CAME BACK, EVEN AFTER HOW I LEFT HER. SHE CAME BACK BECAUSE SHE LOVES ME, AND SHE WANTS TO HELP ME.
I'VE PUT DOWN THE BURDEN OF DAREDEVIL. DESPITE THE SHAPE I'M IN, I SHOULD BE HAPPY.
BUT ALL I CAN THINK ABOUT IS HOW AFRAID I AM.
OF EVERYTHING.
THE SAME WAY AT TRUCK BROKE OSE ALL MY OLD WOUNDS--
--IT'S LIKE IT DID THE SAME TO ALL MY FEARS.
I CAN'T HEAR A CAR HORN WITHOUT SEEING THE TRUCK FLASH INTO MY RADAR SENSE. I'M TERRIFIED OF GOING THROUGH RECOVERY. I'M SCARED OF WHAT WILL BE LEFT OF ME WHEN I DO.
FOGGY, I CAN'T WALK. I DON'T KNOW IF I'LL EVER WALK AGAIN.
AND I USED TO FLY.

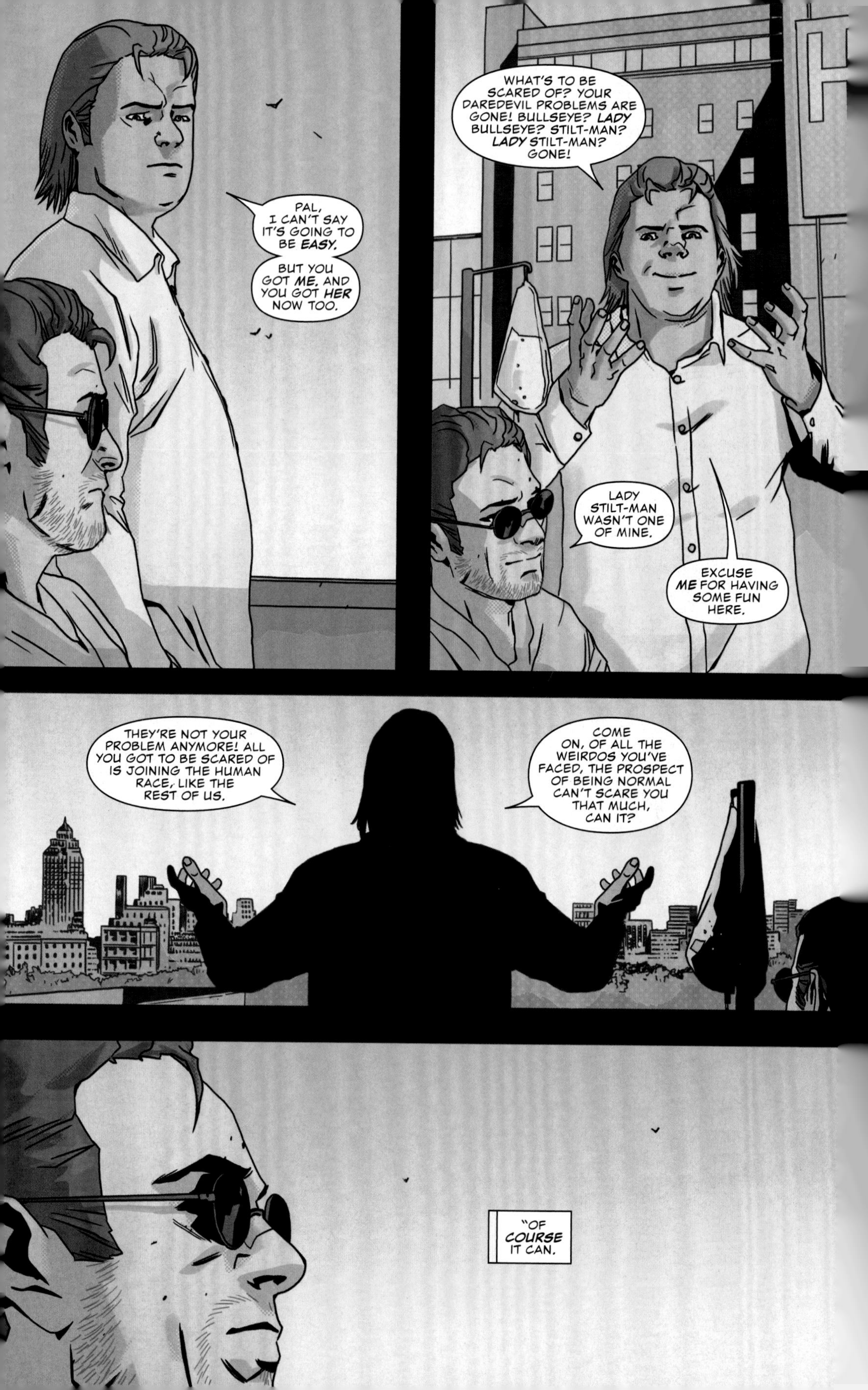
PAL, I CAN'T SAY IT'S GOING TO BE *EASY.*
BUT YOU GOT *ME,* AND YOU GOT *HER* NOW TOO.
WHAT'S TO BE SCARED OF? YOUR DAREDEVIL PROBLEMS ARE GONE! BULLSEYE? *LADY* BULLSEYE? STILT-MAN? *LADY* STILT-MAN? GONE!
LADY STILT-MAN WASN'T ONE OF MINE.
EXCUSE *ME* FOR HAVING SOME FUN HERE.
THEY'RE NOT YOUR PROBLEM ANYMORE! ALL YOU GOT TO BE SCARED OF IS JOINING THE HUMAN RACE, LIKE THE REST OF US.
COME ON, OF ALL THE WEIRDOS YOU'VE FACED, THE PROSPECT OF BEING NORMAL CAN'T SCARE YOU THAT MUCH, CAN IT?
"OF *COURSE* IT CAN.

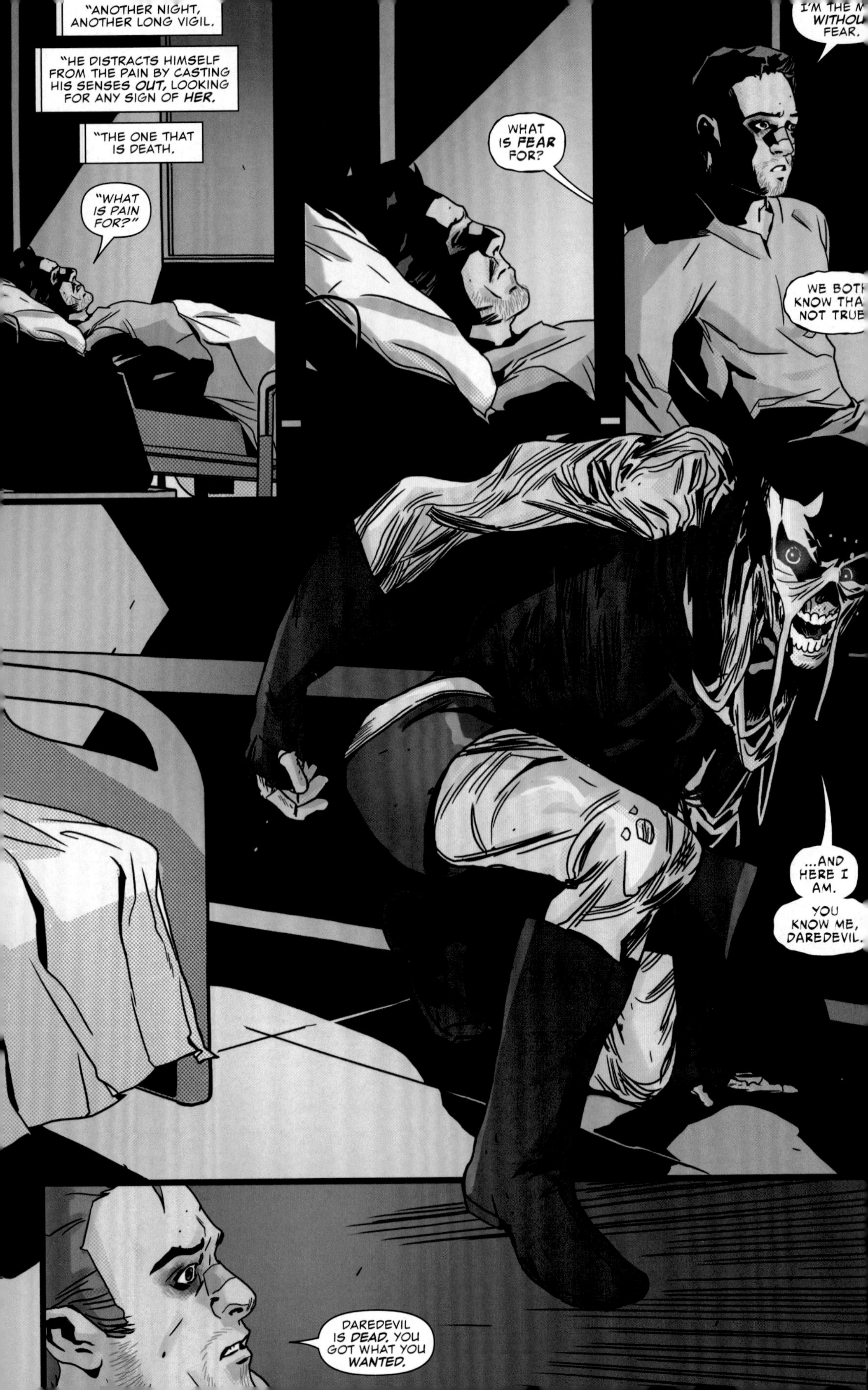
"ANOTHER NIGHT, ANOTHER LONG VIGIL.
"HE DISTRACTS HIMSELF FROM THE PAIN BY CASTING HIS SENSES *OUT*, LOOKING FOR ANY SIGN OF *HER*.
"THE ONE THAT IS DEATH.
"WHAT IS PAIN FOR?"
WHAT IS **FEAR** FOR?
I'M THE M WITHOU FEAR.
WE BOT KNOW THA NOT TRUE
...AND HERE I AM.
YOU KNOW ME, DAREDEVIL.
DAREDEVIL IS *DEAD*. YOU GOT WHAT YOU *WANTED*.

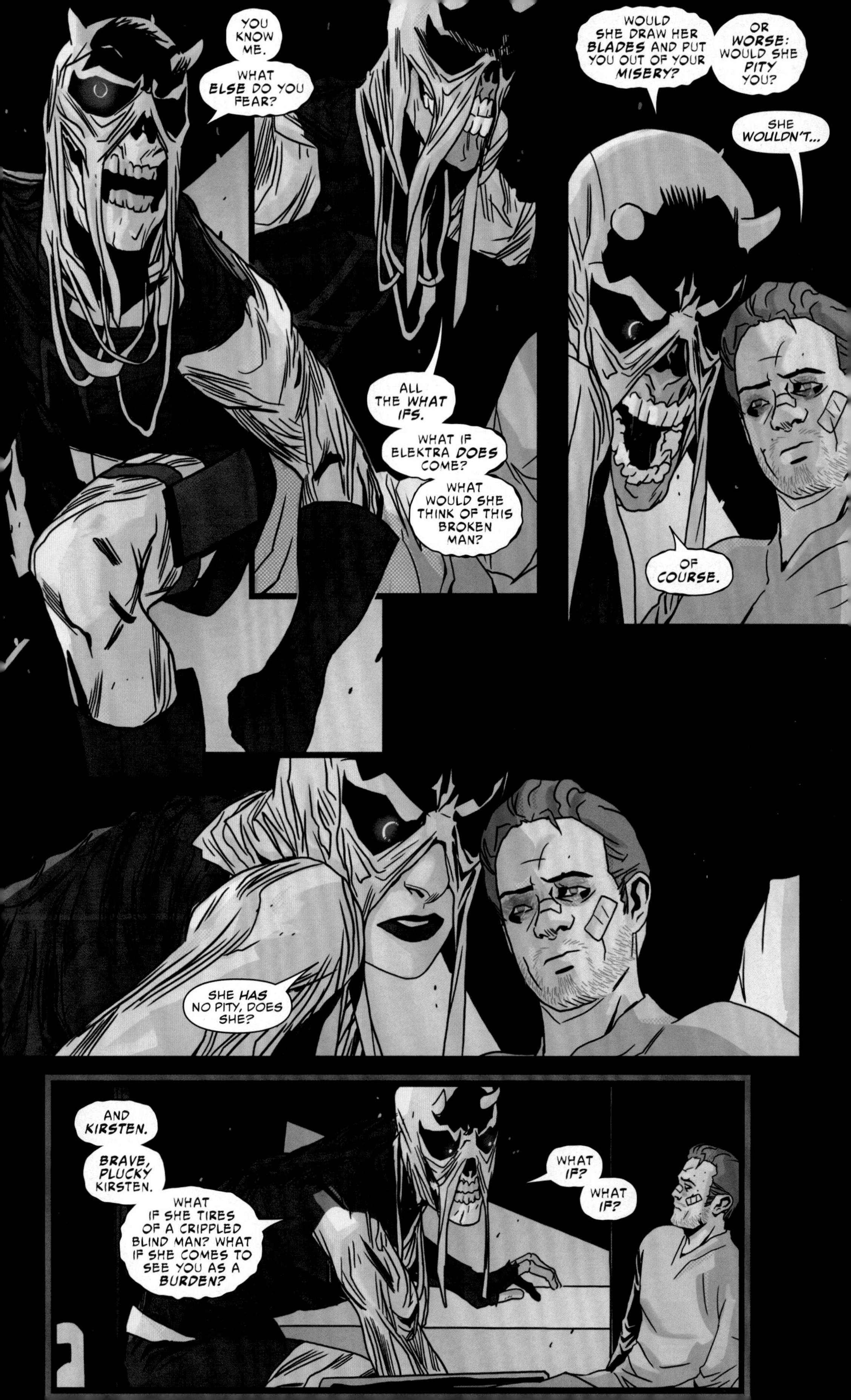
YOU KNOW ME.
WHAT ELSE DO YOU FEAR?
ALL THE WHAT IFS.
WHAT IF ELEKTRA DOES COME?
WHAT WOULD SHE THINK OF THIS BROKEN MAN?
WOULD SHE DRAW HER BLADES AND PUT YOU OUT OF YOUR MISERY?
OR WORSE: WOULD SHE PITY YOU?
SHE WOULDN'T...
OF COURSE.
SHE HAS NO PITY, DOES SHE?
AND KIRSTEN.
BRAVE, PLUCKY KIRSTEN.
WHAT IF SHE TIRES OF A CRIPPLED BLIND MAN? WHAT IF SHE COMES TO SEE YOU AS A BURDEN?
WHAT IF?
WHAT IF?

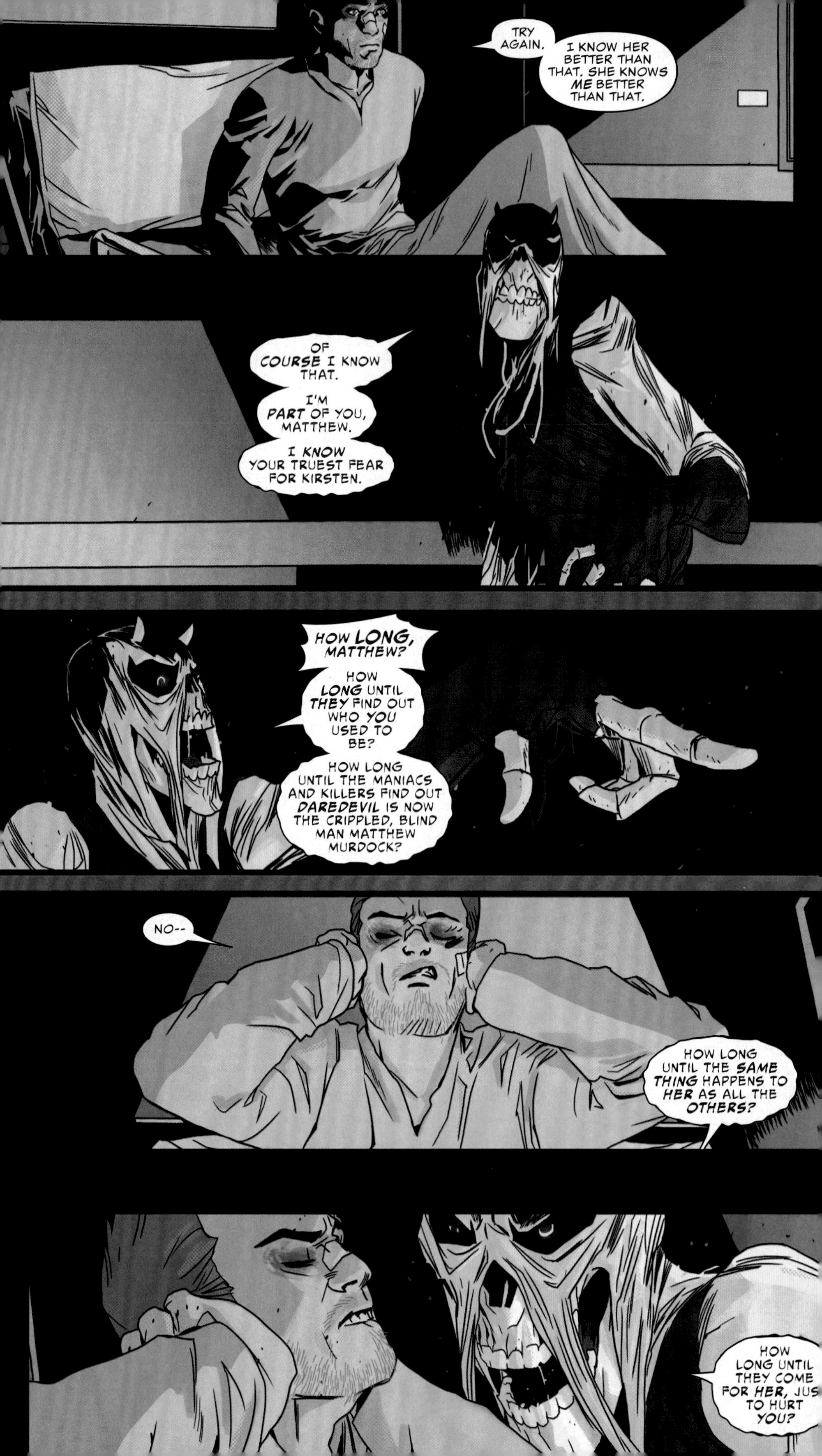
TRY AGAIN.
I KNOW HER BETTER THAN THAT. SHE KNOWS ME BETTER THAN THAT.
OF COURSE I KNOW THAT.
I'M PART OF YOU, MATTHEW.
I KNOW YOUR TRUEST FEAR FOR KIRSTEN.
HOW LONG, MATTHEW?
HOW LONG UNTIL THEY FIND OUT WHO YOU USED TO BE?
HOW LONG UNTIL THE MANIACS AND KILLERS FIND OUT DAREDEVIL IS NOW THE CRIPPLED, BLIND MAN MATTHEW MURDOCK?
NO--
HOW LONG UNTIL THE SAME THING HAPPENS TO HER AS ALL THE OTHERS?
HOW LONG UNTIL THEY COME FOR HER, JUS TO HURT YOU?

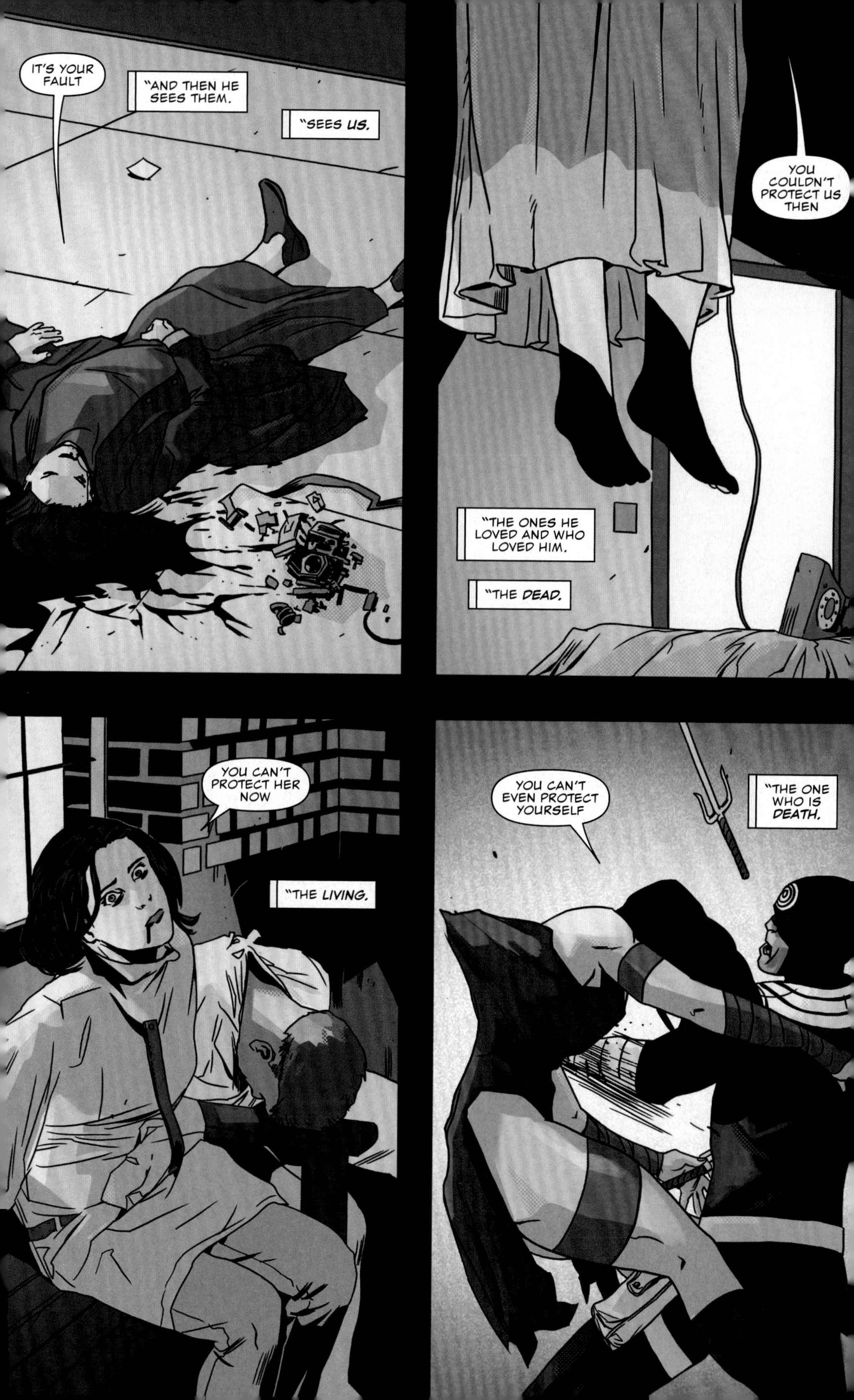
IT'S YOUR FAULT
"AND THEN HE SEES THEM.
"SEES *US.*
YOU COULDN'T PROTECT US THEN
"THE ONES HE LOVED AND WHO LOVED HIM.
"THE *DEAD.*
YOU CAN'T PROTECT HER NOW
"THE *LIVING.*
YOU CAN'T EVEN PROTECT YOURSELF
"THE ONE WHO IS *DEATH.*

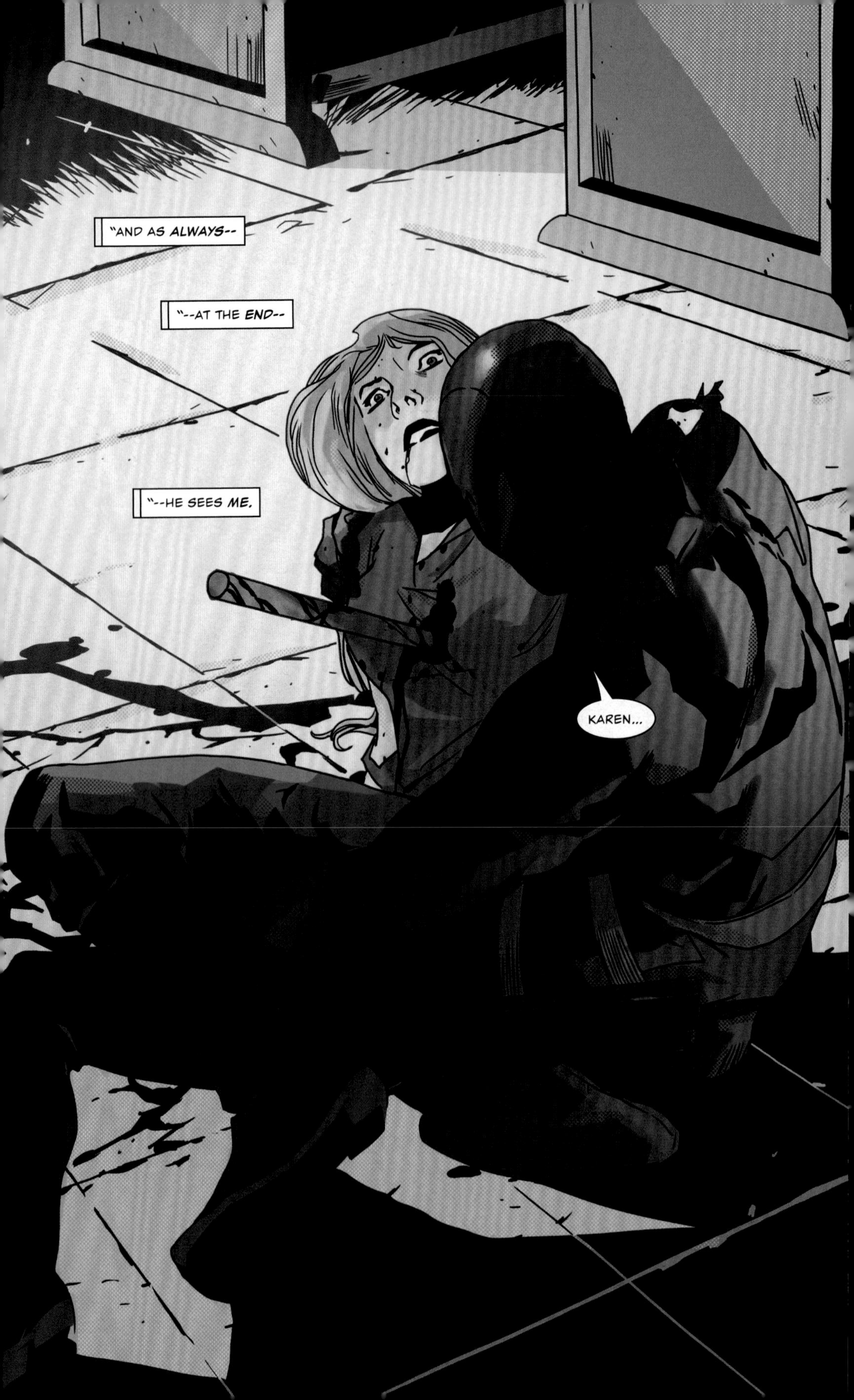
"AND AS ALWAYS--
"--AT THE END--
"--HE SEES ME.
KAREN...

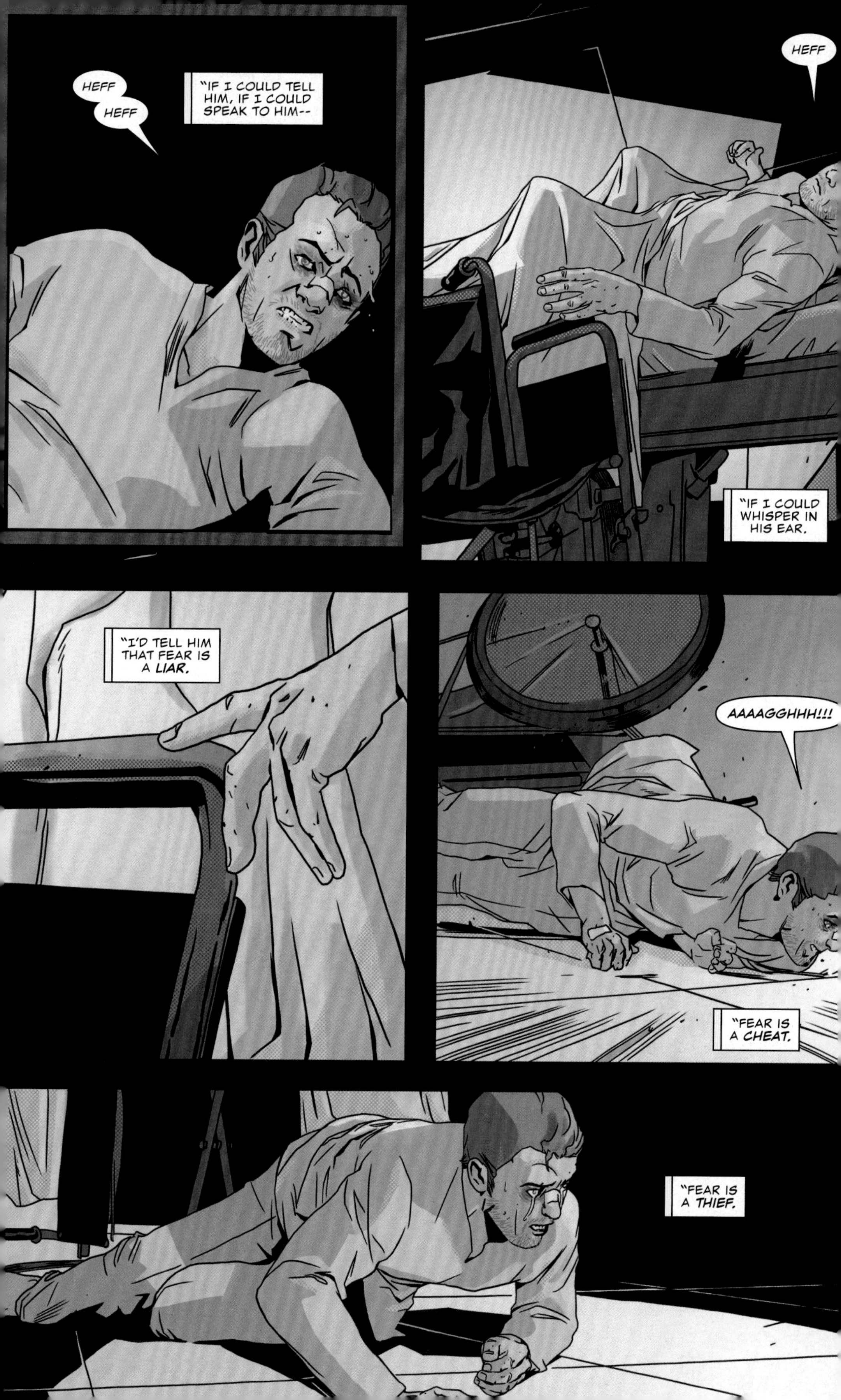
HEFF
HEFF
"IF I COULD TELL HIM, IF I COULD SPEAK TO HIM--
HEFF
"IF I COULD WHISPER IN HIS EAR.
"I'D TELL HIM THAT FEAR IS A LIAR.
AAAAGGHHH!!!
"FEAR IS A CHEAT.
"FEAR IS A THIEF.

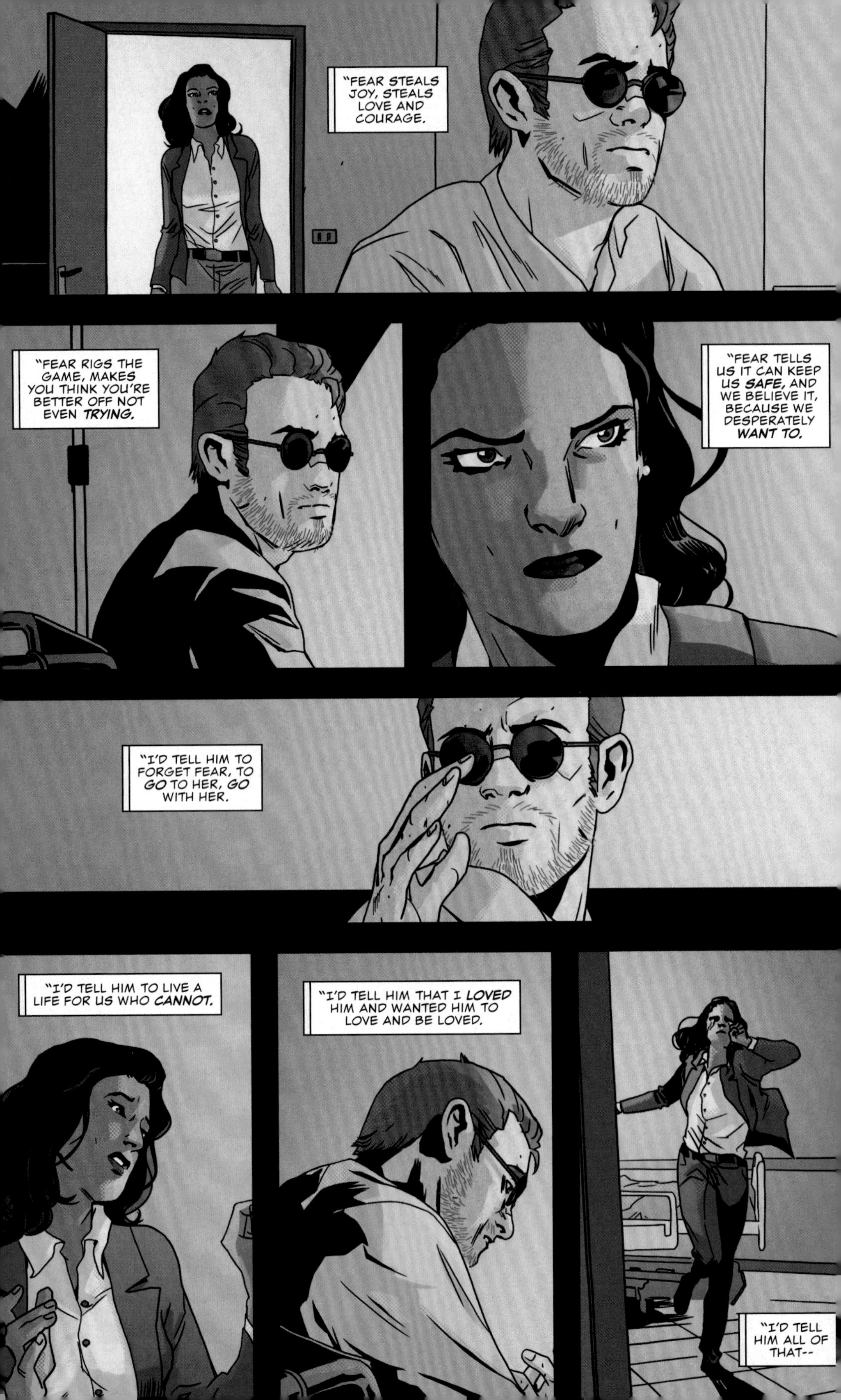
"FEAR STEALS JOY, STEALS LOVE AND COURAGE.
"FEAR RIGS THE GAME, MAKES YOU THINK YOU'RE BETTER OFF NOT EVEN TRYING.
"FEAR TELLS US IT CAN KEEP US SAFE, AND WE BELIEVE IT, BECAUSE WE DESPERATELY WANT TO.
"I'D TELL HIM TO FORGET FEAR, TO GO TO HER, GO WITH HER.
"I'D TELL HIM TO LIVE A LIFE FOR US WHO CANNOT.
"I'D TELL HIM THAT I LOVED HIM AND WANTED HIM TO LOVE AND BE LOVED.
"I'D TELL HIM ALL OF THAT--

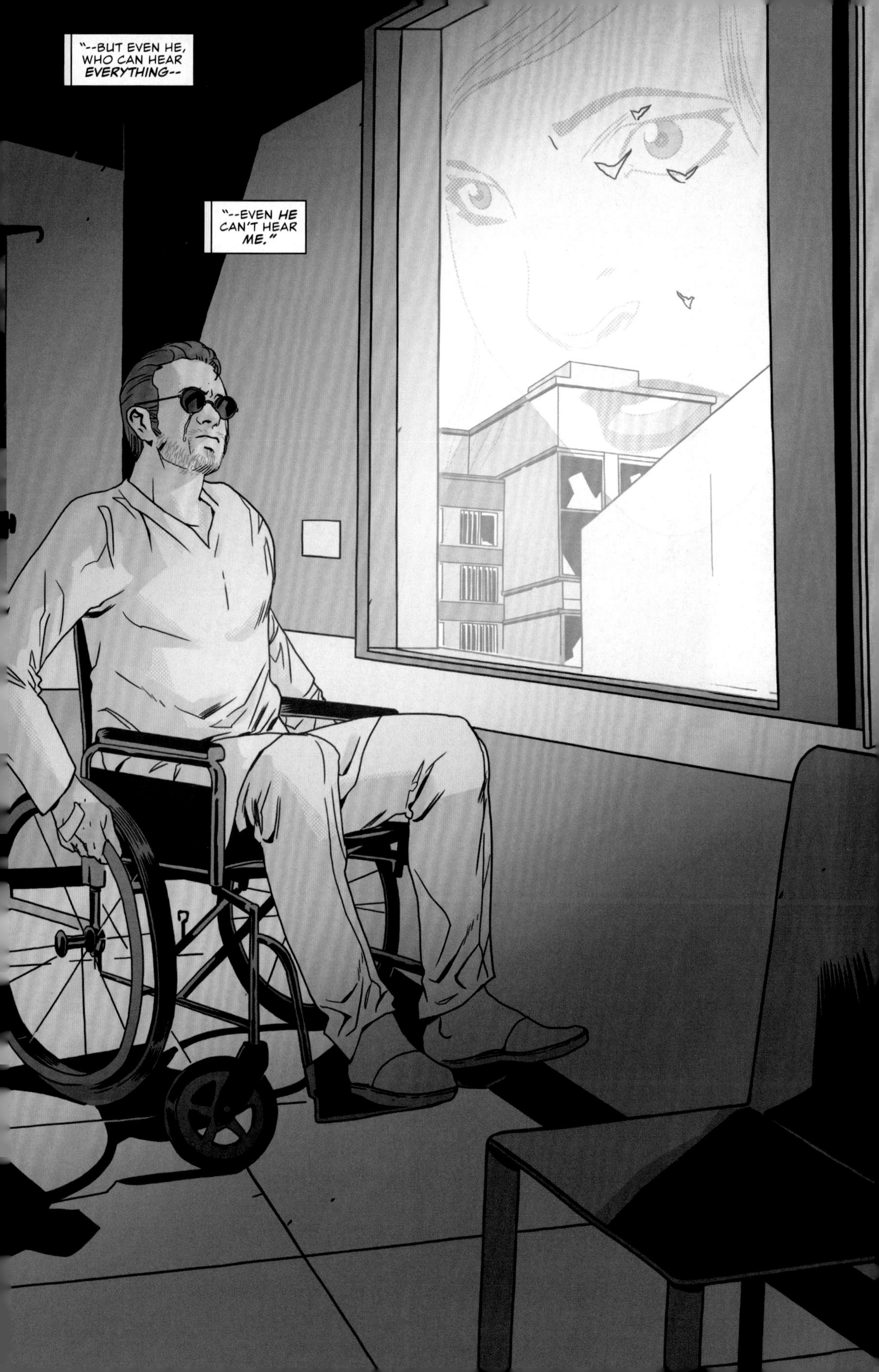
"--BUT EVEN HE, WHO CAN HEAR *EVERYTHING*--
"--EVEN *HE* CAN'T HEAR *ME*."

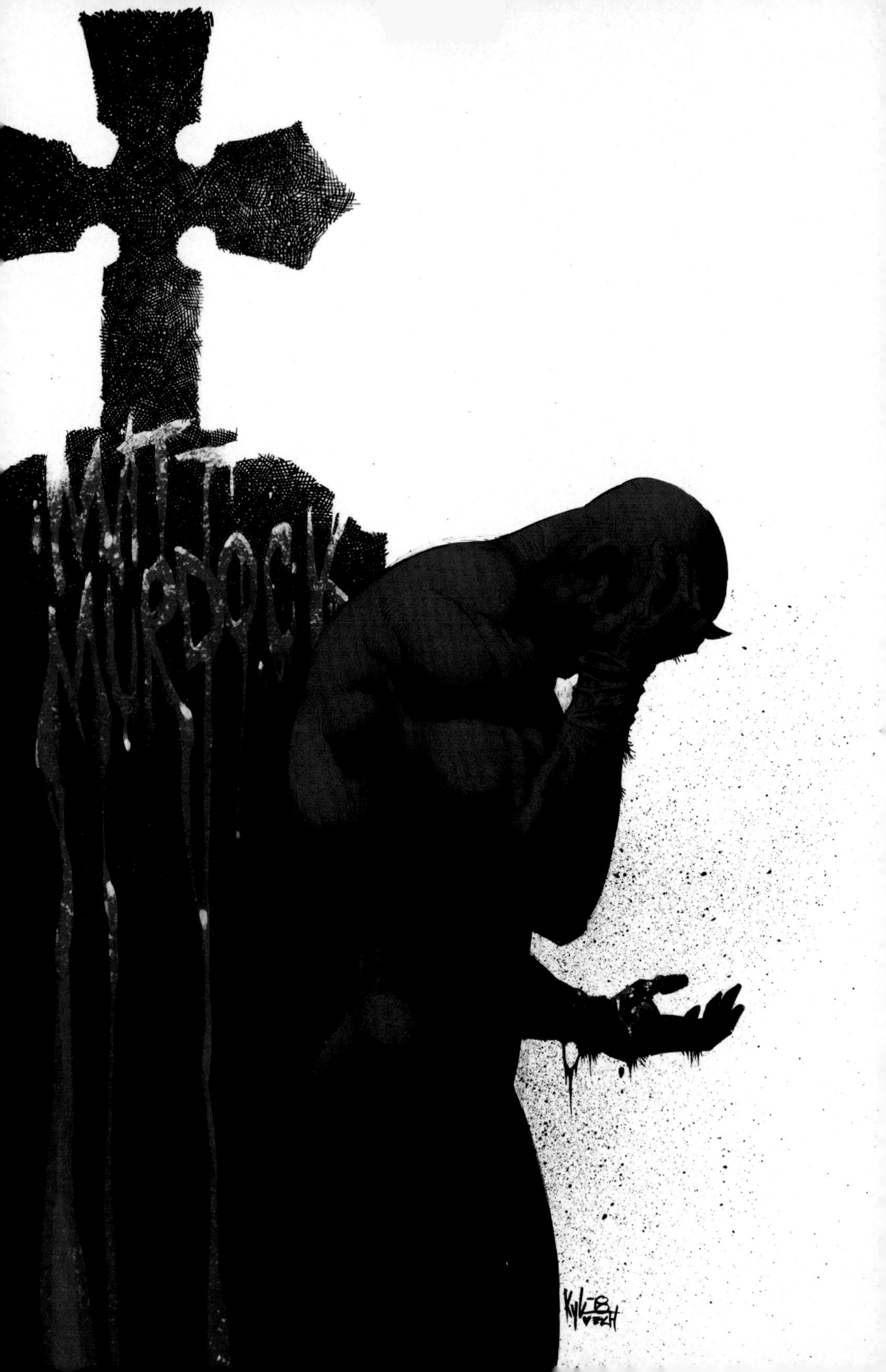
MATT MURDOCK

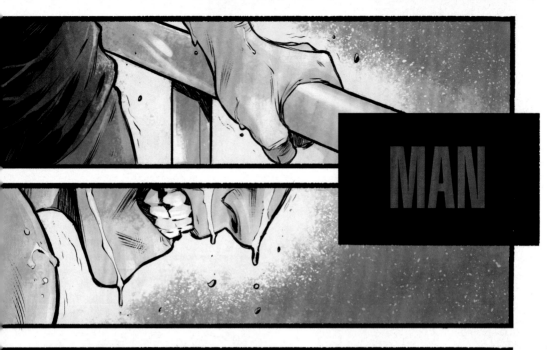

MAN

WITHOUT

FEAR

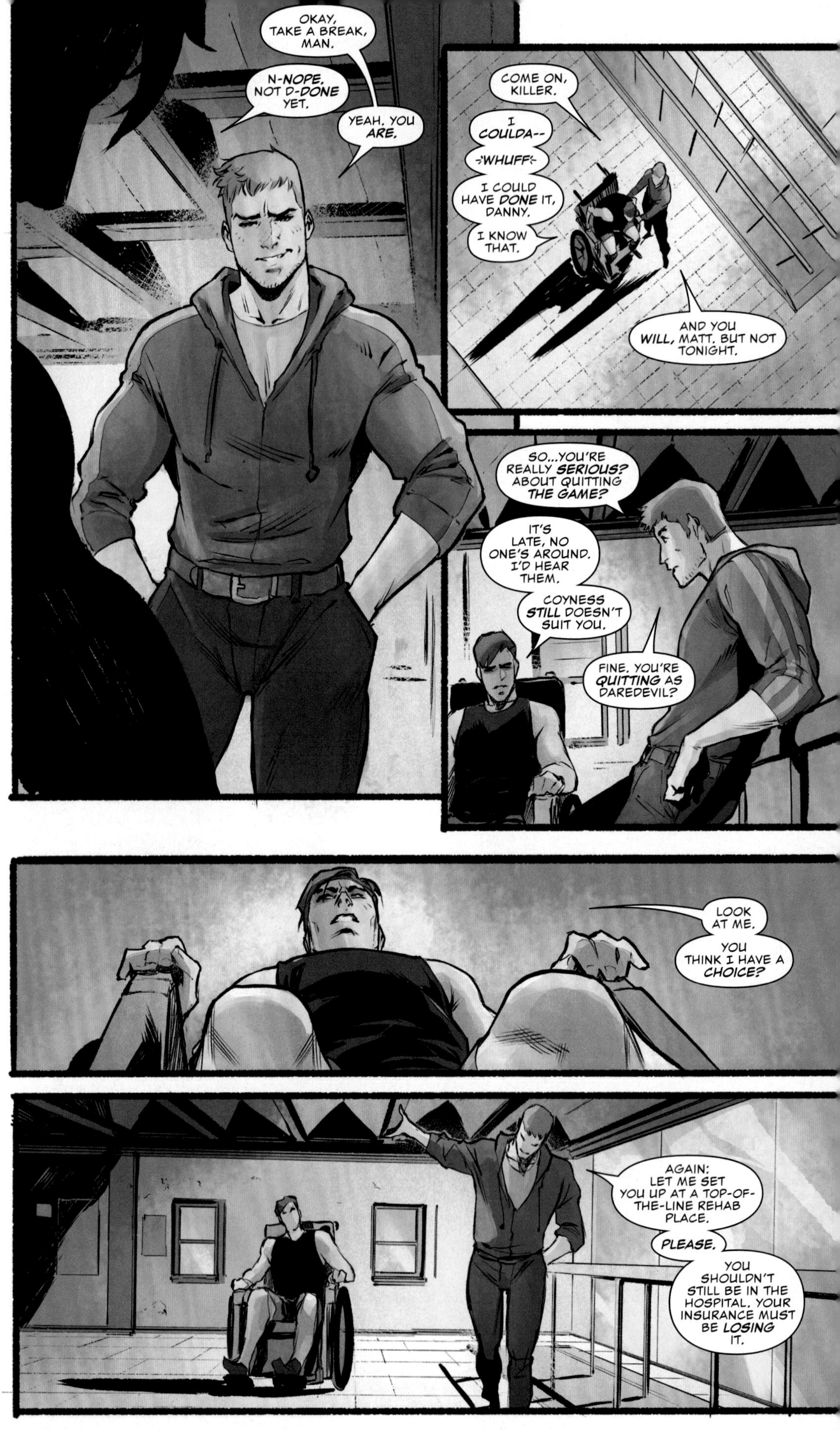
OKAY, TAKE A BREAK, MAN.
N-NOPE. NOT D-DONE YET.
YEAH. YOU ARE.
COME ON, KILLER.
I COULDA--
WHUFF
I COULD HAVE DONE IT, DANNY.
I KNOW THAT.
AND YOU WILL, MATT. BUT NOT TONIGHT.
SO...YOU'RE REALLY SERIOUS? ABOUT QUITTING THE GAME?
IT'S LATE, NO ONE'S AROUND. I'D HEAR THEM.
COYNESS STILL DOESN'T SUIT YOU.
FINE. YOU'RE QUITTING AS DAREDEVIL?
LOOK AT ME.
YOU THINK I HAVE A CHOICE?
AGAIN: LET ME SET YOU UP AT A TOP-OF-THE-LINE REHAB PLACE.
PLEASE.
YOU SHOULDN'T STILL BE IN THE HOSPITAL. YOUR INSURANCE MUST BE LOSING IT.

AGAIN: NO.

"WHEN I WAS A KID, I GREW UP IN CAPUOZZO'S GYM.

"THAT WAS WHERE MY *DAD* TRAINED.

"IT WAS A DUMP. ALL THE KITCHEN WAS A DUMP, REALLY."

THIS IS THE KIND OF PLACE I FEEL AT HOME IN.

NOW HELP ME TO THE BARS.

THEN.

THERE'S A *NEW* FOOLKILLER.

FOOLKILLER
E PLURIBUS UNUM
...RE BORN, WE CRY
...E COME/ TO THIS
...STAGE OF FOOLS.
...HAVE 24 HOURS TO LIVE

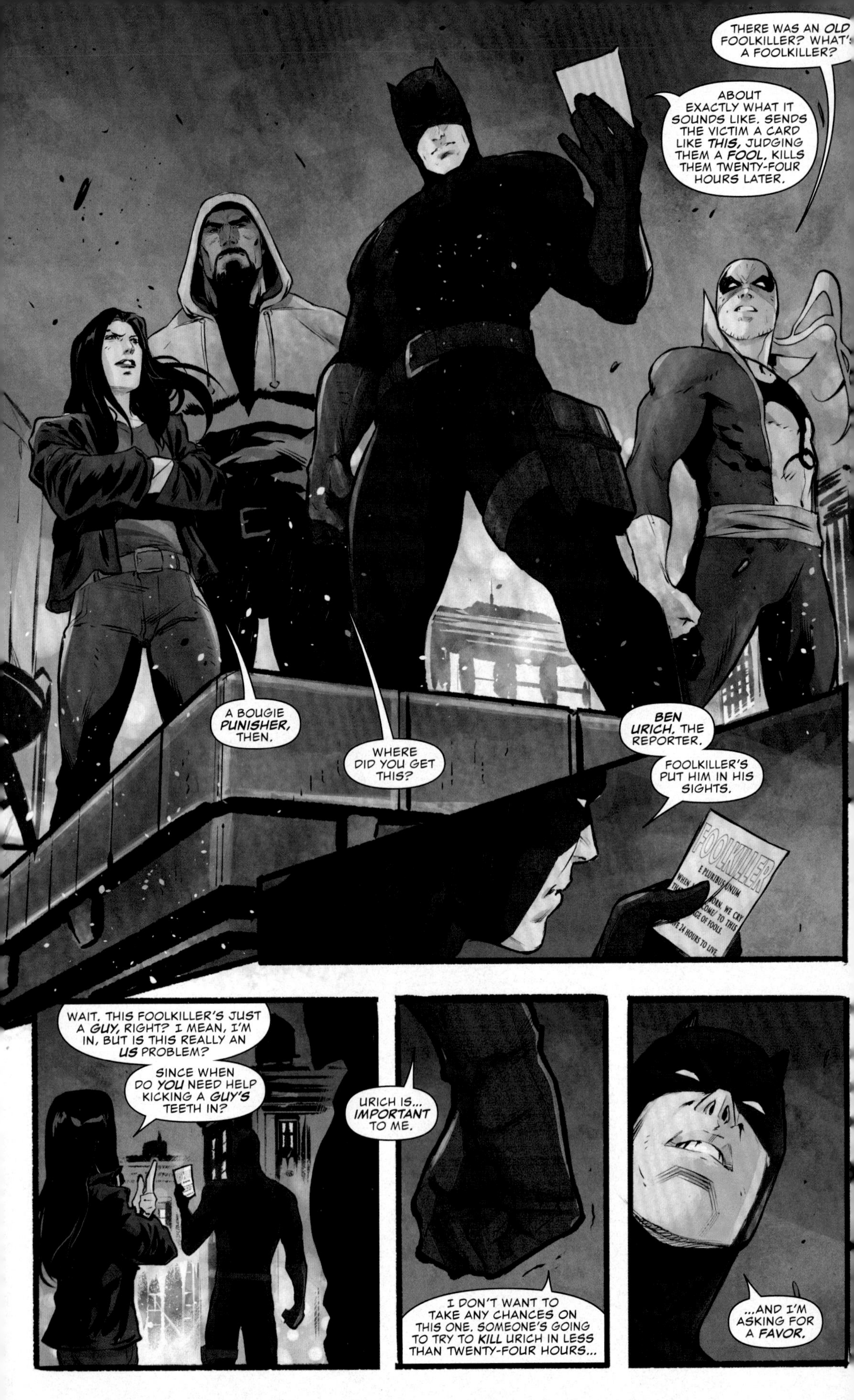
THERE WAS AN *OLD* FOOLKILLER? WHAT'S A FOOLKILLER?
ABOUT EXACTLY WHAT IT SOUNDS LIKE. SENDS THE VICTIM A CARD LIKE *THIS,* JUDGING THEM A *FOOL.* KILLS THEM TWENTY-FOUR HOURS LATER.
A BOUGIE *PUNISHER,* THEN.
WHERE DID YOU GET THIS?
BEN URICH, THE REPORTER.
FOOLKILLER'S PUT HIM IN HIS SIGHTS.
FOOLKILLER
E PLURIBUS UNUM
WAIT. THIS FOOLKILLER'S JUST A *GUY,* RIGHT? I MEAN, I'M IN, BUT IS THIS REALLY AN *US* PROBLEM?
SINCE WHEN DO *YOU* NEED HELP KICKING A *GUY'S* TEETH IN?
URICH IS... *IMPORTANT* TO ME.
I DON'T WANT TO TAKE ANY CHANCES ON THIS ONE. SOMEONE'S GOING TO TRY TO *KILL* URICH IN LESS THAN TWENTY-FOUR HOURS...
...AND I'M ASKING FOR A *FAVOR.*

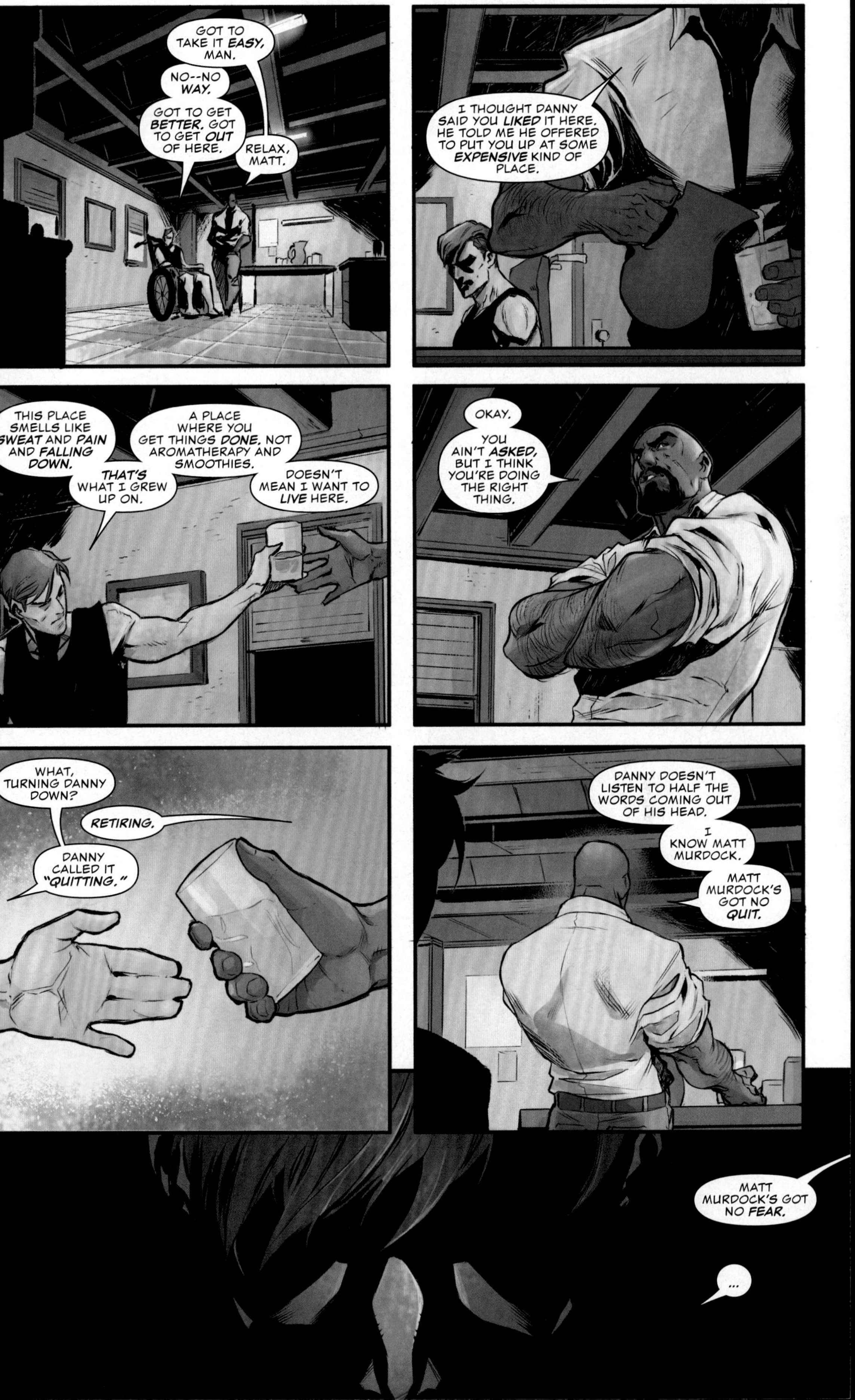

GOT TO TAKE IT EASY, MAN.
NO--NO WAY.
GOT TO GET BETTER. GOT TO GET OUT OF HERE.
RELAX, MATT.
I THOUGHT DANNY SAID YOU LIKED IT HERE. HE TOLD ME HE OFFERED TO PUT YOU UP AT SOME EXPENSIVE KIND OF PLACE.
THIS PLACE SMELLS LIKE SWEAT AND PAIN AND FALLING DOWN.
A PLACE WHERE YOU GET THINGS DONE. NOT AROMATHERAPY AND SMOOTHIES.
THAT'S WHAT I GREW UP ON.
DOESN'T MEAN I WANT TO LIVE HERE.
OKAY.
YOU AIN'T ASKED, BUT I THINK YOU'RE DOING THE RIGHT THING.
WHAT, TURNING DANNY DOWN?
RETIRING.
DANNY CALLED IT "QUITTING."
DANNY DOESN'T LISTEN TO HALF THE WORDS COMING OUT OF HIS HEAD.
I KNOW MATT MURDOCK.
MATT MURDOCK'S GOT NO QUIT.
MATT MURDOCK'S GOT NO FEAR.
...

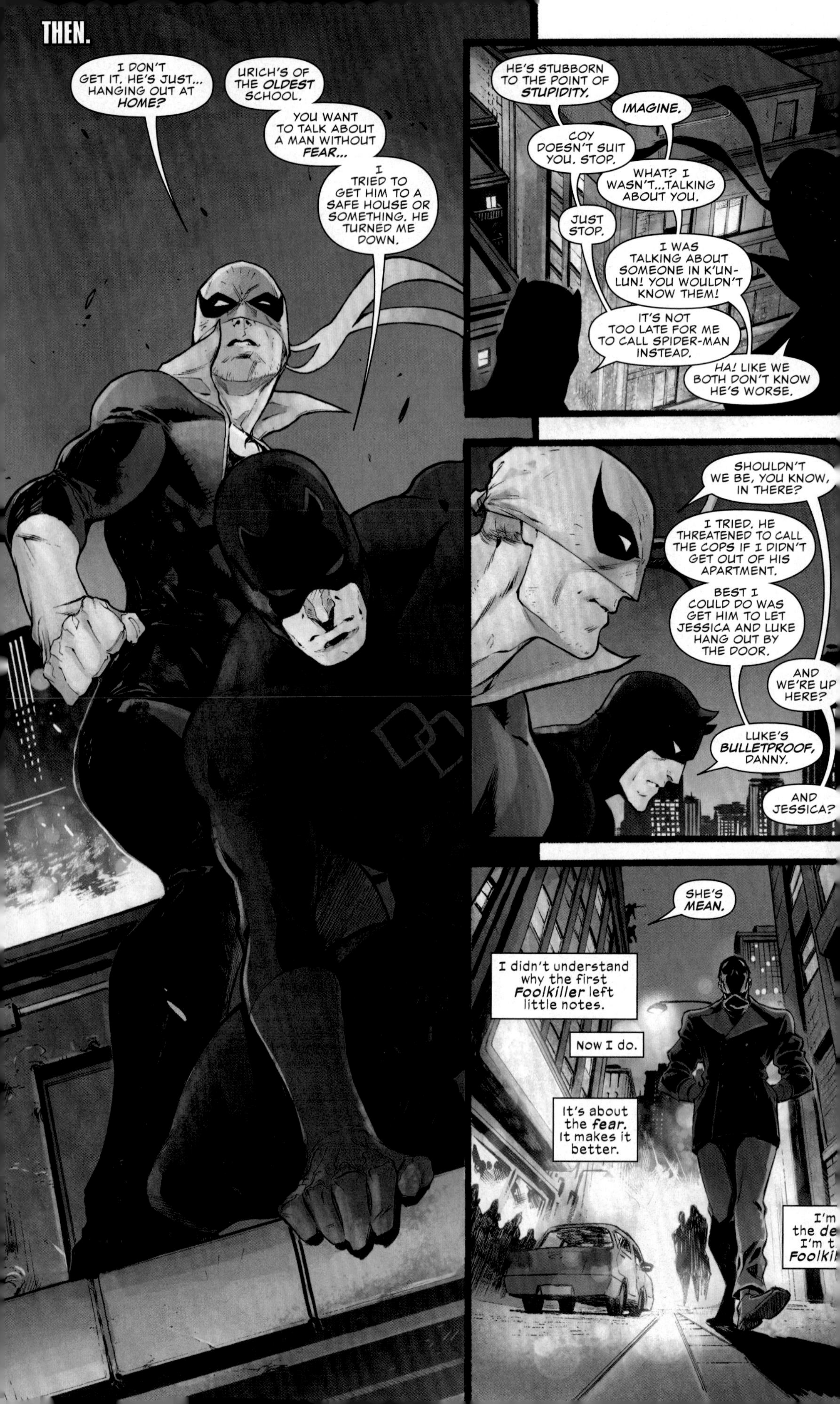

THEN.
I DON'T GET IT. HE'S JUST... HANGING OUT AT HOME?
URICH'S OF THE OLDEST SCHOOL.
YOU WANT TO TALK ABOUT A MAN WITHOUT FEAR...
I TRIED TO GET HIM TO A SAFE HOUSE OR SOMETHING. HE TURNED ME DOWN.
HE'S STUBBORN TO THE POINT OF STUPIDITY.
IMAGINE.
COY DOESN'T SUIT YOU. STOP.
WHAT? I WASN'T...TALKING ABOUT YOU.
JUST STOP.
I WAS TALKING ABOUT SOMEONE IN K'UN-LUN! YOU WOULDN'T KNOW THEM!
IT'S NOT TOO LATE FOR ME TO CALL SPIDER-MAN INSTEAD.
HA! LIKE WE BOTH DON'T KNOW HE'S WORSE.
SHOULDN'T WE BE, YOU KNOW, IN THERE?
I TRIED. HE THREATENED TO CALL THE COPS IF I DIDN'T GET OUT OF HIS APARTMENT.
BEST I COULD DO WAS GET HIM TO LET JESSICA AND LUKE HANG OUT BY THE DOOR.
AND WE'RE UP HERE?
LUKE'S BULLETPROOF, DANNY.
AND JESSICA?
SHE'S MEAN.
I didn't understand why the first Foolkiller left little notes.
Now I do.
It's about the fear. It makes it better.

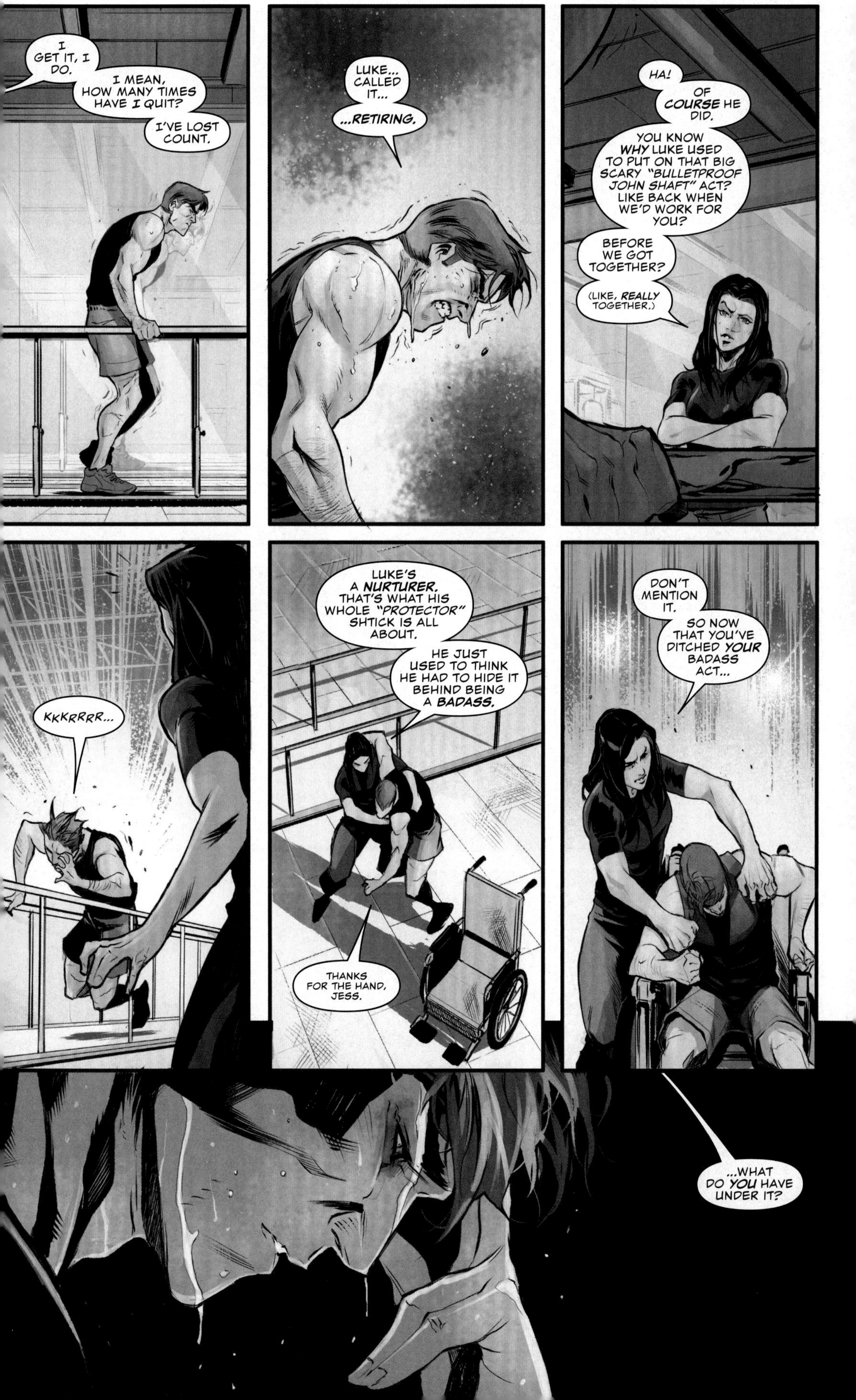
I GET IT, I DO.
I MEAN, HOW MANY TIMES HAVE *I* QUIT?
I'VE LOST COUNT.
LUKE... CALLED IT...
...RETIRING.
HA!
OF *COURSE* HE DID.
YOU KNOW *WHY* LUKE USED TO PUT ON THAT BIG SCARY *"BULLETPROOF JOHN SHAFT"* ACT? LIKE BACK WHEN WE'D WORK FOR YOU?
BEFORE WE GOT TOGETHER?
(LIKE, *REALLY* TOGETHER.)
KKKRRRR...
LUKE'S A *NURTURER.* THAT'S WHAT HIS WHOLE *"PROTECTOR"* SHTICK IS ALL ABOUT.
HE JUST USED TO THINK HE HAD TO HIDE IT BEHIND BEING A *BADASS.*
THANKS FOR THE HAND, JESS.
DON'T MENTION IT.
SO NOW THAT YOU'VE DITCHED *YOUR* BADASS ACT...
...WHAT DO *YOU* HAVE UNDER IT?

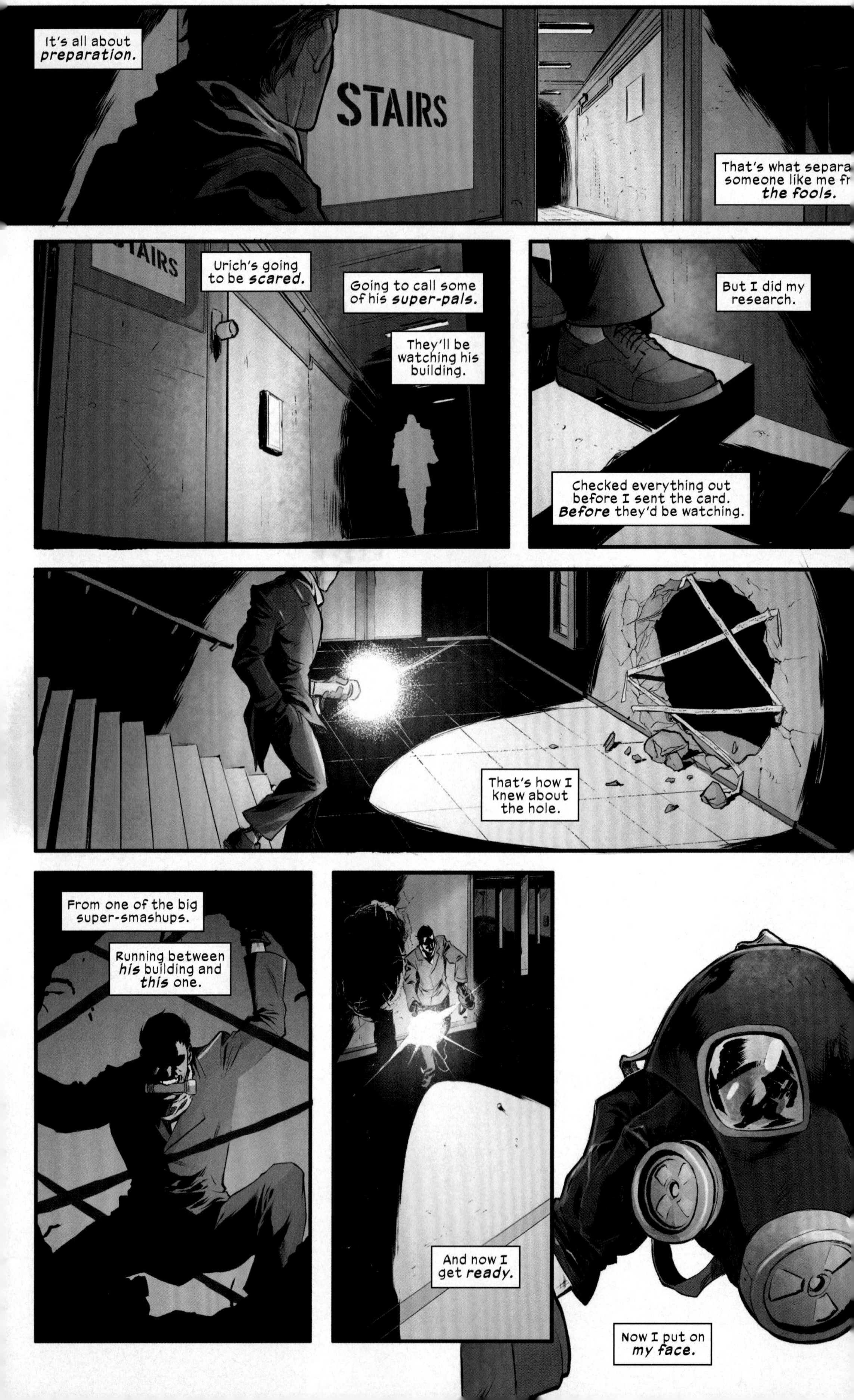
It's all about preparation.
STAIRS
That's what separa someone like me fr the fools.
STAIRS
Urich's going to be scared.
Going to call some of his super-pals.
They'll be watching his building.
But I did my research.
Checked everything out before I sent the card. Before they'd be watching.
That's how I knew about the hole.
From one of the big super-smashups.
Running between his building and this one.
And now I get ready.
Now I put on my face.

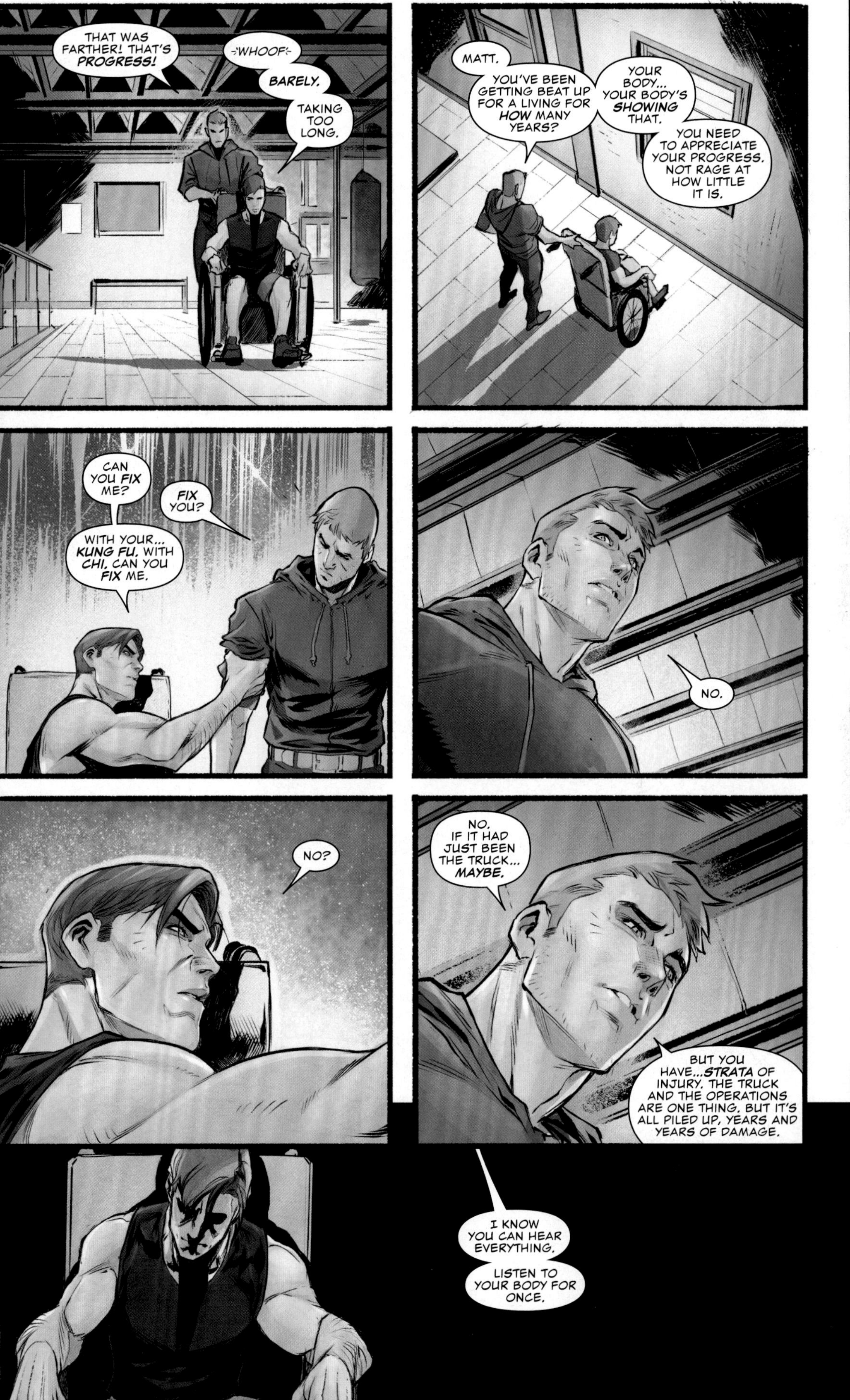

THAT WAS FARTHER! THAT'S PROGRESS!
-WHOOF-
BARELY.
TAKING TOO LONG.
MATT.
YOU'VE BEEN GETTING BEAT UP FOR A LIVING FOR HOW MANY YEARS?
YOUR BODY... YOUR BODY'S SHOWING THAT.
YOU NEED TO APPRECIATE YOUR PROGRESS, NOT RAGE AT HOW LITTLE IT IS.
CAN YOU FIX ME?
FIX YOU?
WITH YOUR... KUNG FU. WITH CHI. CAN YOU FIX ME.
NO.
NO?
NO. IF IT HAD JUST BEEN THE TRUCK... MAYBE.
BUT YOU HAVE...STRATA OF INJURY. THE TRUCK AND THE OPERATIONS ARE ONE THING, BUT IT'S ALL PILED UP, YEARS AND YEARS OF DAMAGE.
I KNOW YOU CAN HEAR EVERYTHING.
LISTEN TO YOUR BODY FOR ONCE.

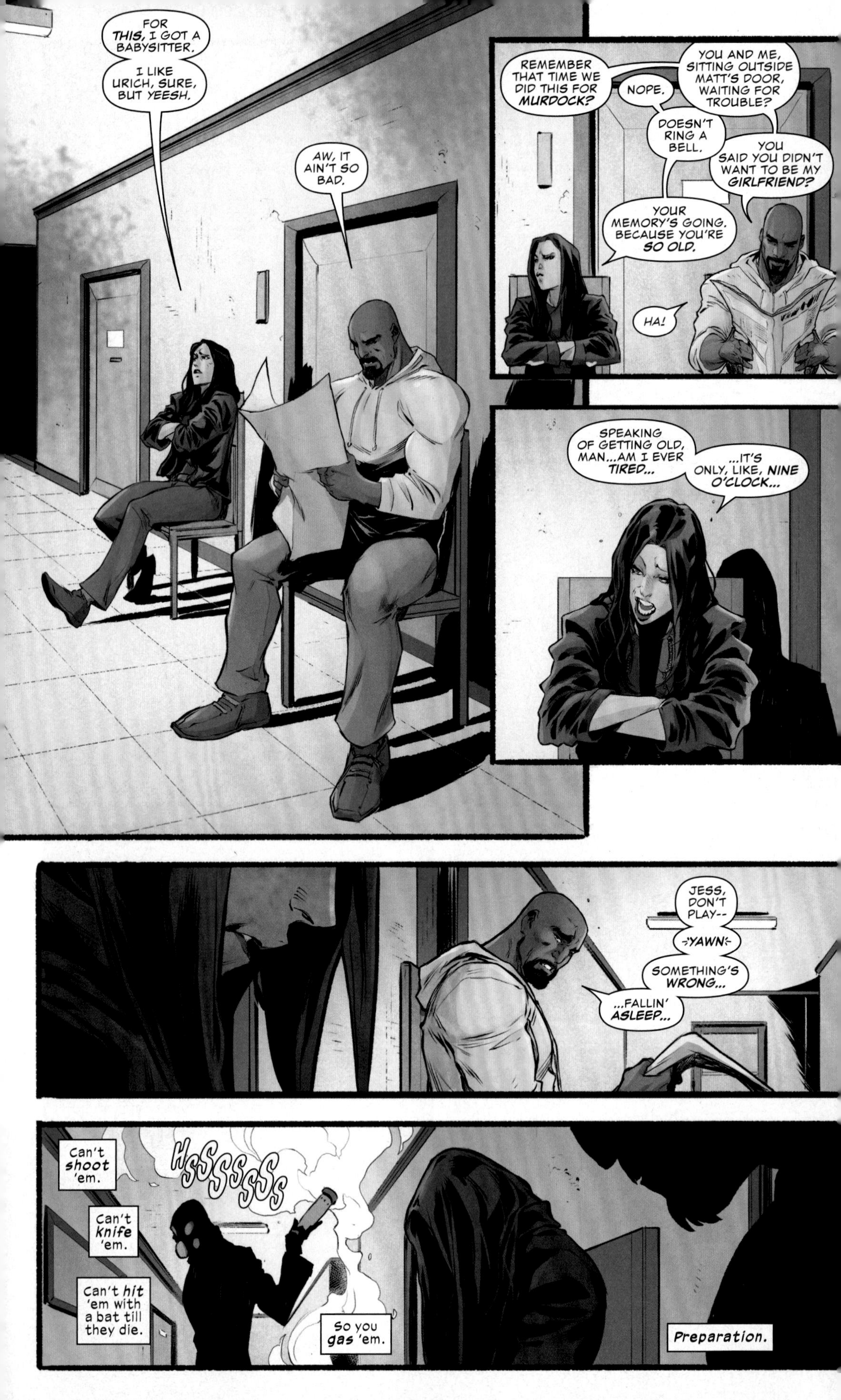

FOR THIS, I GOT A BABYSITTER.
I LIKE URICH, SURE, BUT YEESH.
AW, IT AIN'T SO BAD.
REMEMBER THAT TIME WE DID THIS FOR MURDOCK?
YOU AND ME, SITTING OUTSIDE MATT'S DOOR, WAITING FOR TROUBLE?
NOPE.
DOESN'T RING A BELL.
YOU SAID YOU DIDN'T WANT TO BE MY GIRLFRIEND?
YOUR MEMORY'S GOING. BECAUSE YOU'RE SO OLD.
HA!
SPEAKING OF GETTING OLD, MAN...AM I EVER TIRED...
...IT'S ONLY, LIKE, NINE O'CLOCK...
JESS, DON'T PLAY--
YAWN
SOMETHING'S WRONG...
...FALLIN' ASLEEP...
Can't shoot 'em.
HSSSSSSSS
Can't knife 'em.
Can't hit 'em with a bat till they die.
So you gas 'em.
Preparation.

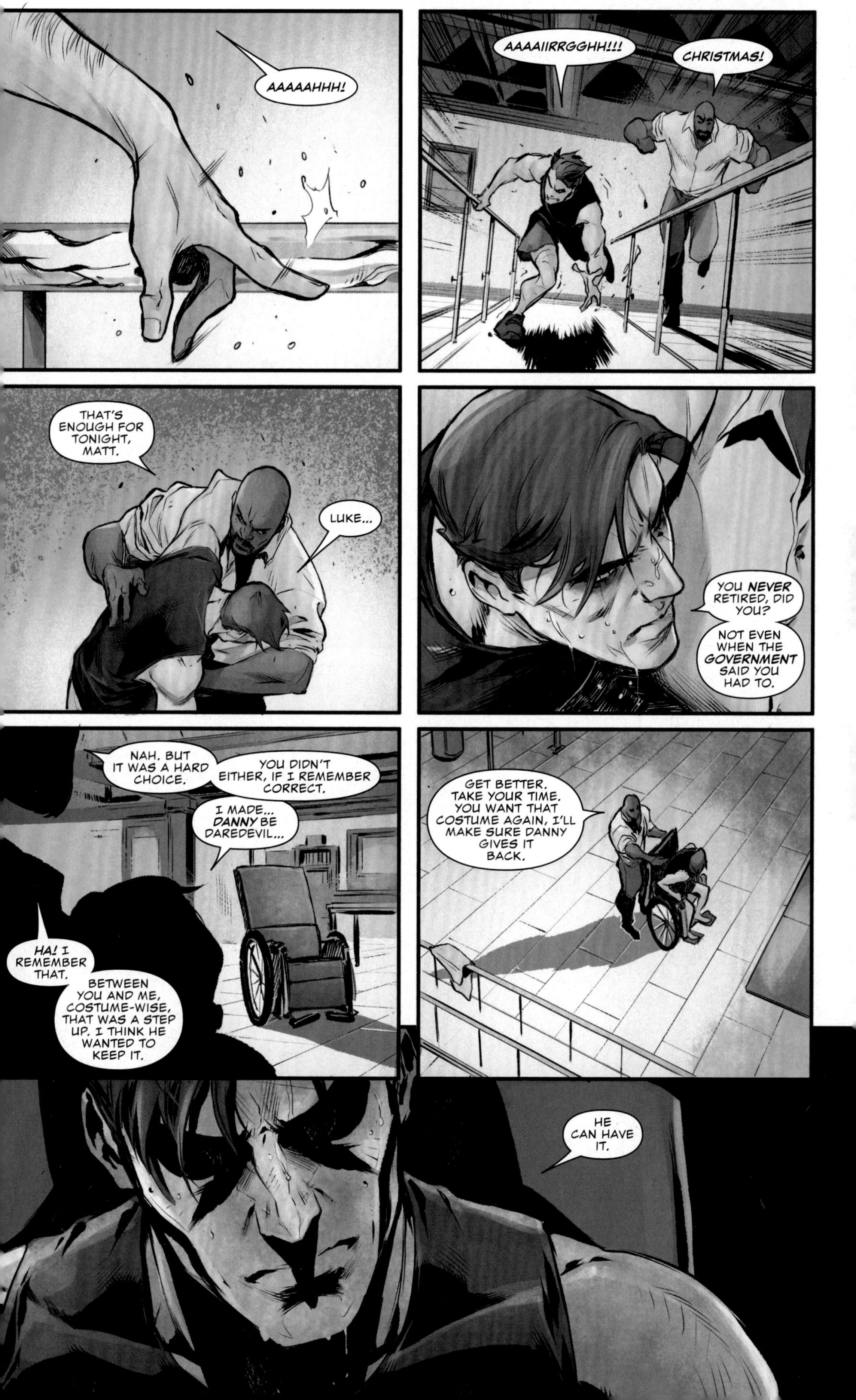

AAAAAHHH!
AAAAIIRRGGHH!!!
CHRISTMAS!
THAT'S ENOUGH FOR TONIGHT, MATT.
LUKE...
YOU NEVER RETIRED, DID YOU?
NOT EVEN WHEN THE GOVERNMENT SAID YOU HAD TO.
NAH. BUT IT WAS A HARD CHOICE.
YOU DIDN'T EITHER, IF I REMEMBER CORRECT.
I MADE... DANNY BE DAREDEVIL...
HA! I REMEMBER THAT.
BETWEEN YOU AND ME, COSTUME-WISE, THAT WAS A STEP UP. I THINK HE WANTED TO KEEP IT.
GET BETTER. TAKE YOUR TIME. YOU WANT THAT COSTUME AGAIN, I'LL MAKE SURE DANNY GIVES IT BACK.
HE CAN HAVE IT.

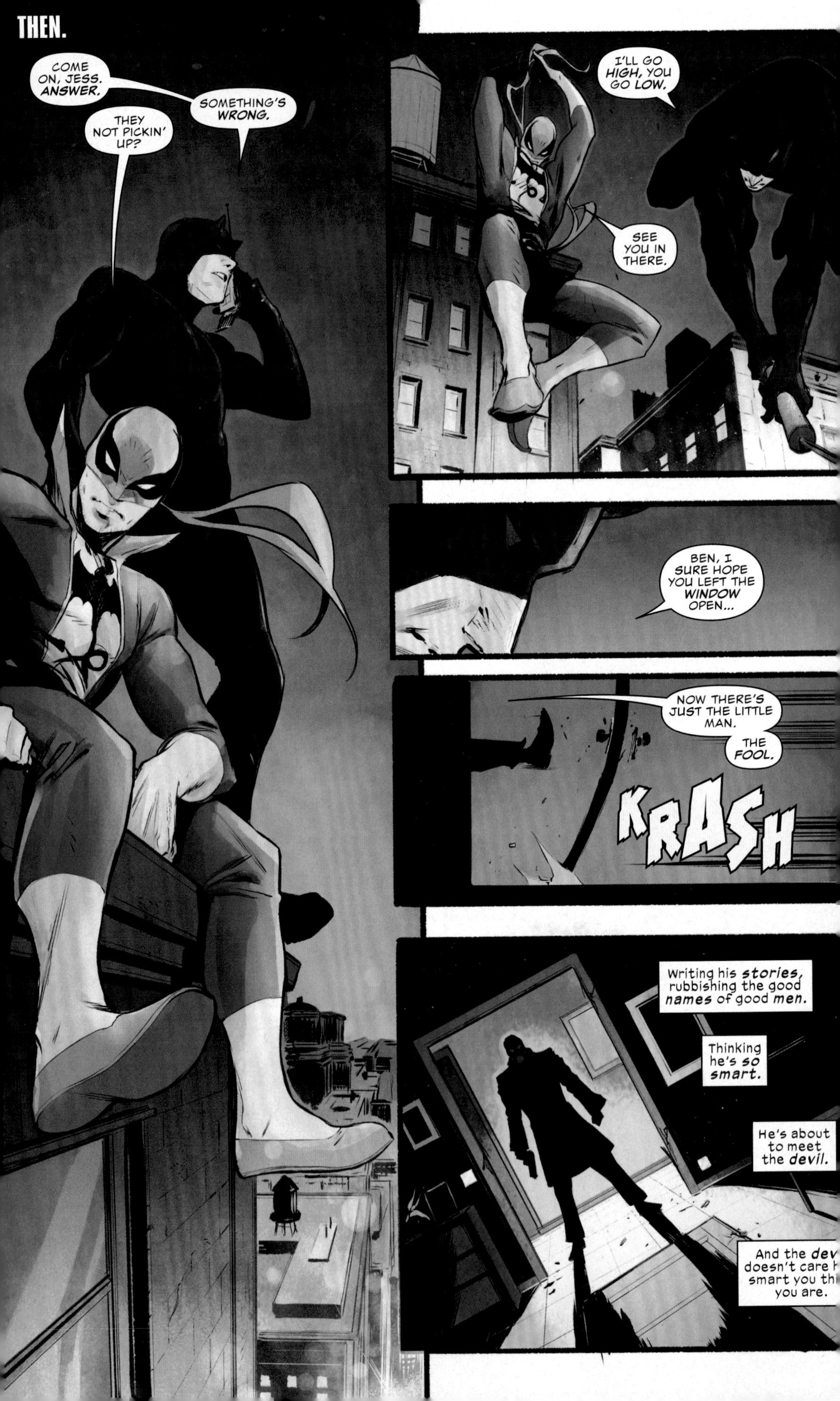
THEN.
COME ON, JESS. ANSWER.
SOMETHING'S WRONG.
THEY NOT PICKIN' UP?
I'LL GO HIGH, YOU GO LOW.
SEE YOU IN THERE.
BEN, I SURE HOPE YOU LEFT THE WINDOW OPEN...
NOW THERE'S JUST THE LITTLE MAN.
THE FOOL.
KRASH
Writing his stories, rubbishing the good names of good men.
Thinking he's so smart.
He's about to meet the devil.
And the dev
doesn't care h
smart you th
you are.

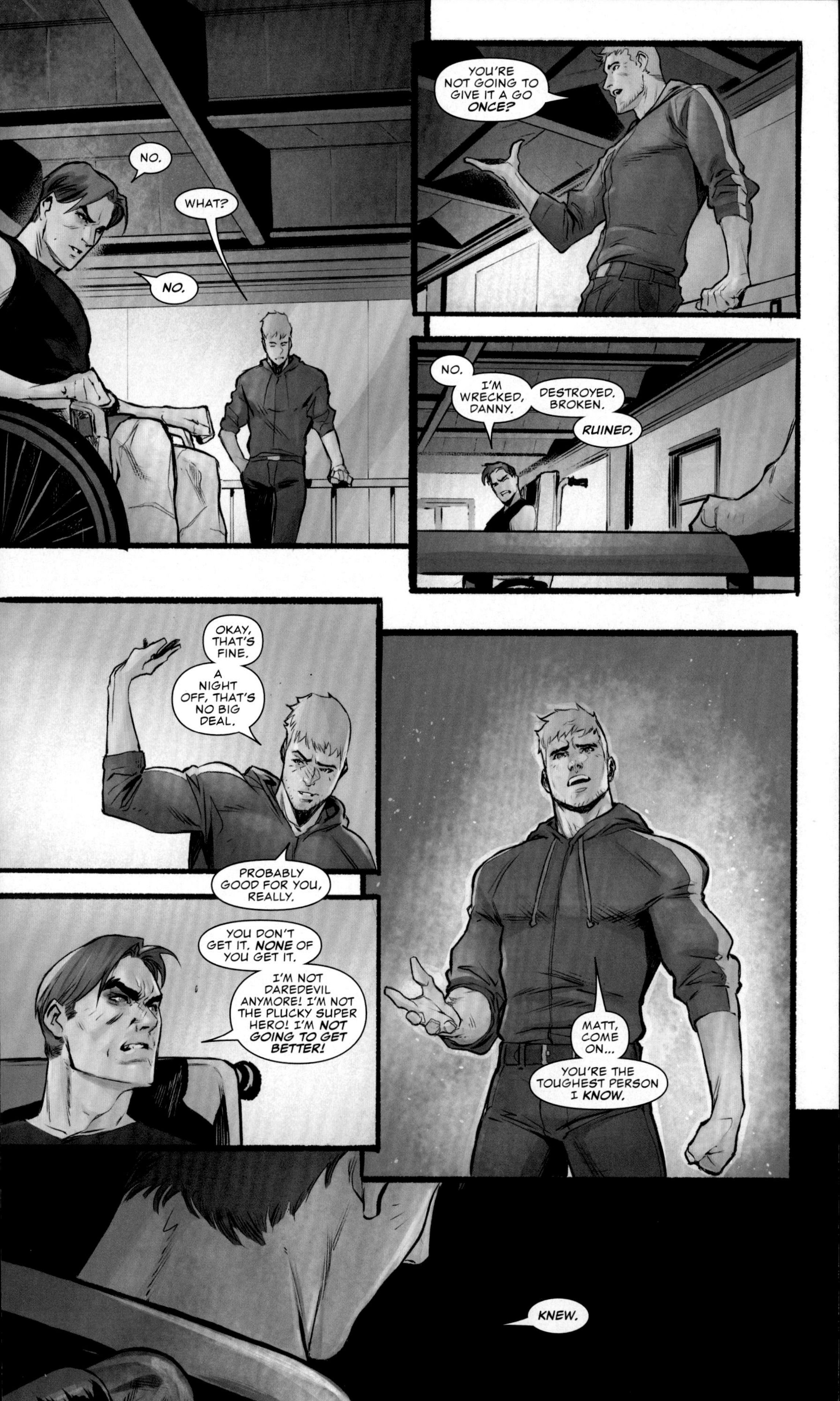

NO.
WHAT?
NO.
YOU'RE NOT GOING TO GIVE IT A GO ONCE?
NO.
I'M WRECKED, DANNY.
DESTROYED. BROKEN.
RUINED.
OKAY, THAT'S FINE.
A NIGHT OFF, THAT'S NO BIG DEAL.
PROBABLY GOOD FOR YOU, REALLY.
YOU DON'T GET IT. NONE OF YOU GET IT.
I'M NOT DAREDEVIL ANYMORE! I'M NOT THE PLUCKY SUPER HERO! I'M NOT GOING TO GET BETTER!
MATT, COME ON...
YOU'RE THE TOUGHEST PERSON I KNOW.
KNEW.

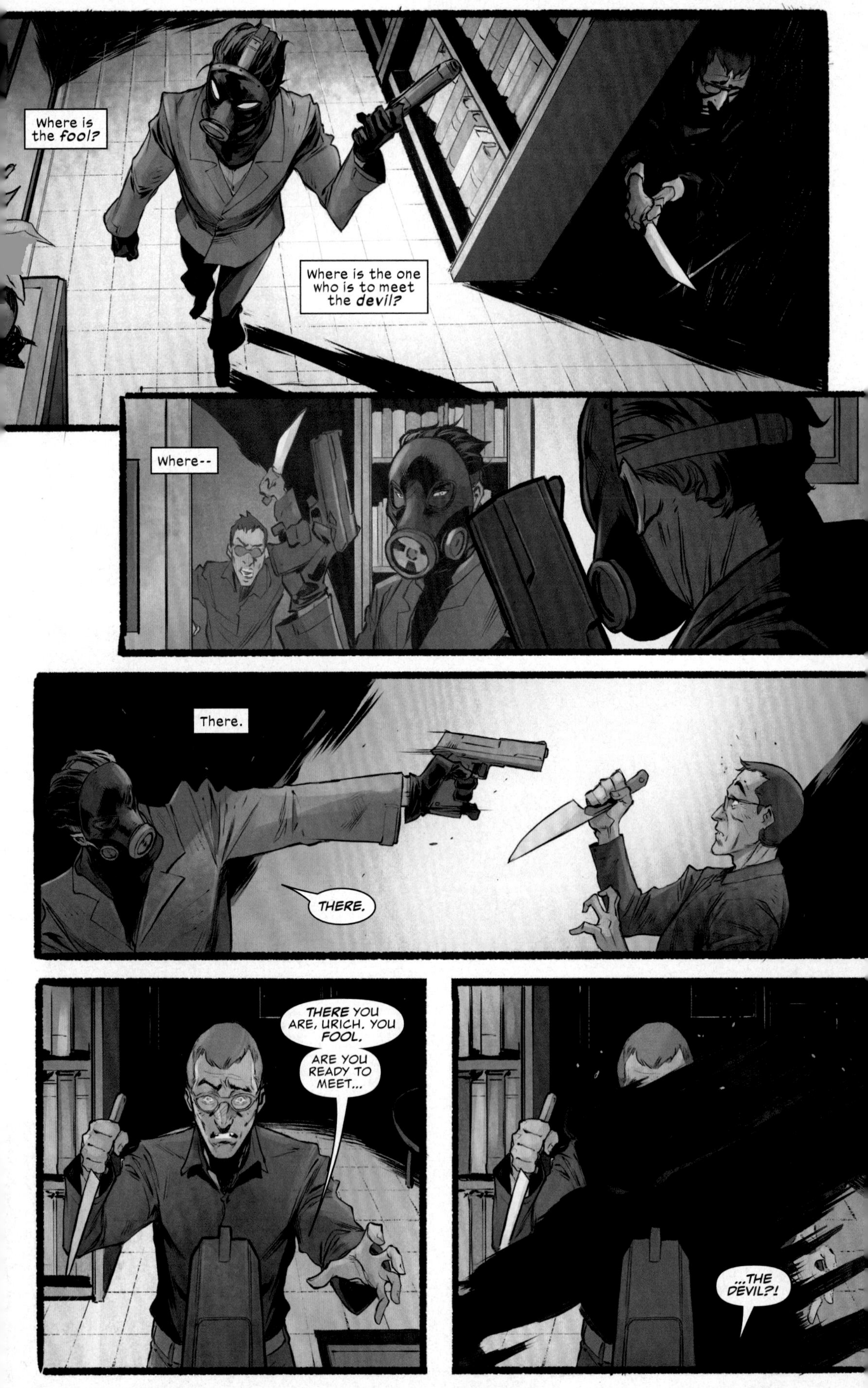

Where is the *fool?*
Where is the one who is to meet the *devil?*
Where--
There.
THERE.
THERE YOU ARE, URICH. YOU *FOOL.*
ARE YOU READY TO MEET...
...THE *DEVIL?!*

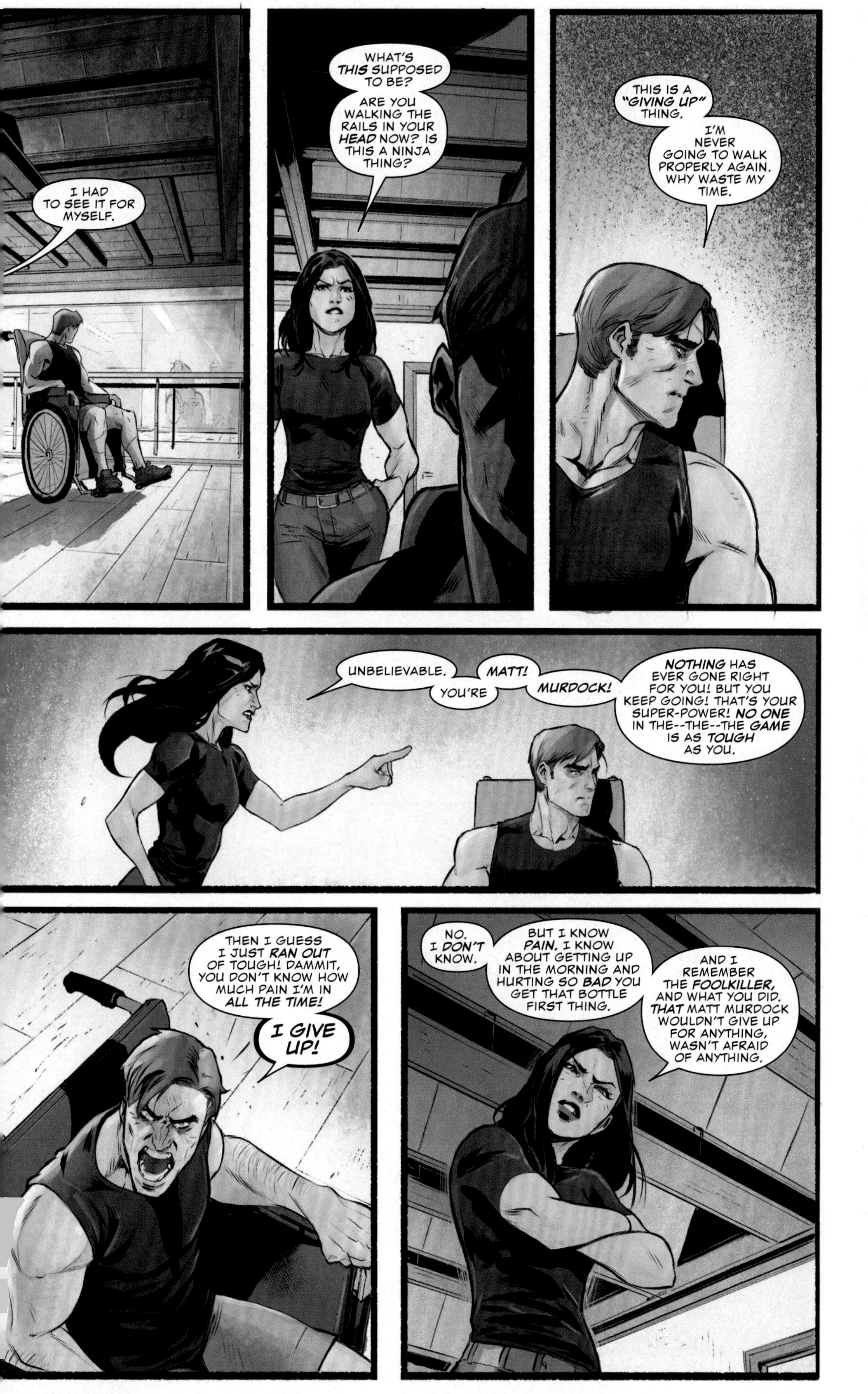

I HAD TO SEE IT FOR MYSELF.
WHAT'S *THIS* SUPPOSED TO BE?
ARE YOU WALKING THE RAILS IN YOUR *HEAD* NOW? IS THIS A NINJA THING?
THIS IS A *"GIVING UP"* THING.
I'M NEVER GOING TO WALK PROPERLY AGAIN. WHY WASTE MY TIME.
UNBELIEVABLE.
YOU'RE
MATT!
MURDOCK!
NOTHING HAS EVER GONE RIGHT FOR YOU! BUT YOU KEEP GOING! THAT'S YOUR SUPER-POWER! *NO ONE* IN THE--THE--THE *GAME* IS AS *TOUGH* AS YOU.
THEN I GUESS I JUST *RAN OUT* OF TOUGH! DAMMIT, YOU DON'T KNOW HOW MUCH PAIN I'M IN *ALL THE TIME!*
I GIVE UP!
NO, I *DON'T* KNOW.
BUT I KNOW *PAIN.* I KNOW ABOUT GETTING UP IN THE MORNING AND HURTING SO *BAD* YOU GET THAT BOTTLE FIRST THING.
AND I REMEMBER THE *FOOLKILLER,* AND WHAT YOU DID. *THAT* MATT MURDOCK WOULDN'T GIVE UP FOR ANYTHING, WASN'T AFRAID OF ANYTHING.

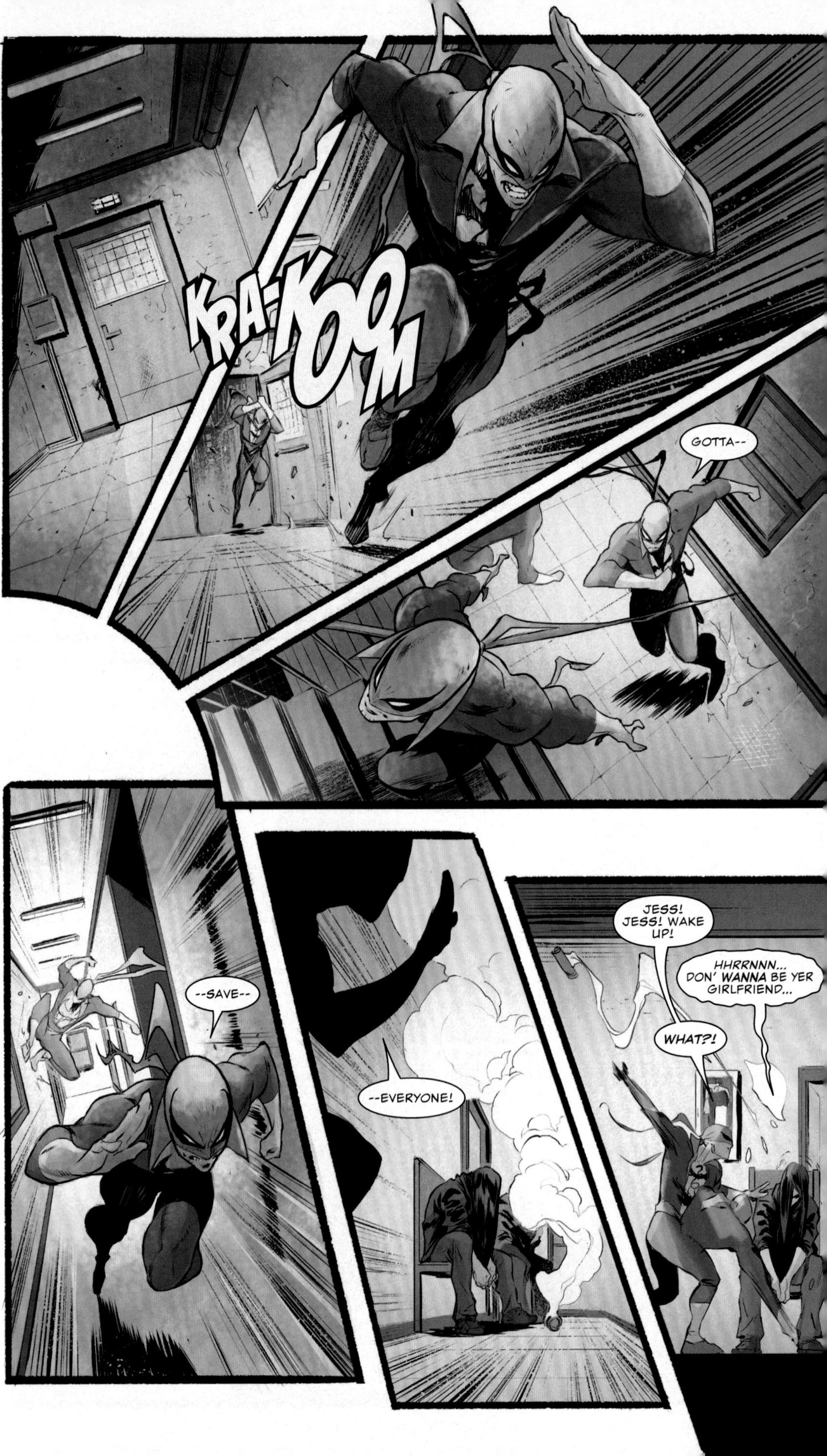
KRA-KOOM
GOTTA--
--SAVE--
--EVERYONE!
JESS! JESS! WAKE UP!
HHRRNNN... DON' WANNA BE YER GIRLFRIEND...
WHAT?!

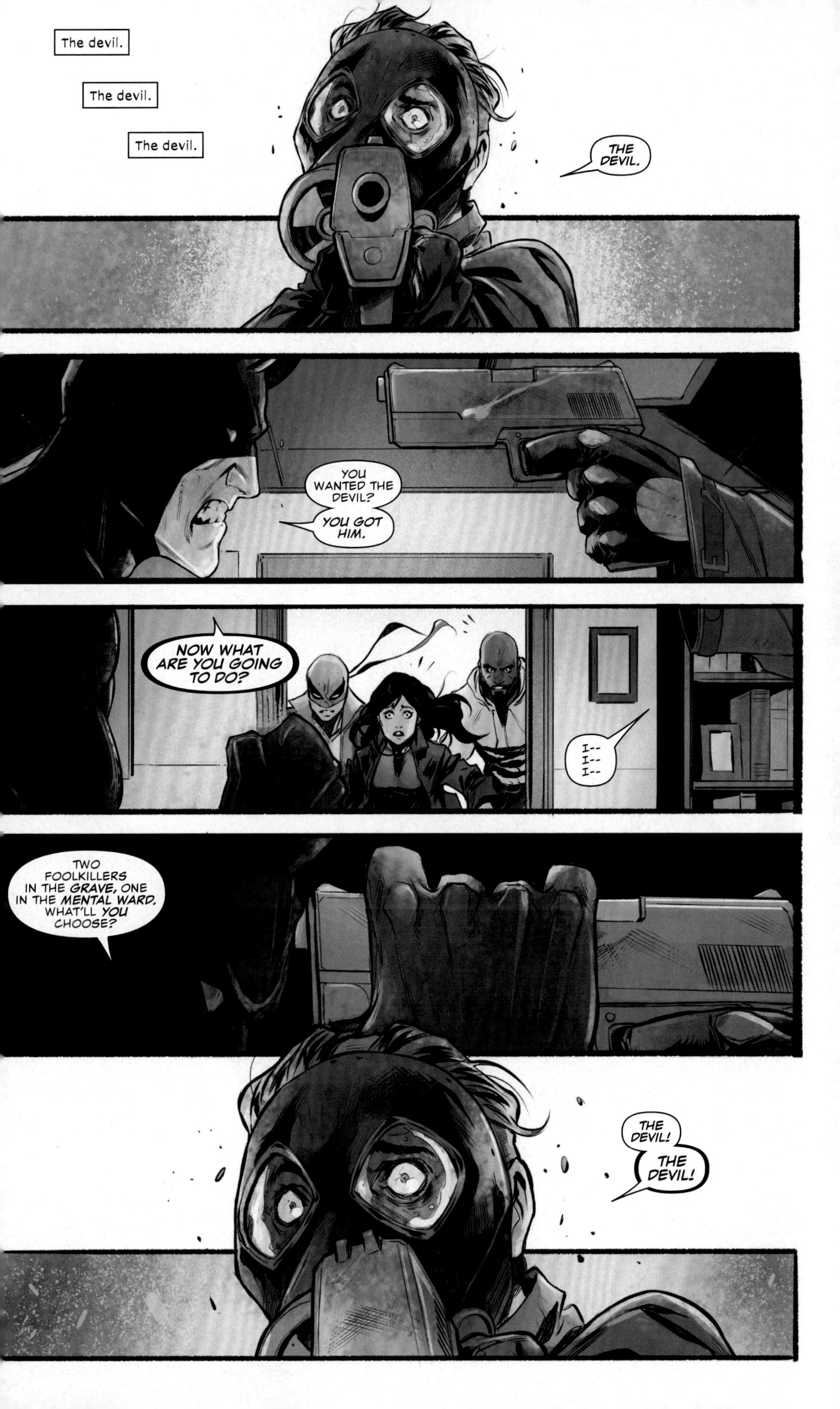
The devil.
The devil.
The devil.
THE DEVIL.
YOU WANTED THE DEVIL?
YOU GOT HIM.
NOW WHAT ARE YOU GOING TO DO?
I-- I-- I--
TWO FOOLKILLERS IN THE GRAVE, ONE IN THE MENTAL WARD. WHAT'LL YOU CHOOSE?
THE DEVIL!
THE DEVIL!

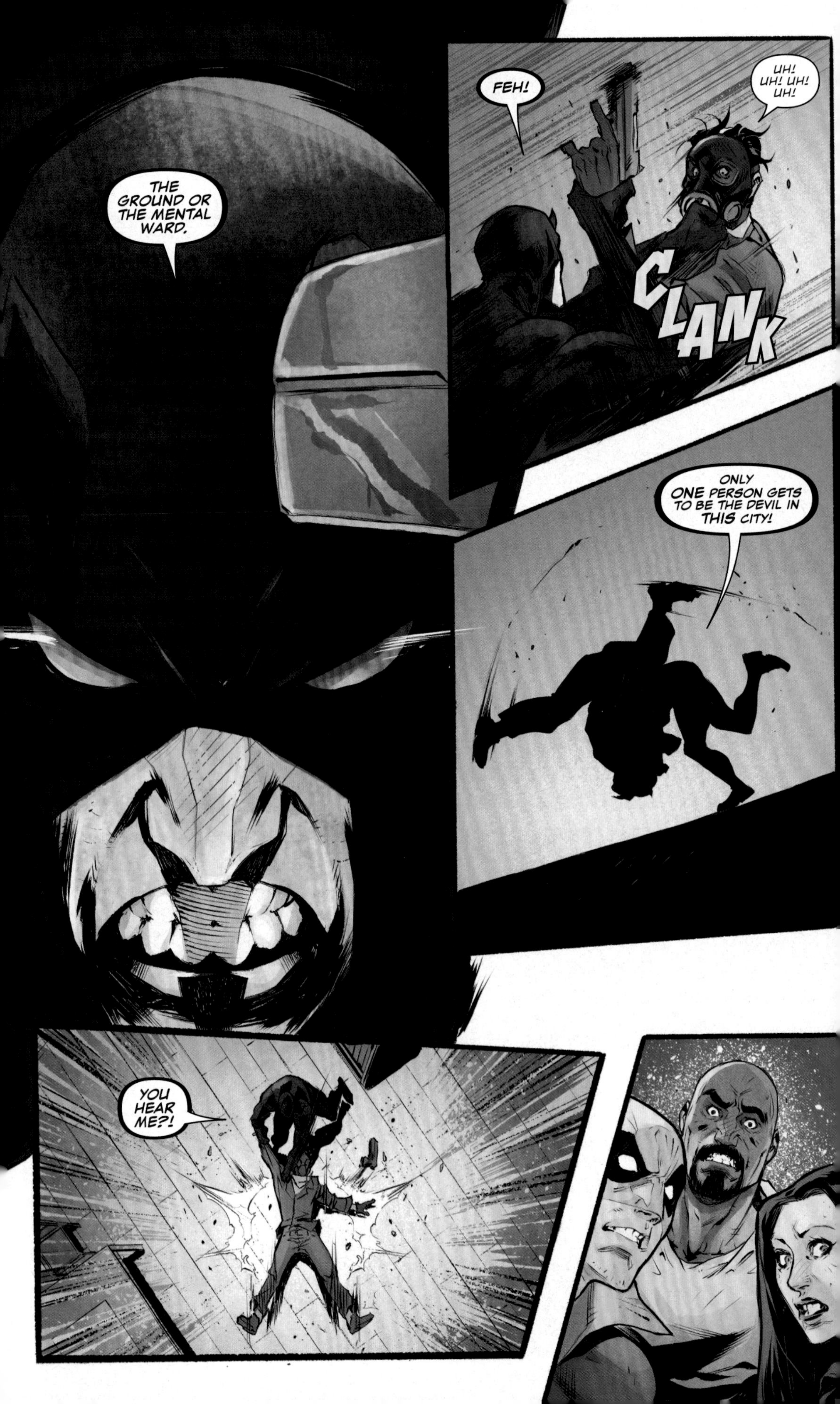
THE GROUND OR THE MENTAL WARD.
FEH!
UH! UH! UH! UH!
CLANK
ONLY ONE PERSON GETS TO BE THE DEVIL IN THIS CITY!
YOU HEAR ME?!

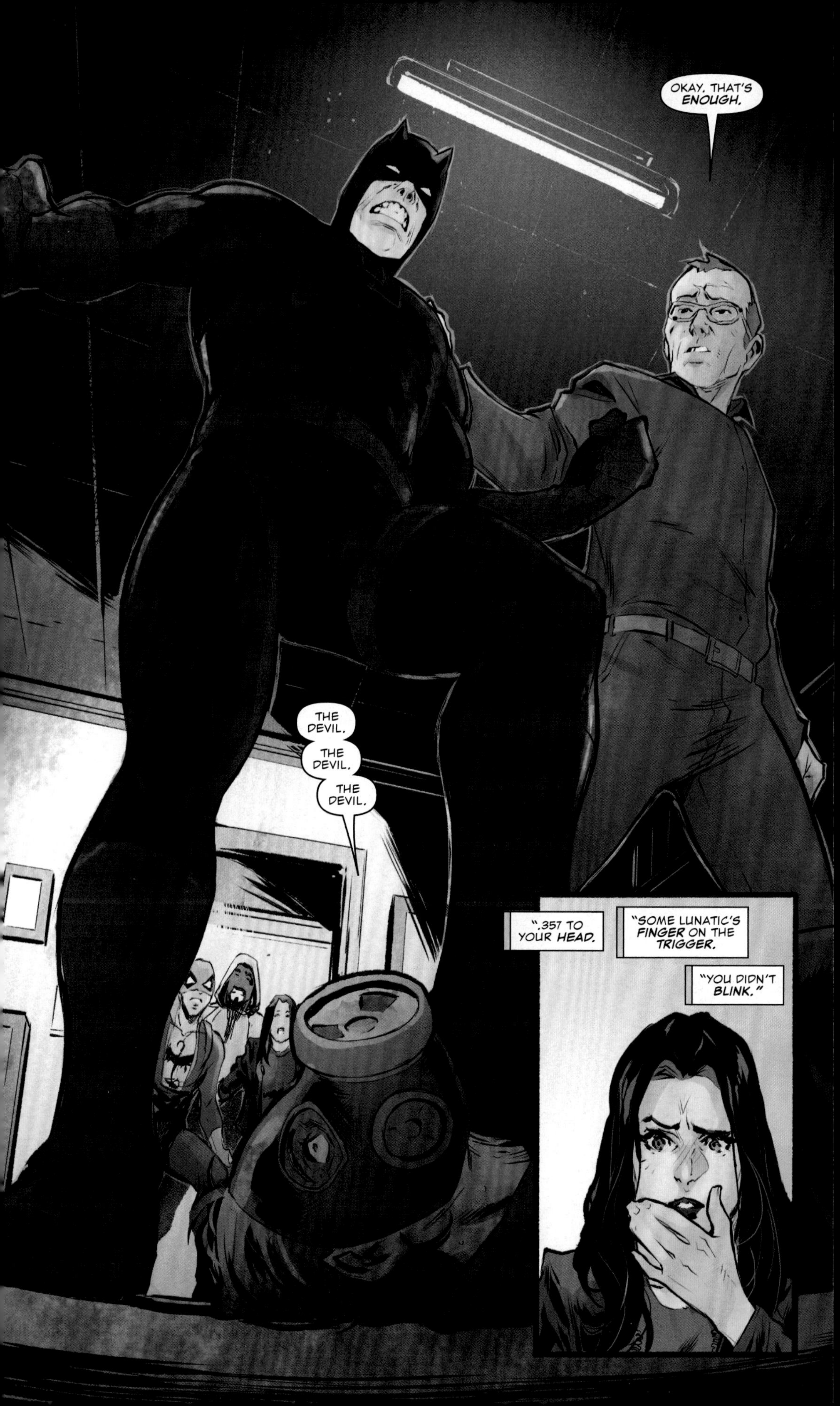

OKAY. THAT'S ENOUGH.
THE DEVIL.
THE DEVIL.
THE DEVIL.
".357 TO YOUR HEAD.
"SOME LUNATIC'S FINGER ON THE TRIGGER.
"YOU DIDN'T BLINK."

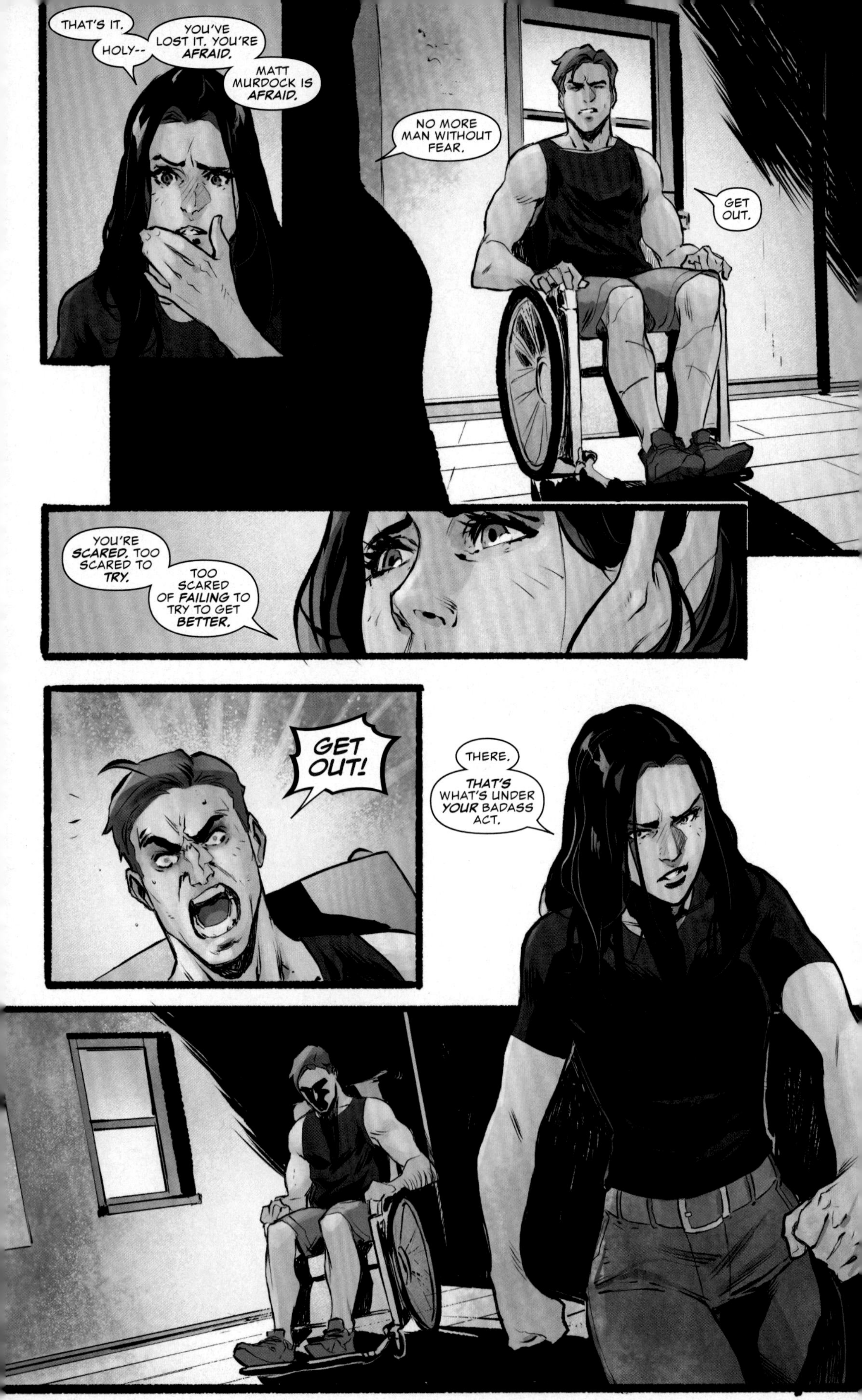
THAT'S IT.
HOLY--
YOU'VE LOST IT. YOU'RE AFRAID.
MATT MURDOCK IS AFRAID.
NO MORE MAN WITHOUT FEAR.
GET OUT.
YOU'RE SCARED. TOO SCARED TO TRY.
TOO SCARED OF FAILING TO TRY TO GET BETTER.
GET OUT!
THERE.
THAT'S WHAT'S UNDER YOUR BADASS ACT.

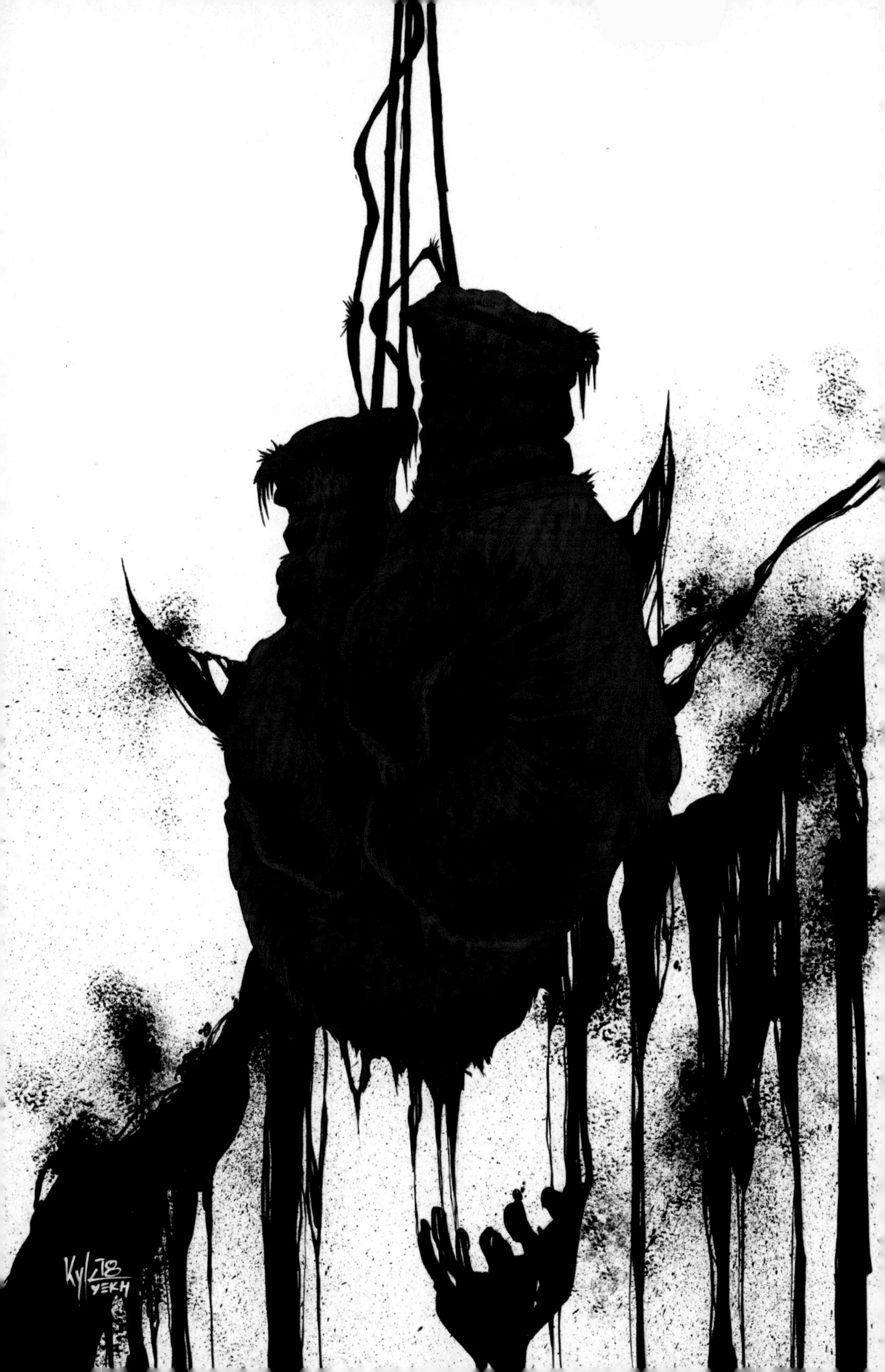

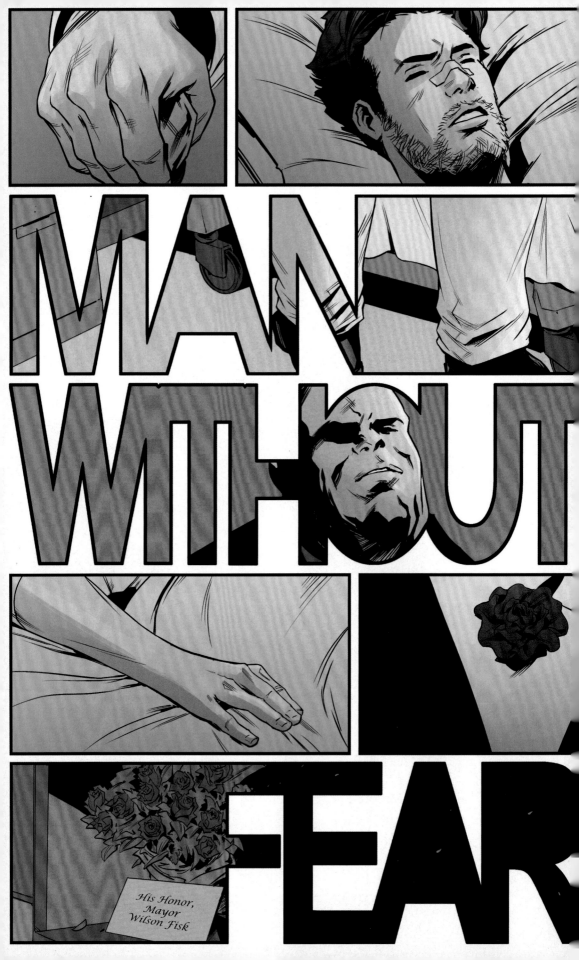

His Honor,
Mayor
Wilson Fisk

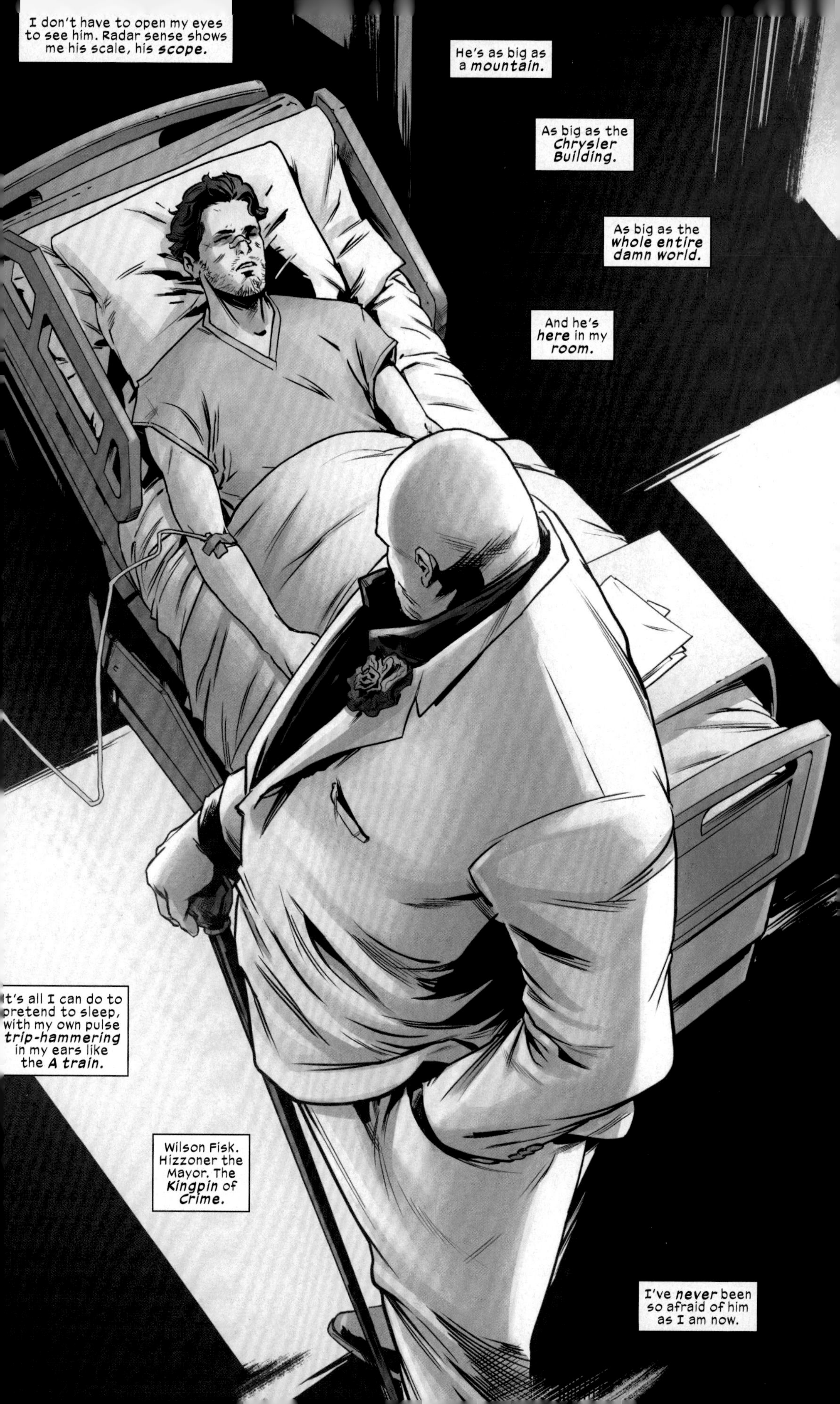

I don't have to open my eyes to see him. Radar sense shows me his scale, his *scope.*
He's as big as a *mountain.*
As big as the *Chrysler Building.*
As big as the *whole entire damn world.*
And he's *here* in my *room.*
It's all I can do to pretend to sleep, with my own pulse *trip-hammering* in my ears like the *A train.*
Wilson Fisk. Hizzoner the Mayor. The *Kingpin* of *Crime.*
I've *never* been so afraid of him as I am now.

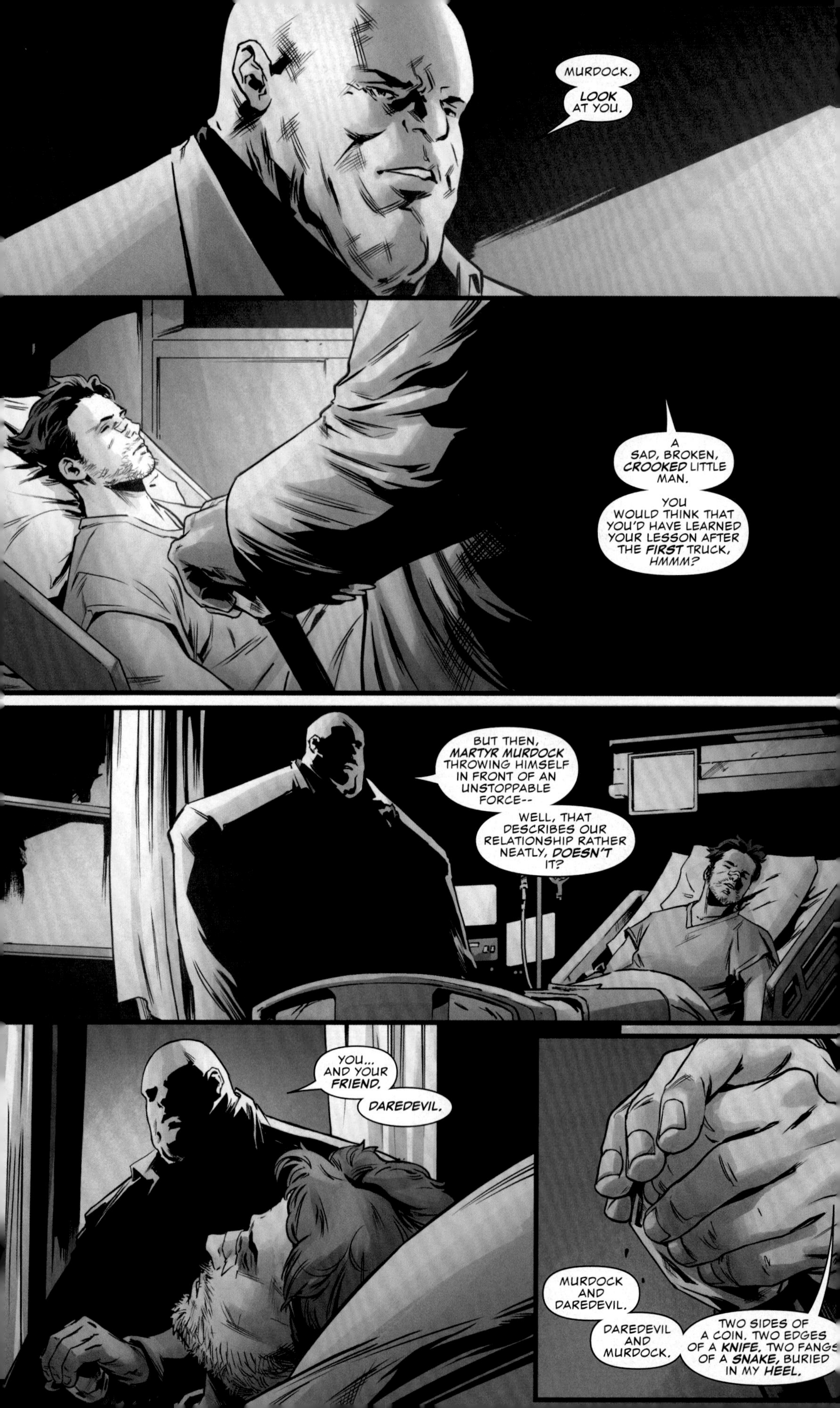
MURDOCK.
LOOK AT YOU.
A SAD, BROKEN, CROOKED LITTLE MAN.
YOU WOULD THINK THAT YOU'D HAVE LEARNED YOUR LESSON AFTER THE FIRST TRUCK, HMMM?
BUT THEN, MARTYR MURDOCK THROWING HIMSELF IN FRONT OF AN UNSTOPPABLE FORCE--
WELL, THAT DESCRIBES OUR RELATIONSHIP RATHER NEATLY, DOESN'T IT?
YOU... AND YOUR FRIEND.
DAREDEVIL.
MURDOCK AND DAREDEVIL.
DAREDEVIL AND MURDOCK.
TWO SIDES OF A COIN. TWO EDGES OF A KNIFE. TWO FANGS OF A SNAKE, BURIED IN MY HEEL.

THOUGH ACCORDING TO [YO]UR FILE...IT WOULD [A]PPEAR THAT YOUR [E]DGE HAS BEEN... DULLED.

YOUR FANGS PULLED.

Of *course* he has my confidential medical file.

He's the *Kingpin.*

He gets whatever he wants.

GIVEN UP ON YOUR PHYSICAL THERAPY, HAVE YOU, MURDOCK? OVERCOME WITH *DESPAIR?* PUSHING YOUR *FRIENDS* AWAY?

HOW *DELICIOUS.*

And what he wants right now...

...is to *gloat.*

That's him all over.

Petty. Cruel. Vindictive, under that veneer of civility.

It's how he shows what he *really is.*

No one smells like him.

His cologne is *bespoke,* made for him in *France.*

Five hundred bucks an *ounce.* But that's not what I mean.

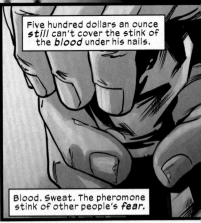

Five hundred dollars an ounce *still* can't cover the stink of the *blood* under his nails.

Blood. Sweat. The pheromone stink of other people's *fear.*

That's what Fisk smells like. What he really is.

And *that's* why I'm so afraid of him.

HNH.

I LOVE A NIGHT LIKE THIS.

I ALWAYS HAVE, EVER SINCE YOUR *FRIEND* JOINED US.

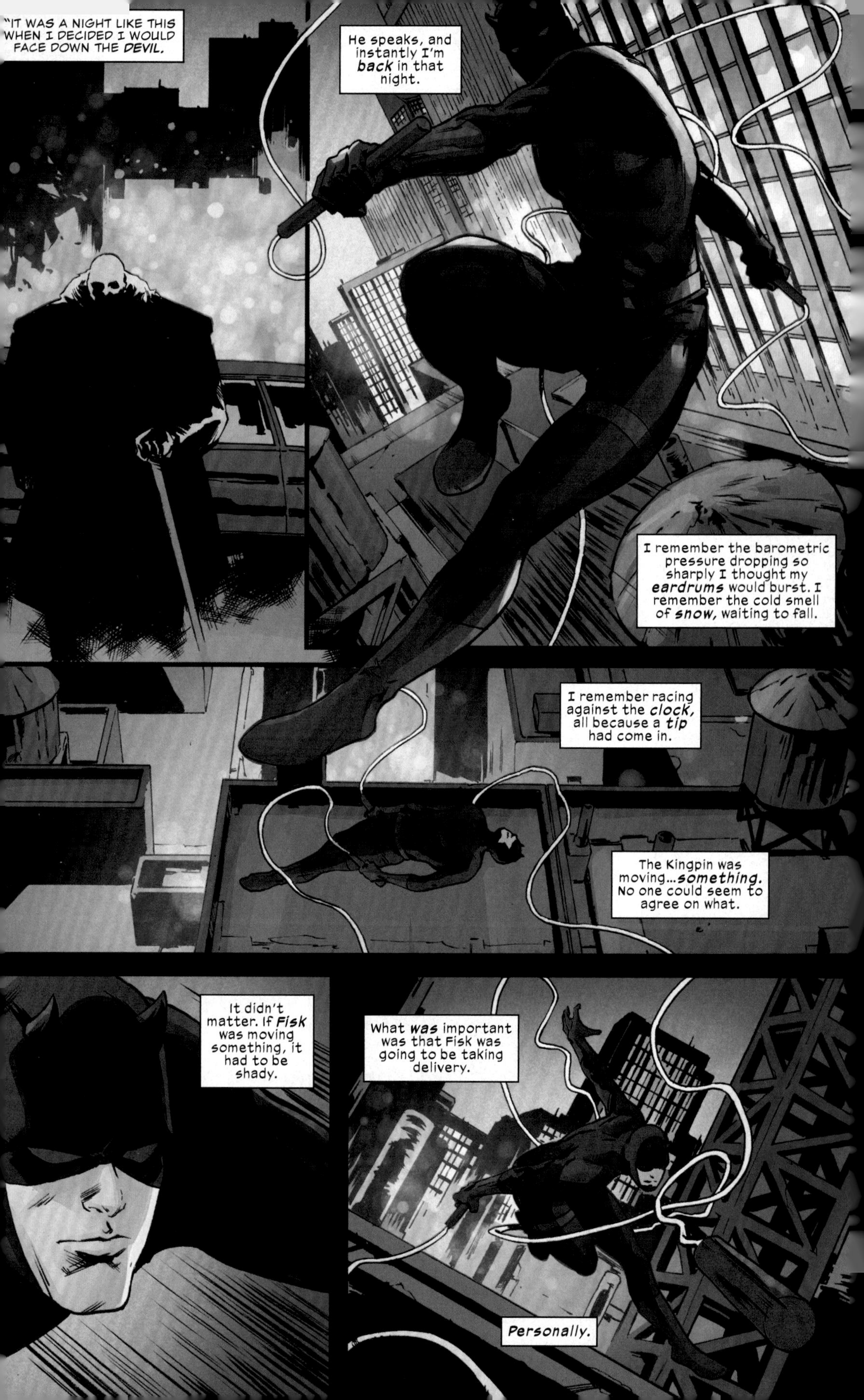
"IT WAS A NIGHT LIKE THIS WHEN I DECIDED I WOULD FACE DOWN THE *DEVIL.*
He speaks, and instantly I'm *back* in that night.
I remember the barometric pressure dropping so sharply I thought my *eardrums* would burst. I remember the cold smell of *snow,* waiting to fall.
I remember racing against the *clock,* all because a *tip* had come in.
The Kingpin was moving...*something.* No one could seem to agree on what.
It didn't matter. If *Fisk* was moving something, it had to be shady.
What *was* important was that Fisk was going to be taking delivery.
Personally.

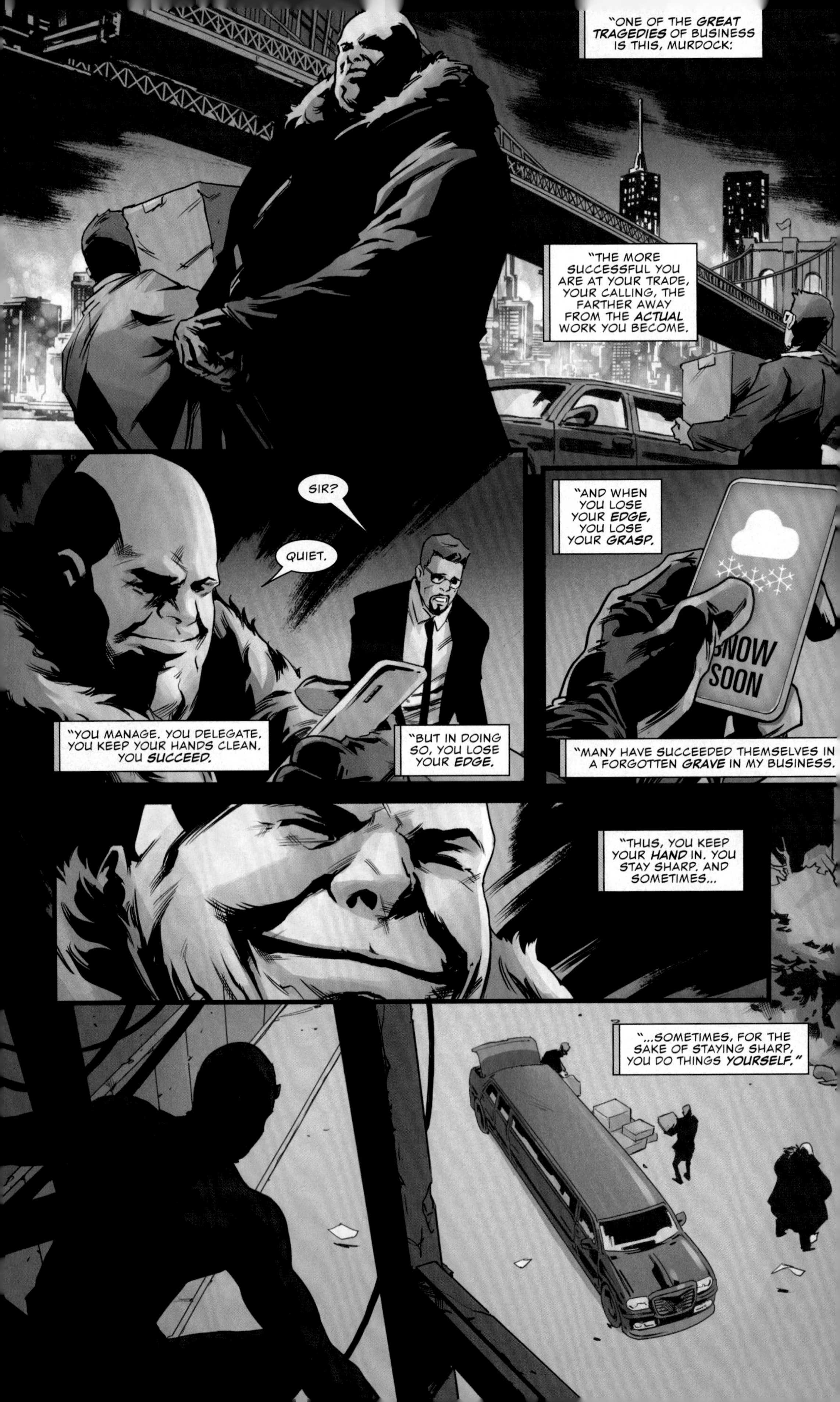
"ONE OF THE GREAT TRAGEDIES OF BUSINESS IS THIS, MURDOCK:
"THE MORE SUCCESSFUL YOU ARE AT YOUR TRADE, YOUR CALLING, THE FARTHER AWAY FROM THE ACTUAL WORK YOU BECOME.
SIR?
QUIET.
"YOU MANAGE. YOU DELEGATE. YOU KEEP YOUR HANDS CLEAN. YOU SUCCEED.
"BUT IN DOING SO, YOU LOSE YOUR EDGE.
"AND WHEN YOU LOSE YOUR EDGE, YOU LOSE YOUR GRASP.
SOON
"MANY HAVE SUCCEEDED THEMSELVES IN A FORGOTTEN GRAVE IN MY BUSINESS.
"THUS, YOU KEEP YOUR HAND IN. YOU STAY SHARP. AND SOMETIMES...
"...SOMETIMES, FOR THE SAKE OF STAYING SHARP, YOU DO THINGS YOURSELF."

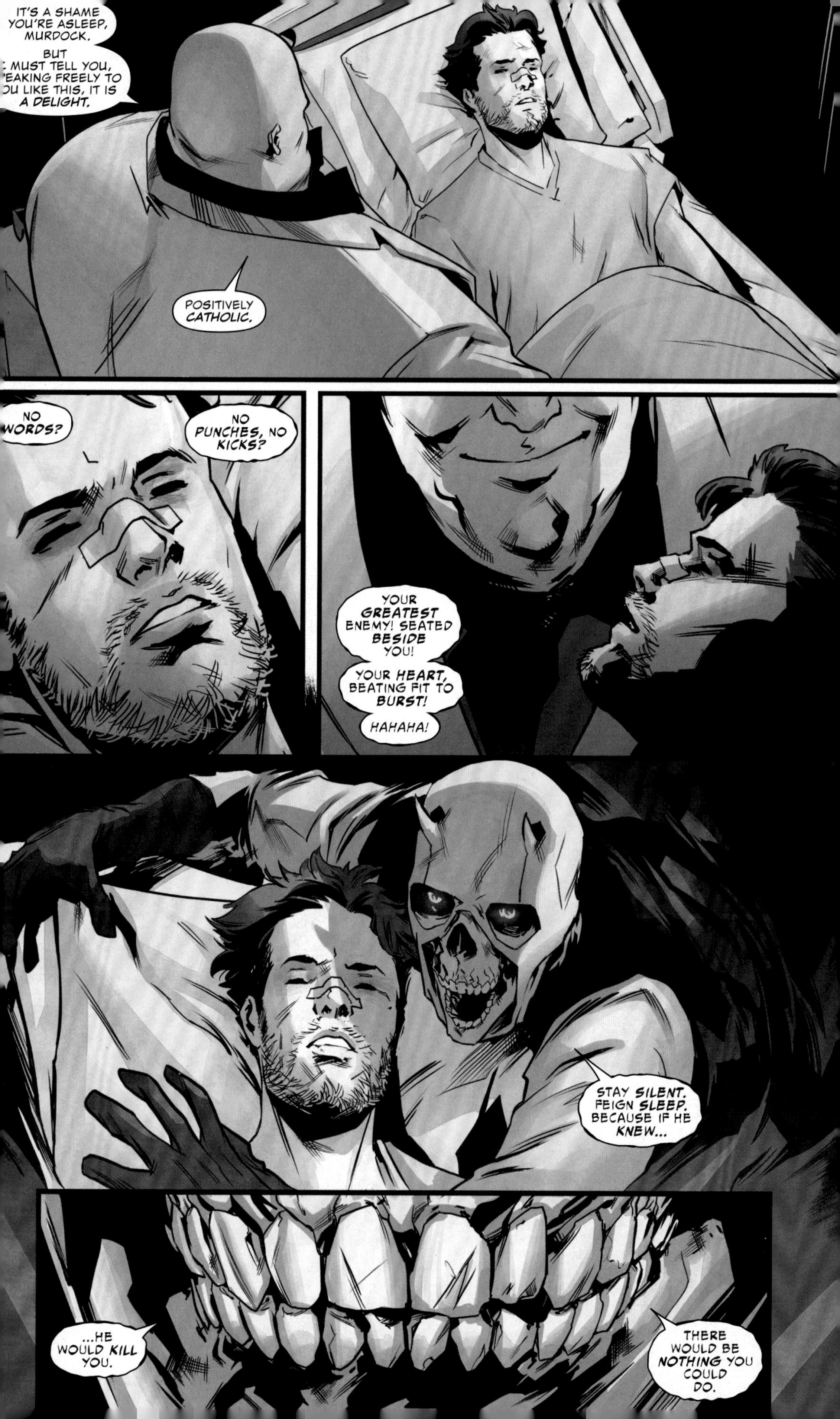

IT'S A SHAME YOU'RE ASLEEP, MURDOCK.
BUT I MUST TELL YOU, SPEAKING FREELY TO YOU LIKE THIS, IT IS A DELIGHT.
POSITIVELY CATHOLIC.
NO WORDS?
NO PUNCHES, NO KICKS?
YOUR GREATEST ENEMY! SEATED BESIDE YOU!
YOUR HEART, BEATING FIT TO BURST!
HAHAHA!
STAY SILENT. FEIGN SLEEP. BECAUSE IF HE KNEW...
...HE WOULD KILL YOU.
THERE WOULD BE NOTHING YOU COULD DO.

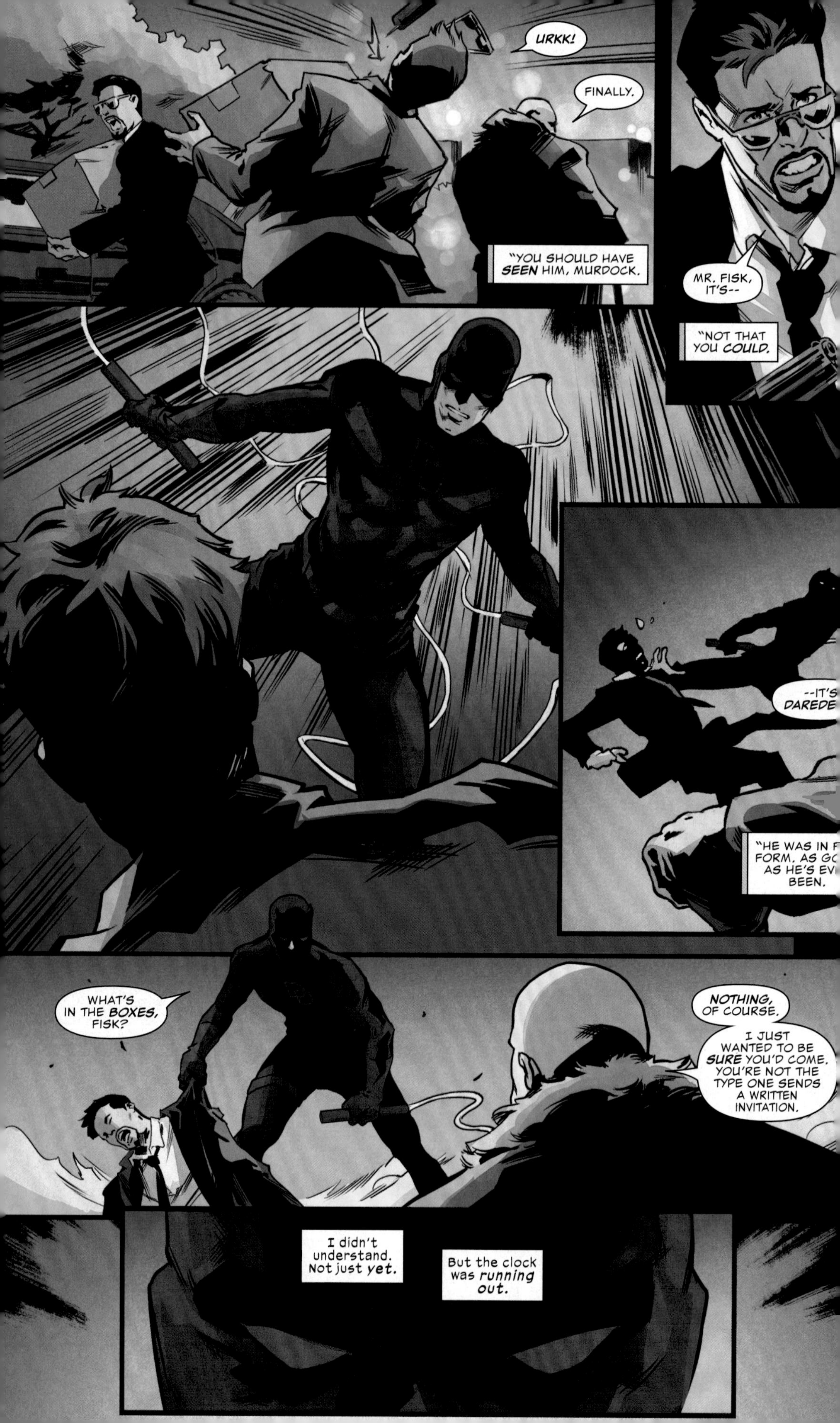
URKK!
FINALLY.
"YOU SHOULD HAVE SEEN HIM, MURDOCK.
MR. FISK, IT'S--
"NOT THAT YOU COULD.
--IT'S DAREDE
"HE WAS IN F FORM, AS GO AS HE'S EV BEEN.
WHAT'S IN THE BOXES, FISK?
NOTHING, OF COURSE.
I JUST WANTED TO BE SURE YOU'D COME. YOU'RE NOT THE TYPE ONE SENDS A WRITTEN INVITATION.
I didn't understand. Not just yet.
But the clock was running out.

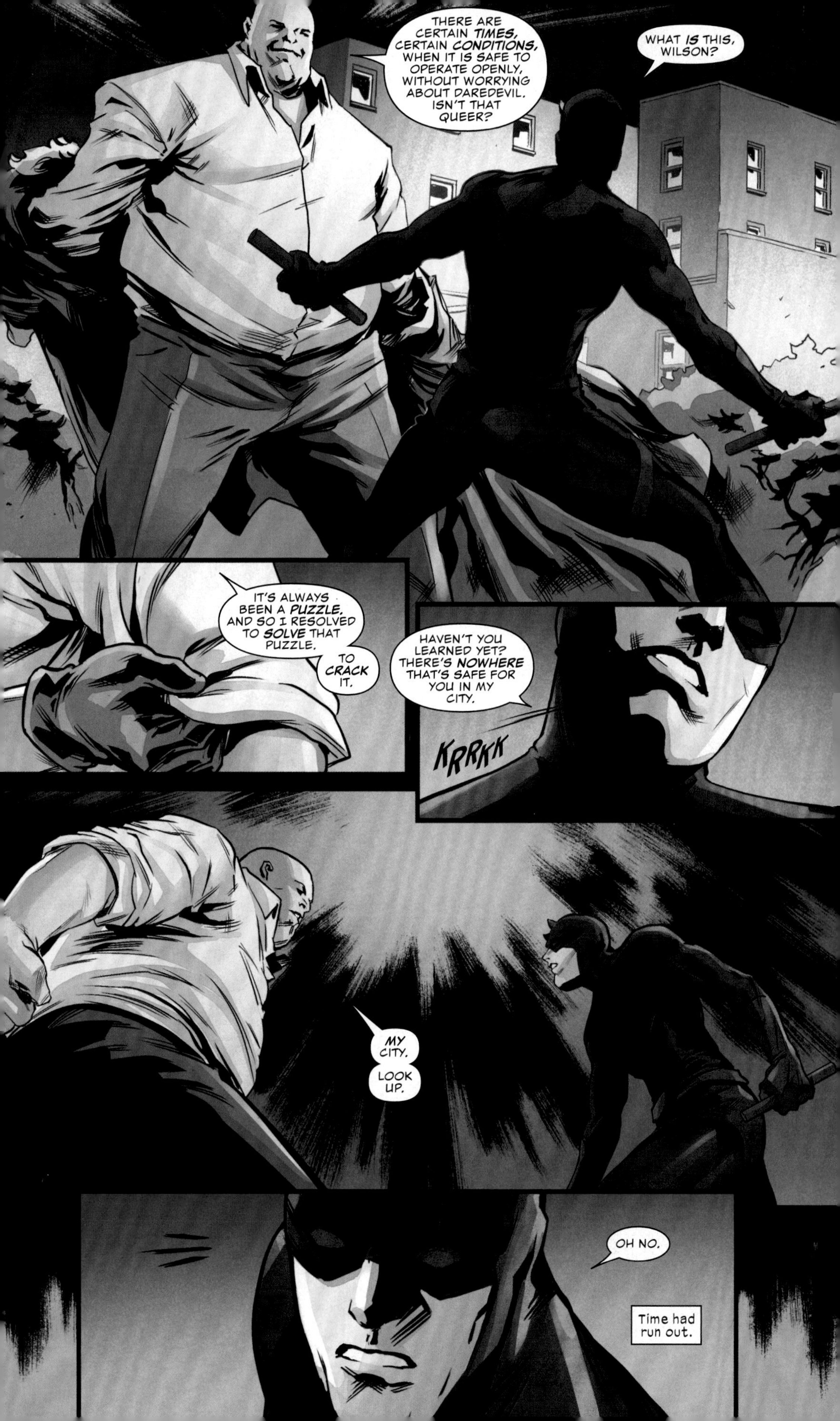
THERE ARE CERTAIN TIMES, CERTAIN CONDITIONS, WHEN IT IS SAFE TO OPERATE OPENLY, WITHOUT WORRYING ABOUT DAREDEVIL. ISN'T THAT QUEER?
WHAT IS THIS, WILSON?
IT'S ALWAYS BEEN A PUZZLE. AND SO I RESOLVED TO SOLVE THAT PUZZLE.
TO CRACK IT.
HAVEN'T YOU LEARNED YET? THERE'S NOWHERE THAT'S SAFE FOR YOU IN MY CITY.
KRRKK
MY CITY.
LOOK UP.
OH NO.
Time had run out.

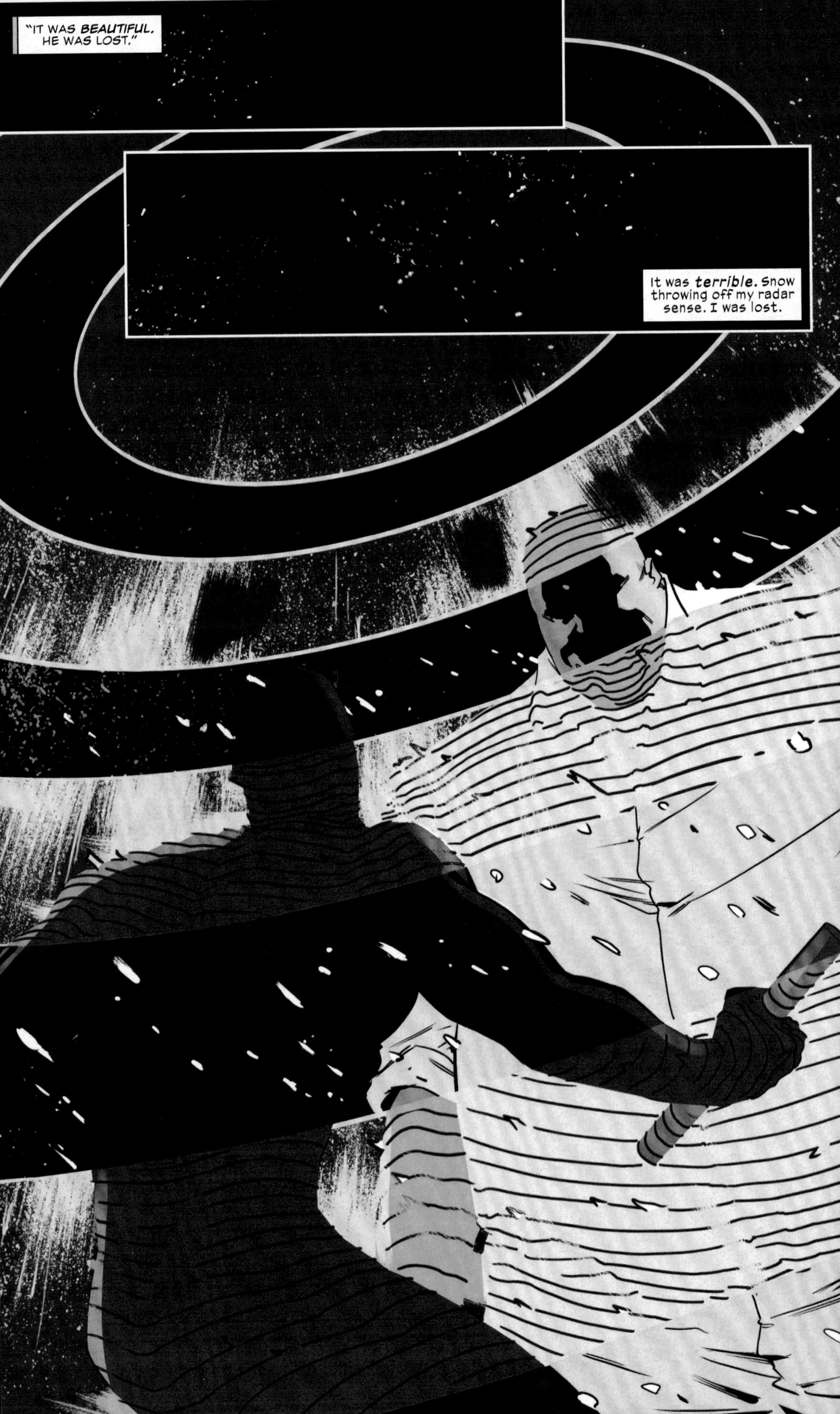
"IT WAS *BEAUTIFUL*. HE WAS LOST."
It was *terrible*. Snow throwing off my radar sense. I was lost.

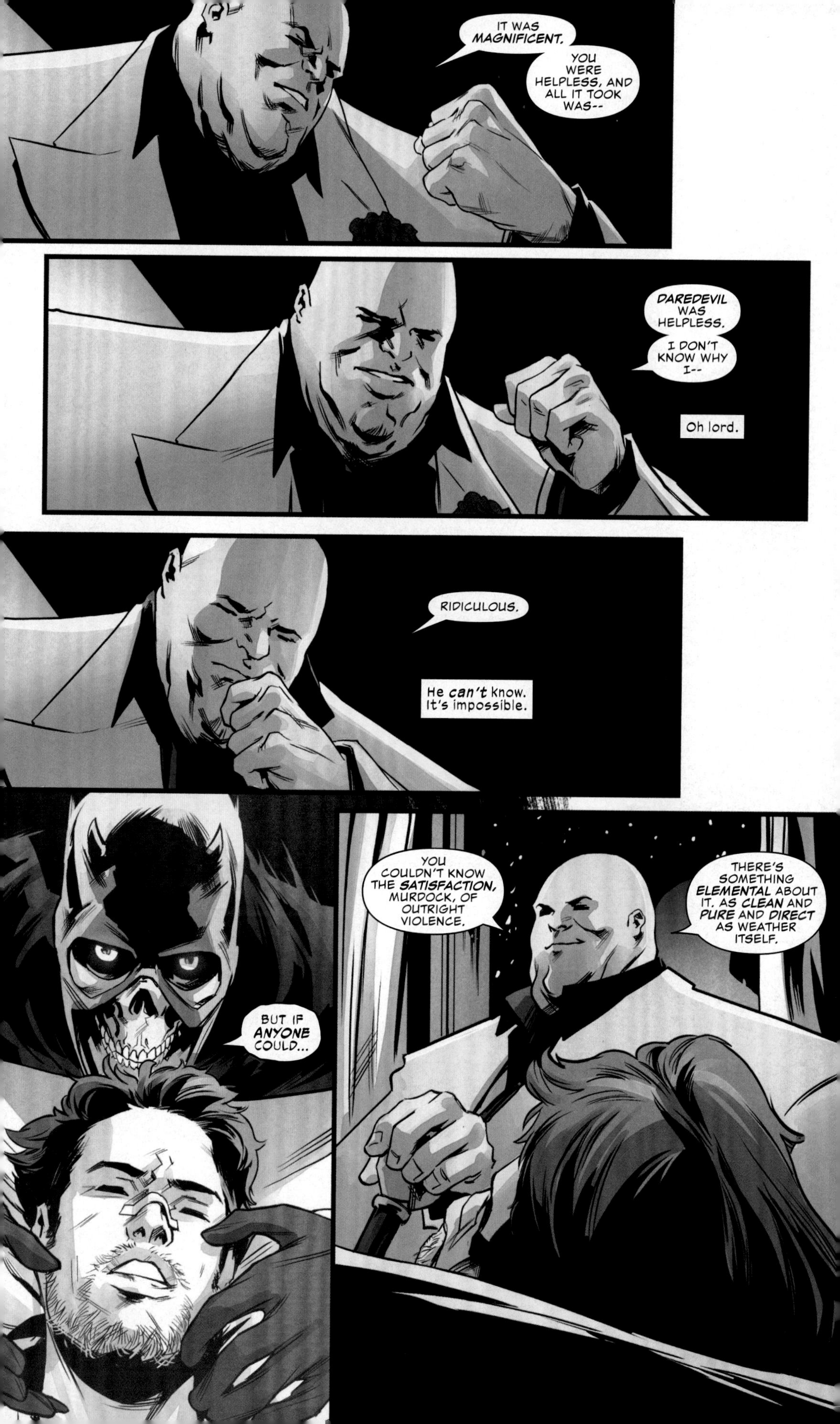
IT WAS MAGNIFICENT.
YOU WERE HELPLESS, AND ALL IT TOOK WAS--
DAREDEVIL WAS HELPLESS.
I DON'T KNOW WHY I--
Oh lord.
RIDICULOUS.
He can't know. It's impossible.
BUT IF ANYONE COULD...
YOU COULDN'T KNOW THE SATISFACTION, MURDOCK, OF OUTRIGHT VIOLENCE.
THERE'S SOMETHING ELEMENTAL ABOUT IT. AS CLEAN AND PURE AND DIRECT AS WEATHER ITSELF.

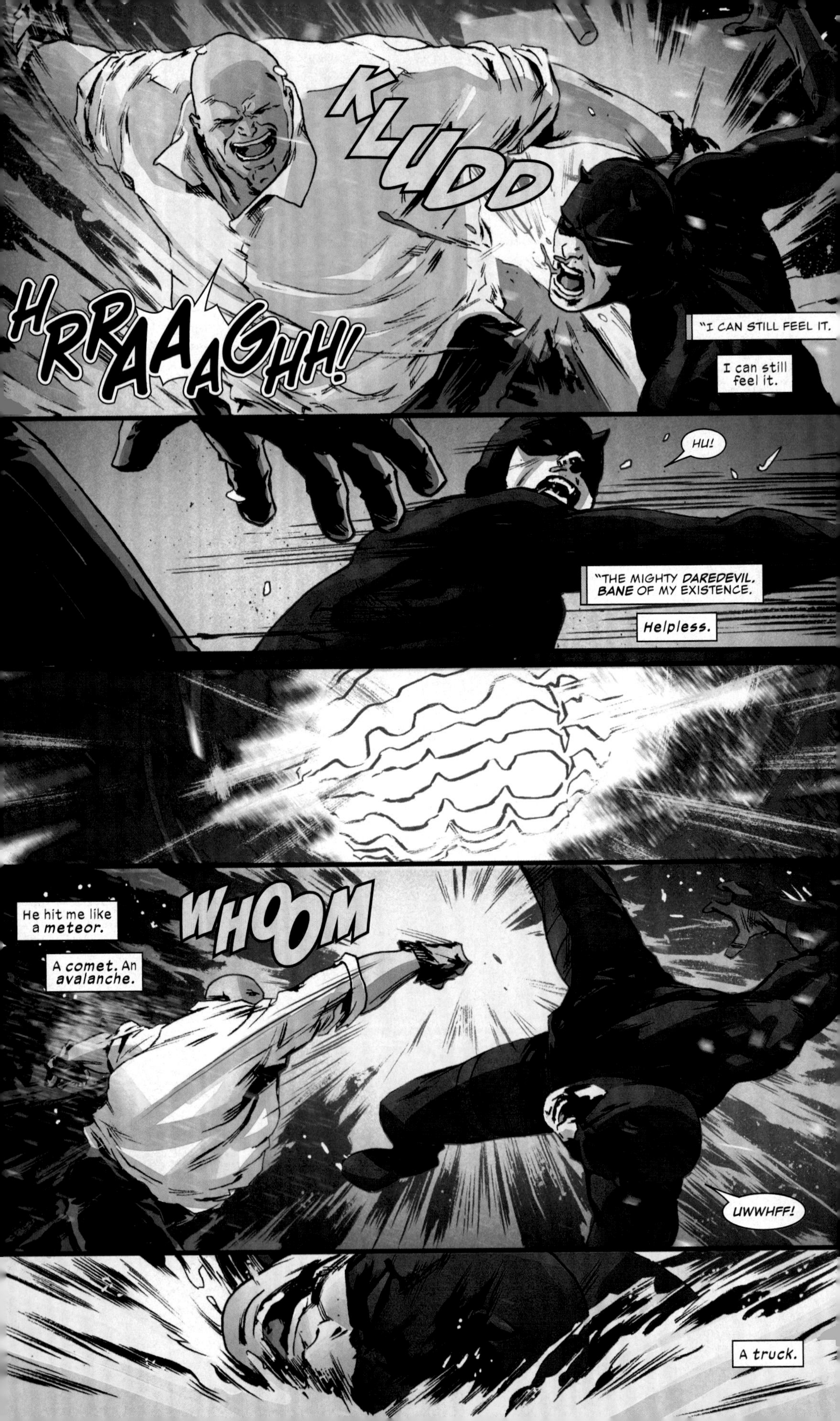

KLUDD
HRRAAAAGHH!
"I CAN STILL FEEL IT.
I can still feel it.
HU!
"THE MIGHTY DAREDEVIL. BANE OF MY EXISTENCE.
Helpless.
He hit me like a meteor.
A comet. An avalanche.
WHOOM
UWWHFF!
A truck.

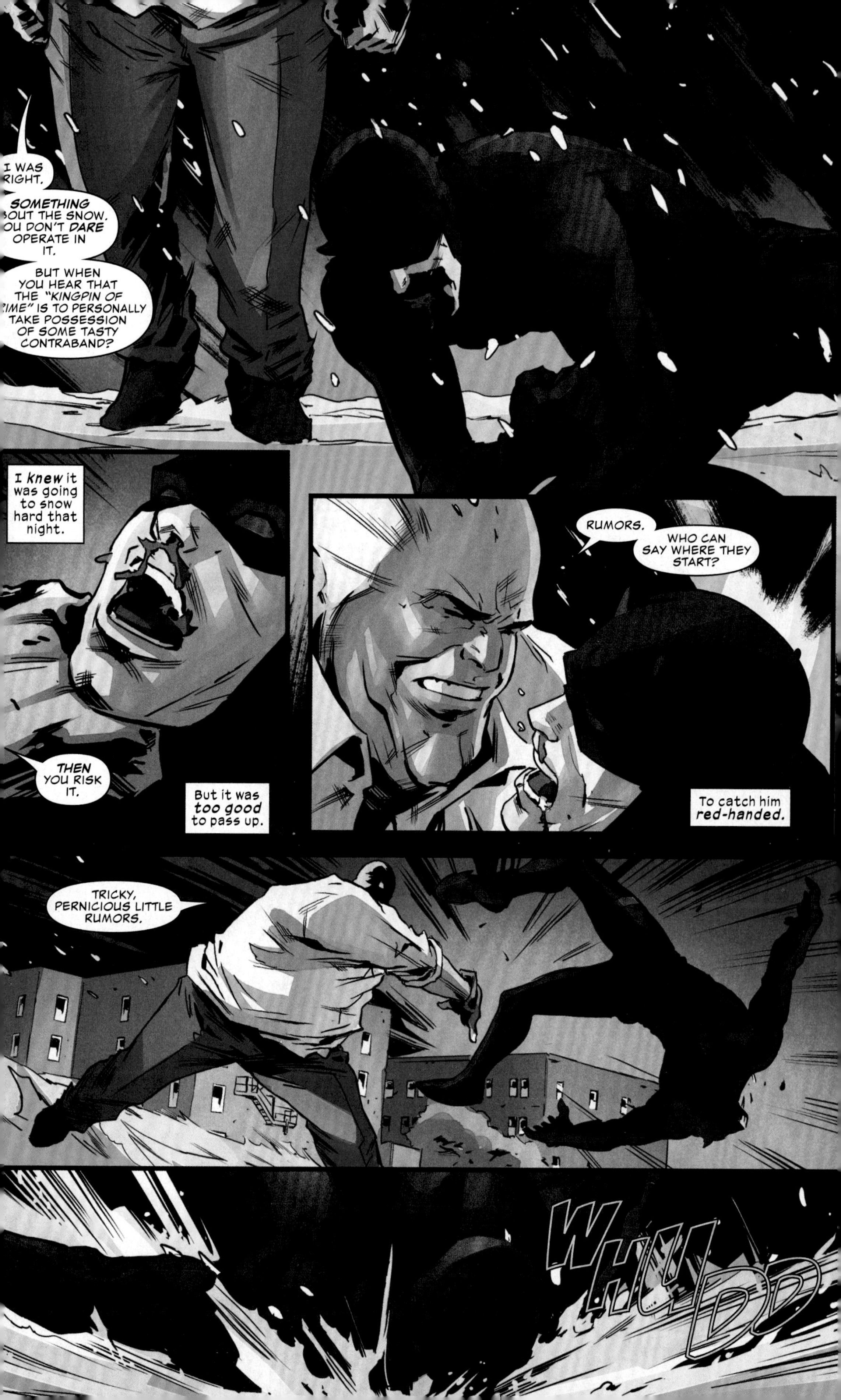
I WAS RIGHT.
SOMETHING BOUT THE SNOW. OU DON'T DARE OPERATE IN IT.
BUT WHEN YOU HEAR THAT THE "KINGPIN OF RIME" IS TO PERSONALLY TAKE POSSESSION OF SOME TASTY CONTRABAND?
I knew it was going to snow hard that night.
THEN YOU RISK IT.
But it was too good to pass up.
RUMORS.
WHO CAN SAY WHERE THEY START?
To catch him red-handed.
TRICKY, PERNICIOUS LITTLE RUMORS.
WHUDD

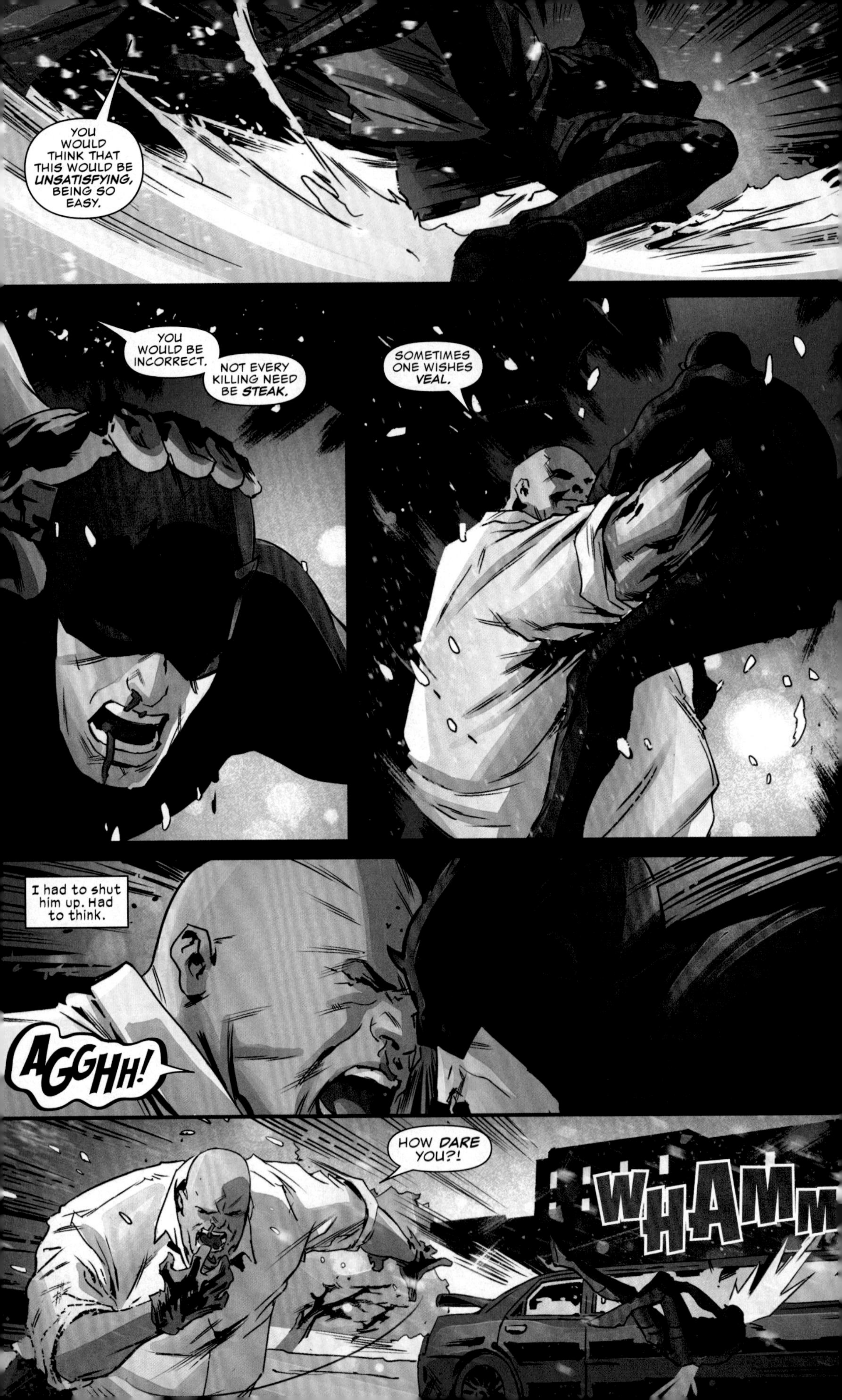
YOU WOULD THINK THAT THIS WOULD BE UNSATISFYING, BEING SO EASY.
YOU WOULD BE INCORRECT.
NOT EVERY KILLING NEED BE STEAK.
SOMETIMES ONE WISHES VEAL.
I had to shut him up. Had to think.
AGGHH!
HOW DARE YOU?!
WHAMM

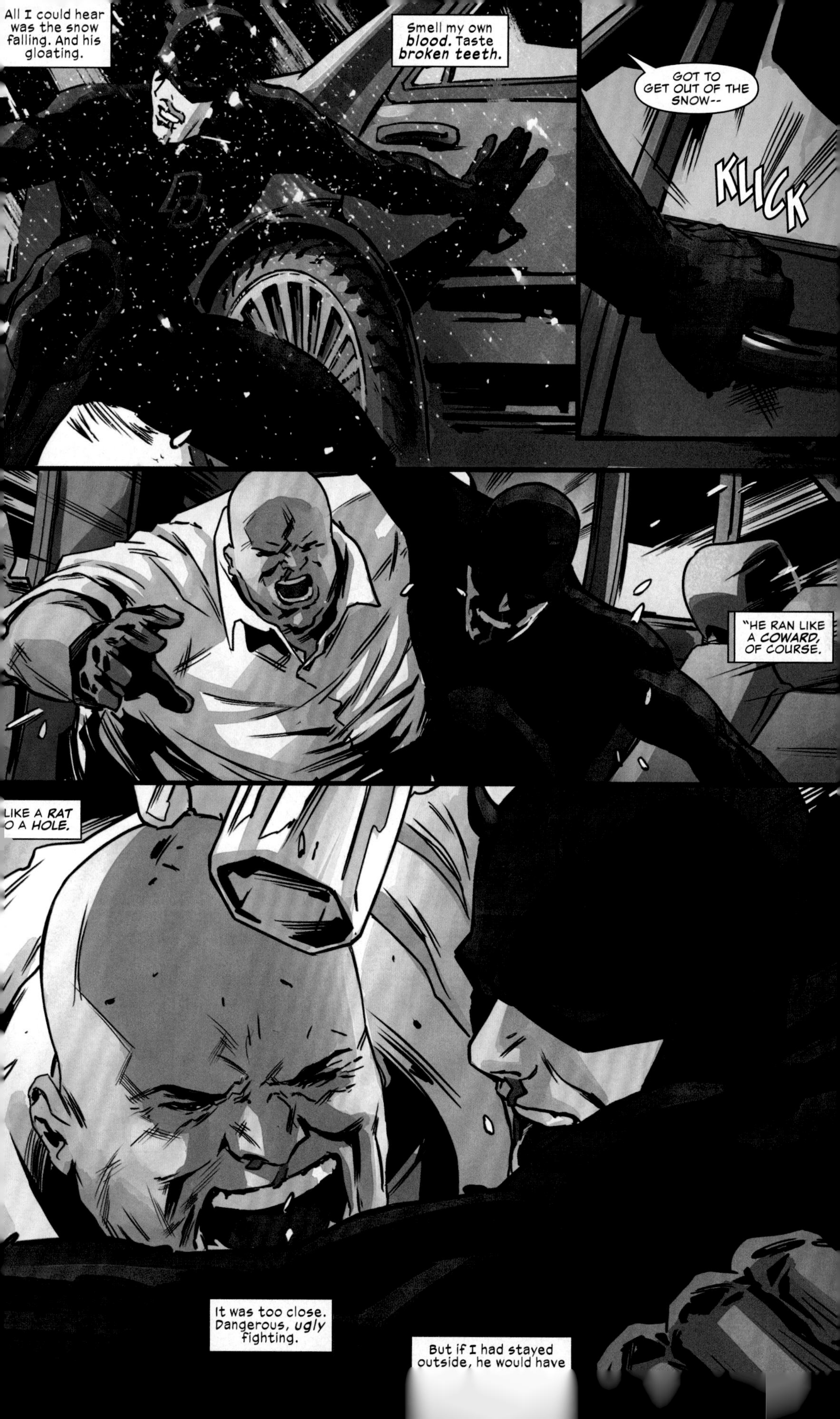
All I could hear was the snow falling. And his gloating.
Smell my own *blood.* Taste *broken teeth.*
GOT TO GET OUT OF THE SNOW--
KLICK
"HE RAN LIKE A *COWARD,* OF COURSE.
LIKE A *RAT*
O A *HOLE.*
It was too close. Dangerous, *ugly* fighting.
But if I had stayed outside, he would have

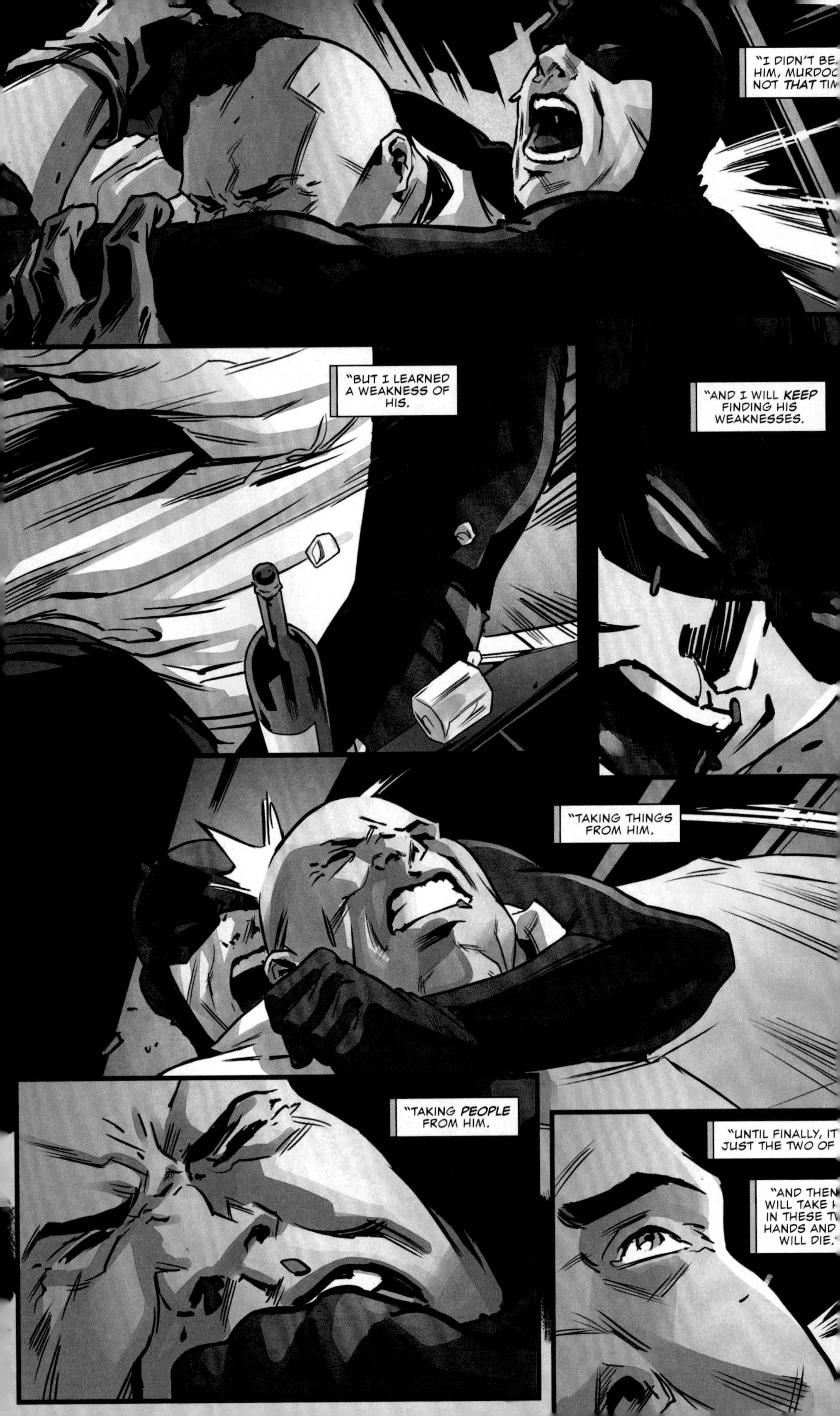
"I DIDN'T BE
HIM, MURDOC
NOT *THAT* TIM
"BUT I LEARNED A WEAKNESS OF HIS.
"AND I WILL *KEEP* FINDING HIS WEAKNESSES.
"TAKING THINGS FROM HIM.
"TAKING *PEOPLE* FROM HIM.
"UNTIL FINALLY, IT
JUST THE TWO OF
"AND THEN
WILL TAKE
IN THESE T
HANDS AND
WILL DIE."

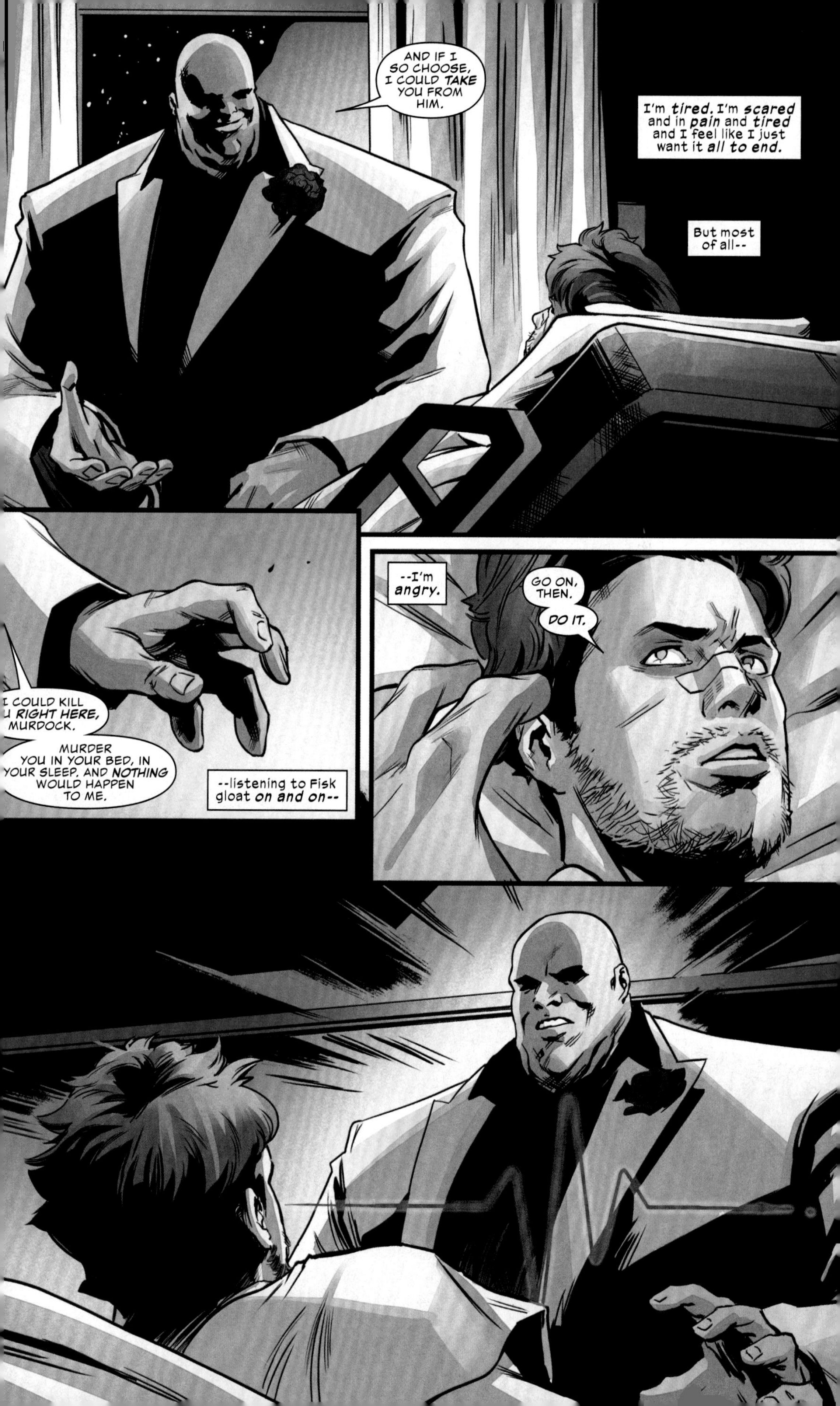
AND IF I SO CHOOSE, I COULD TAKE YOU FROM HIM.
I'm tired. I'm scared and in pain and tired and I feel like I just want it all to end.
But most of all--
I COULD KILL U RIGHT HERE, MURDOCK.
MURDER YOU IN YOUR BED, IN YOUR SLEEP. AND NOTHING WOULD HAPPEN TO ME.
--listening to Fisk gloat on and on--
--I'm angry.
GO ON, THEN.
DO IT.

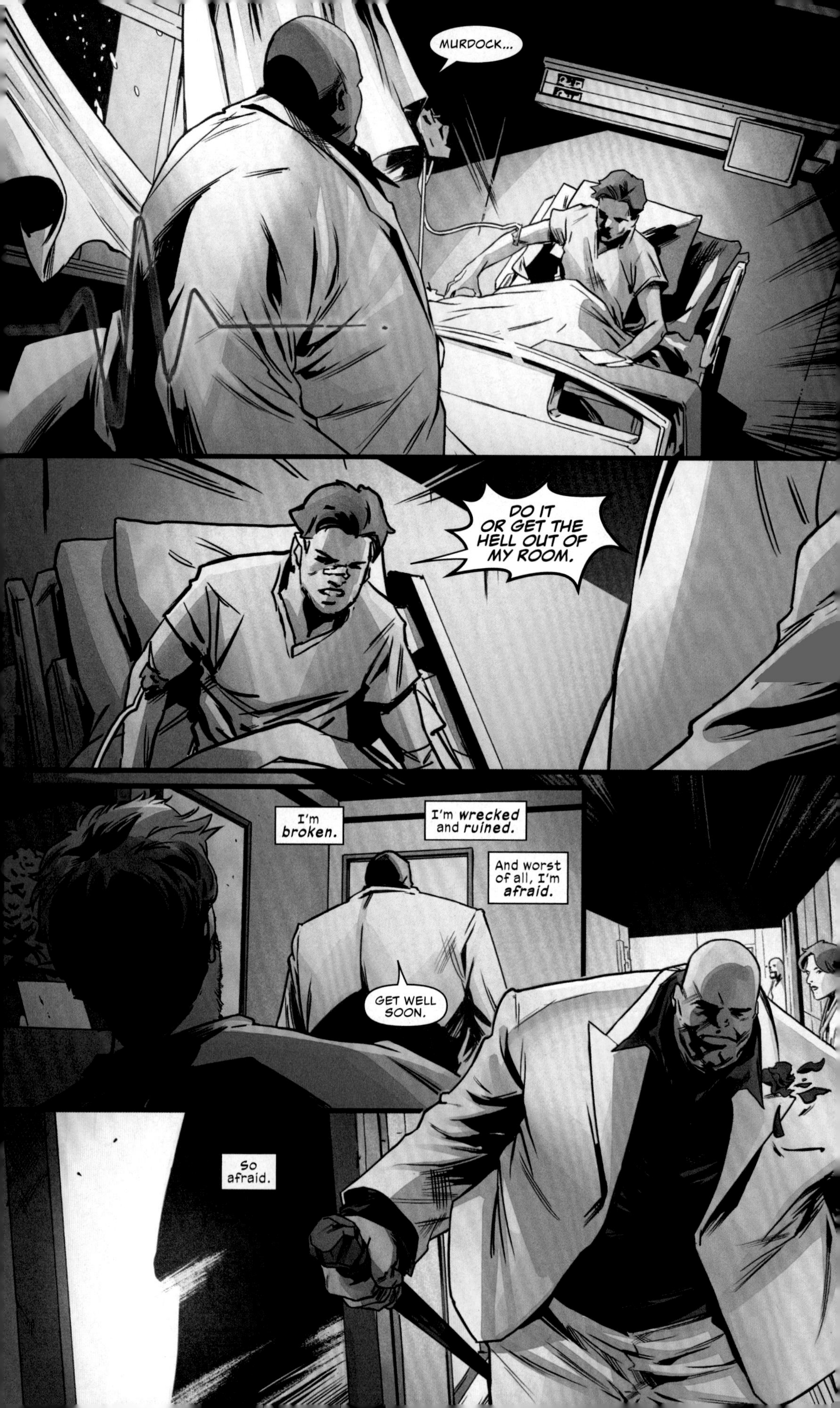
MURDOCK...
DO IT OR GET THE HELL OUT OF MY ROOM.
I'm *broken*.
I'm *wrecked* and *ruined*.
And worst of all, I'm *afraid*.
GET WELL SOON.
So afraid.

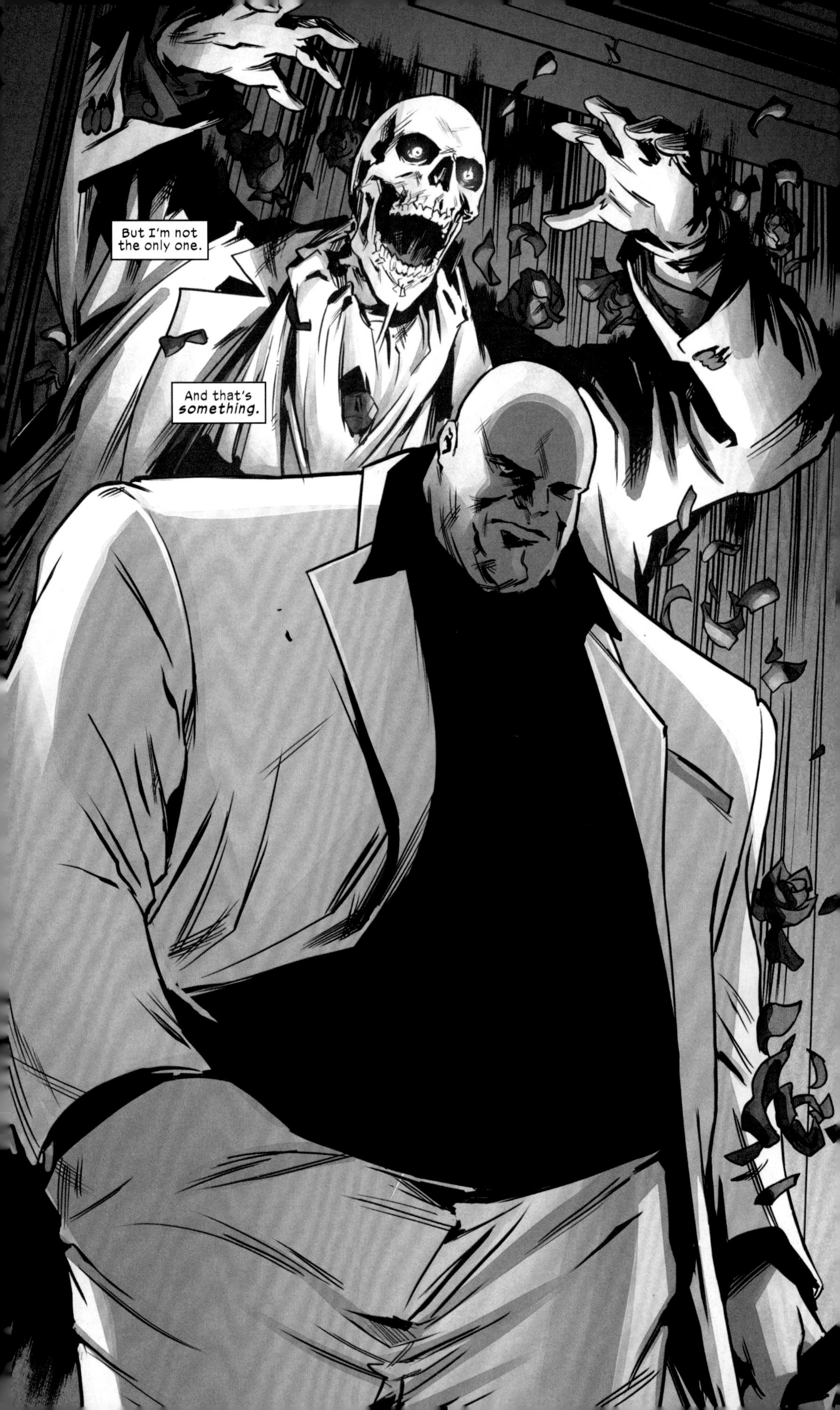

But I'm not the only one.
And that's *something.*

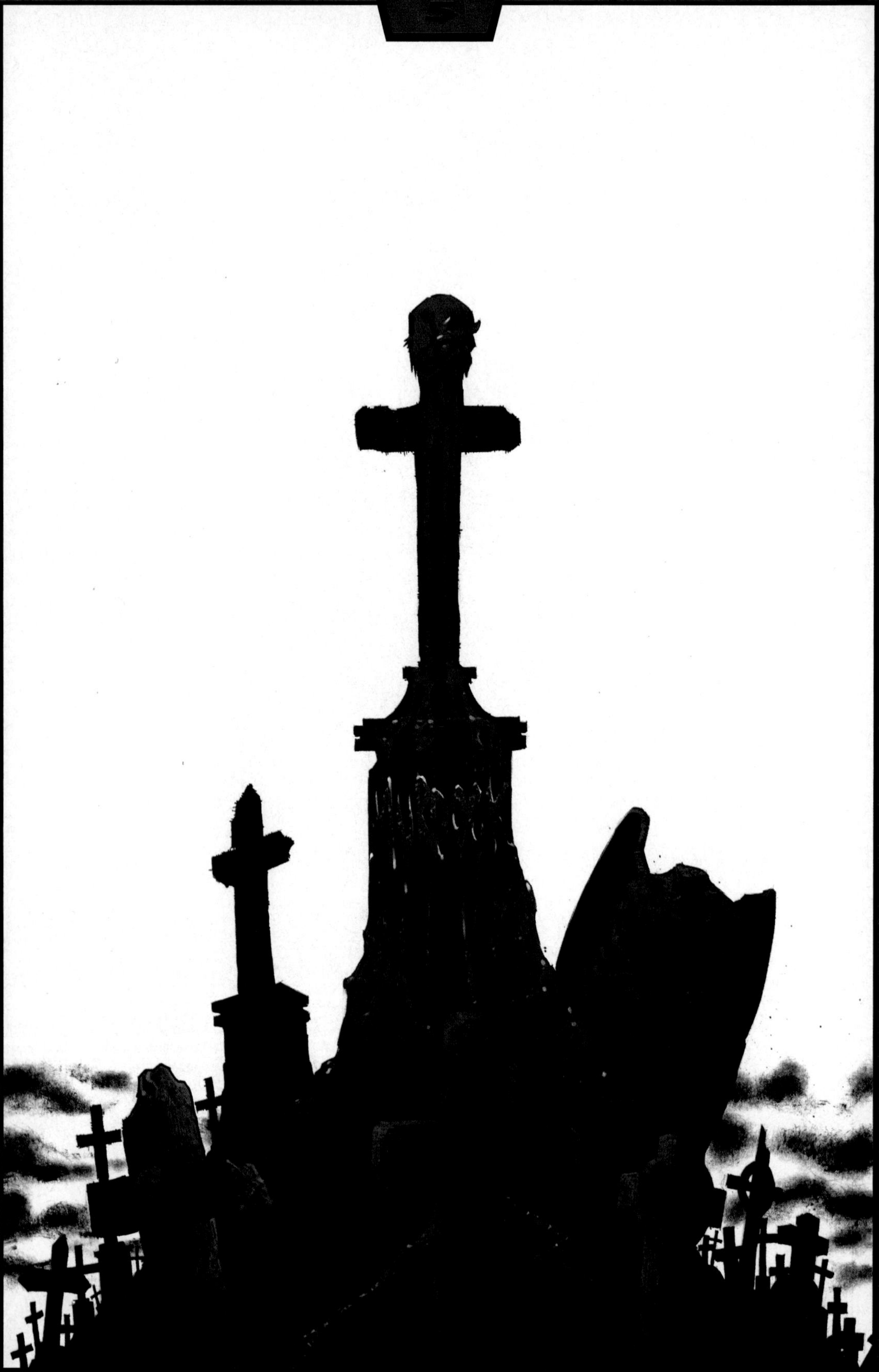

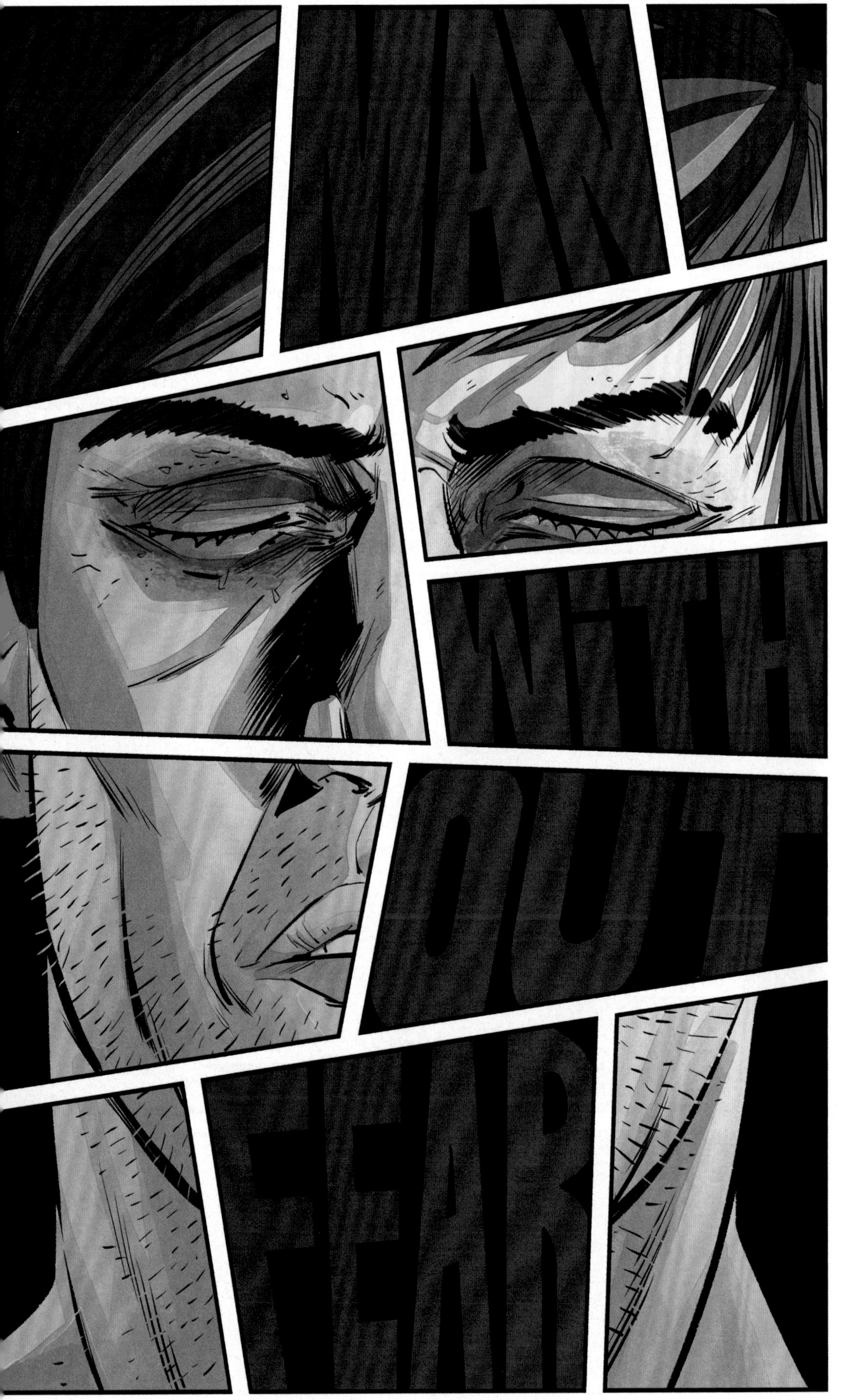
MAN
WITH
OUT
FEAR

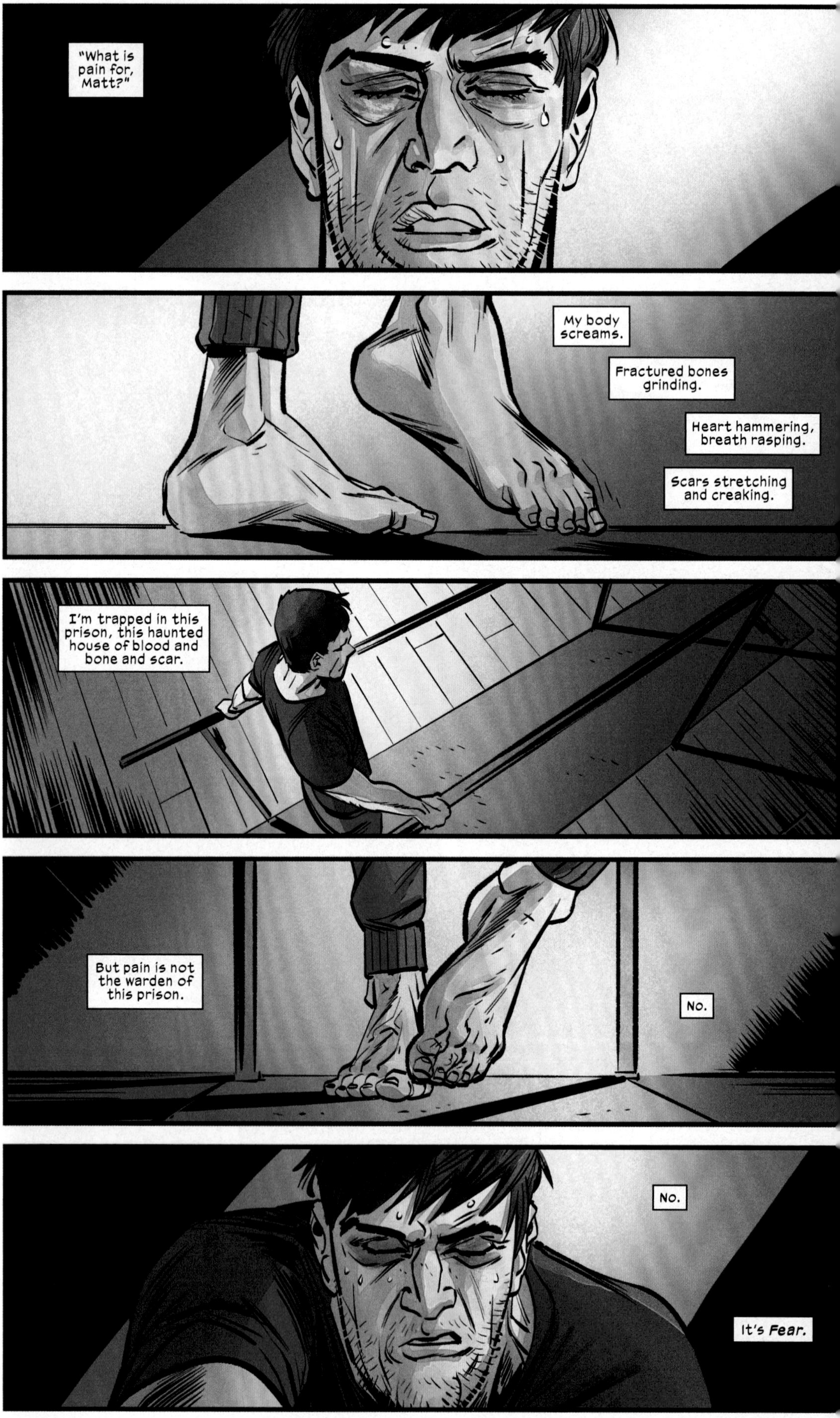
"What is pain for, Matt?"
My body screams.
Fractured bones grinding.
Heart hammering, breath rasping.
Scars stretching and creaking.
I'm trapped in this prison, this haunted house of blood and bone and scar.
But pain is not the warden of this prison.
No.
No.
It's *Fear.*

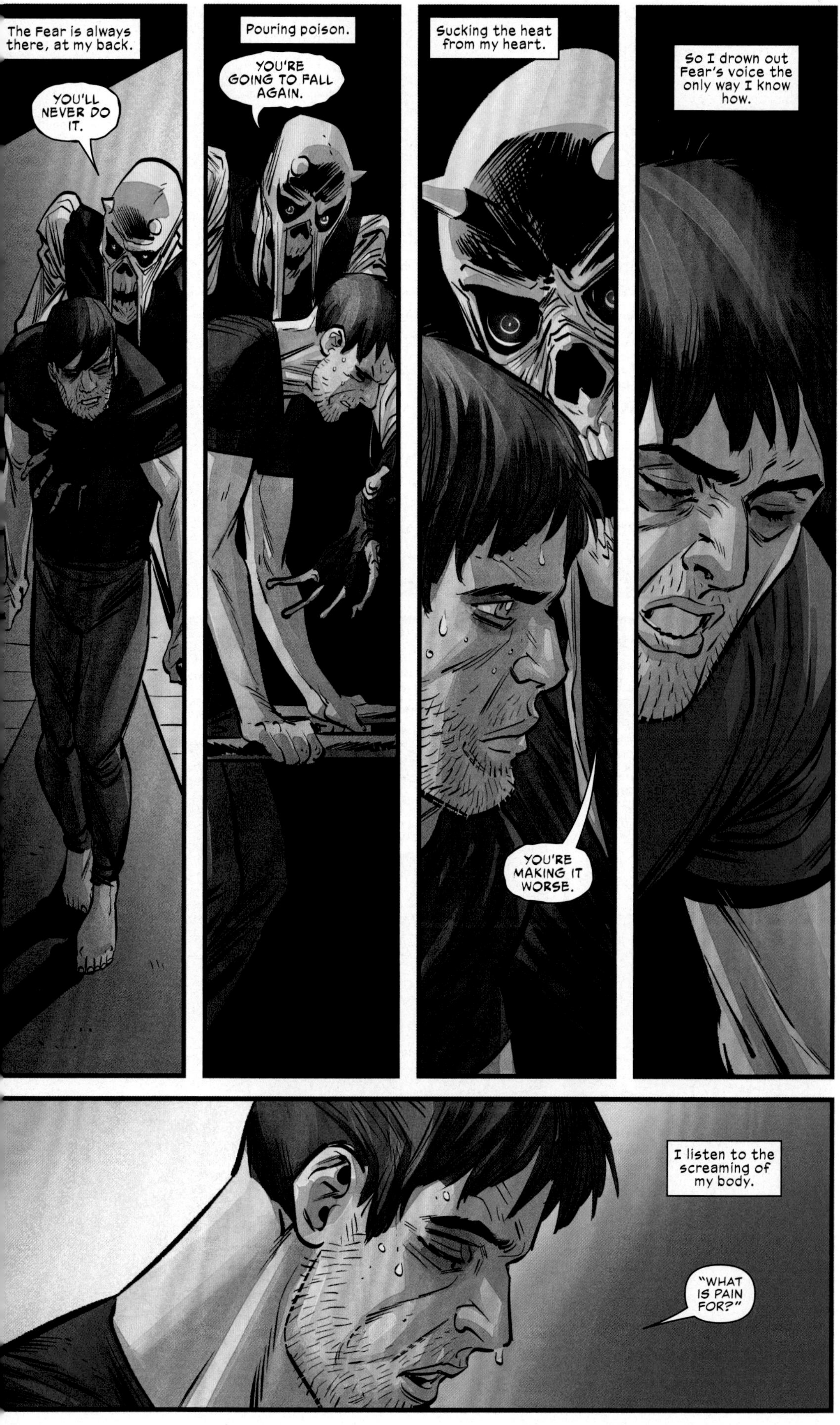
The Fear is always there, at my back.
YOU'LL NEVER DO IT.
Pouring poison.
YOU'RE GOING TO FALL AGAIN.
Sucking the heat from my heart.
YOU'RE MAKING IT WORSE.
So I drown out Fear's voice the only way I know how.
I listen to the screaming of my body.
"WHAT IS PAIN FOR?"

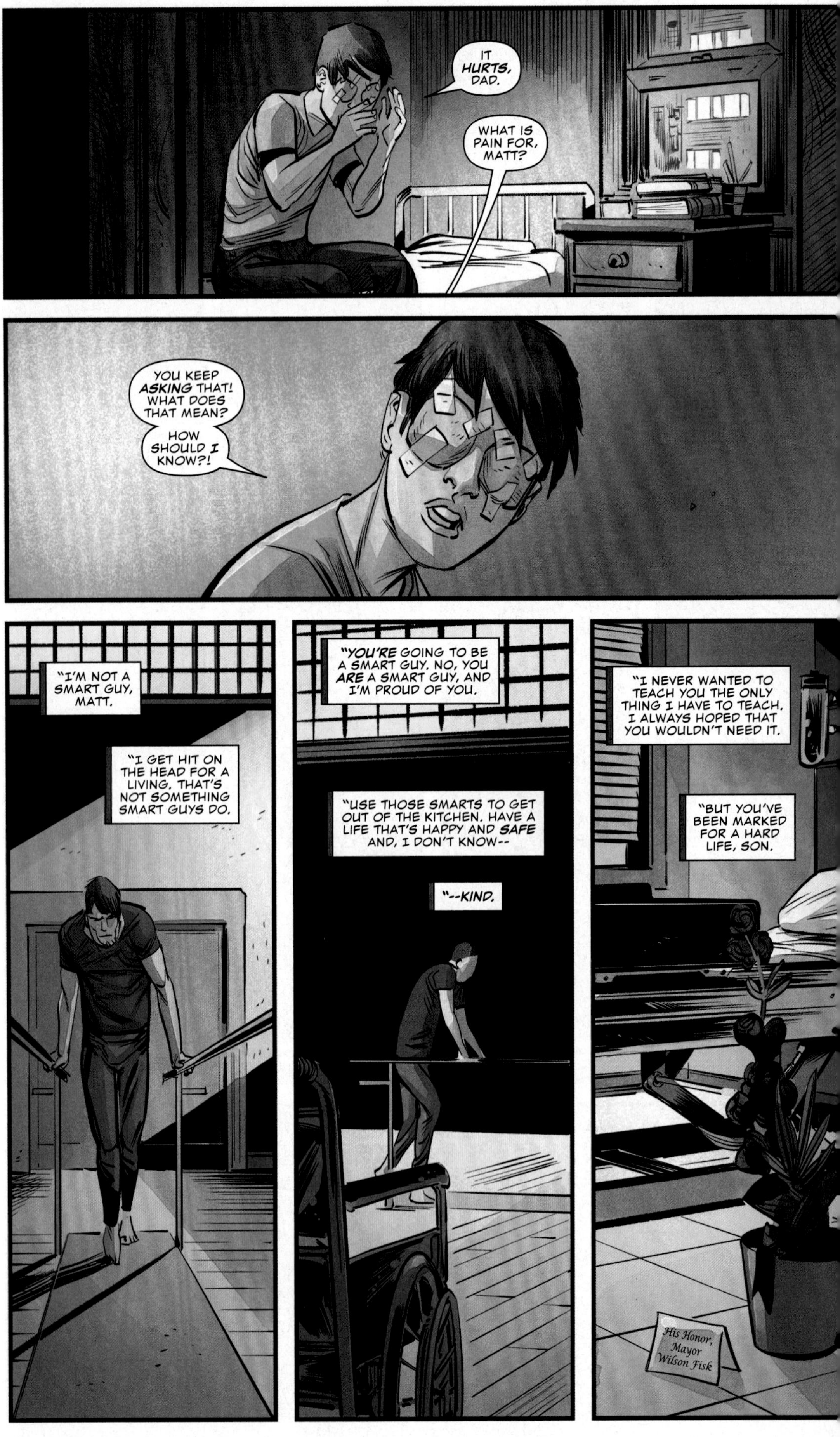
IT HURTS, DAD.
WHAT IS PAIN FOR, MATT?
YOU KEEP ASKING THAT! WHAT DOES THAT MEAN?
HOW SHOULD I KNOW?!
"I'M NOT A SMART GUY, MATT.
"I GET HIT ON THE HEAD FOR A LIVING. THAT'S NOT SOMETHING SMART GUYS DO.
"YOU'RE GOING TO BE A SMART GUY. NO, YOU ARE A SMART GUY, AND I'M PROUD OF YOU.
"USE THOSE SMARTS TO GET OUT OF THE KITCHEN. HAVE A LIFE THAT'S HAPPY AND SAFE AND, I DON'T KNOW--
"--KIND.
"I NEVER WANTED TO TEACH YOU THE ONLY THING I HAVE TO TEACH. I ALWAYS HOPED THAT YOU WOULDN'T NEED IT.
"BUT YOU'VE BEEN MARKED FOR A HARD LIFE, SON.
His Honor, Mayor Wilson Fisk

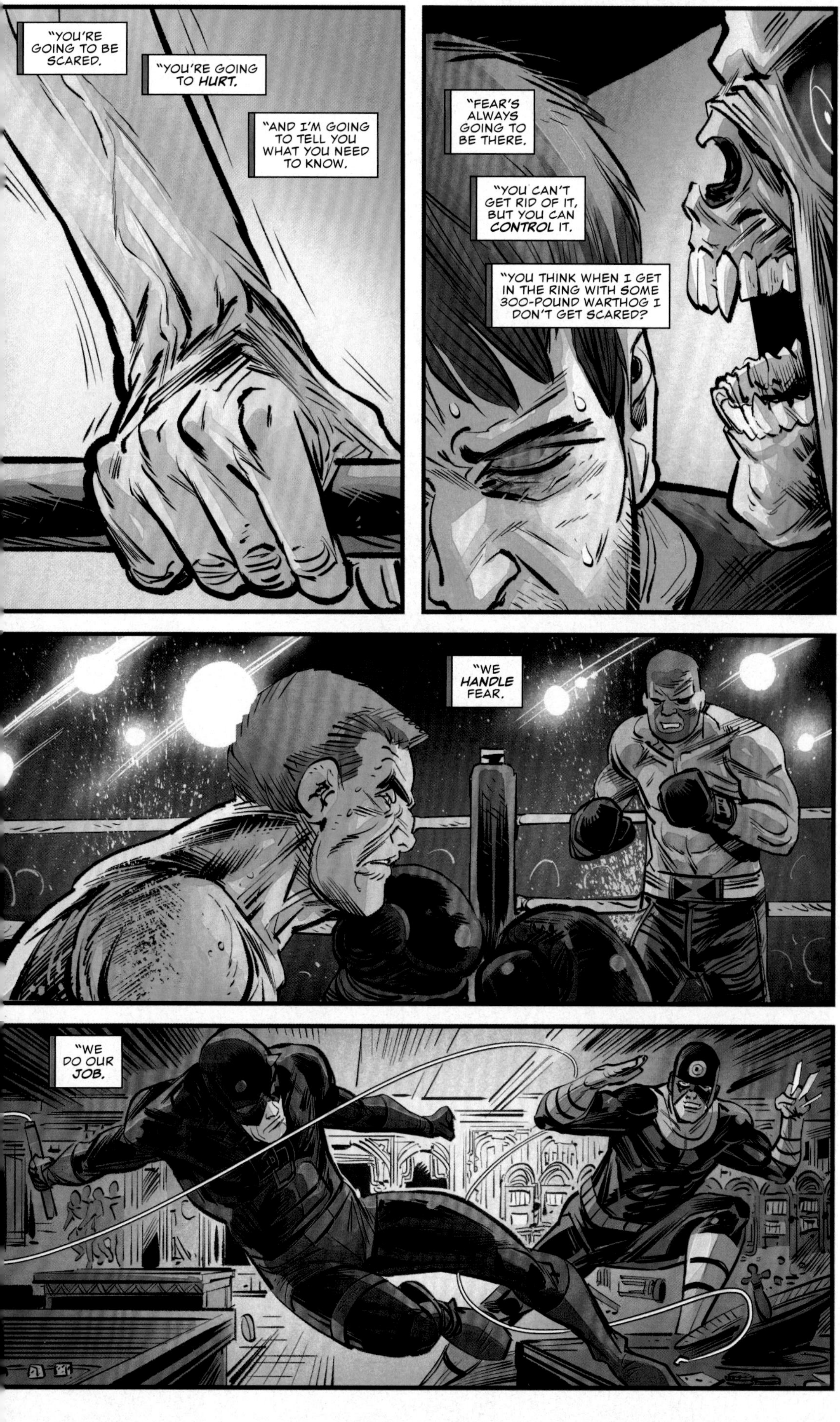
"YOU'RE GOING TO BE SCARED.
"YOU'RE GOING TO HURT.
"AND I'M GOING TO TELL YOU WHAT YOU NEED TO KNOW.
"FEAR'S ALWAYS GOING TO BE THERE.
"YOU CAN'T GET RID OF IT, BUT YOU CAN CONTROL IT.
"YOU THINK WHEN I GET IN THE RING WITH SOME 300-POUND WARTHOG I DON'T GET SCARED?
"WE HANDLE FEAR.
"WE DO OUR JOB.

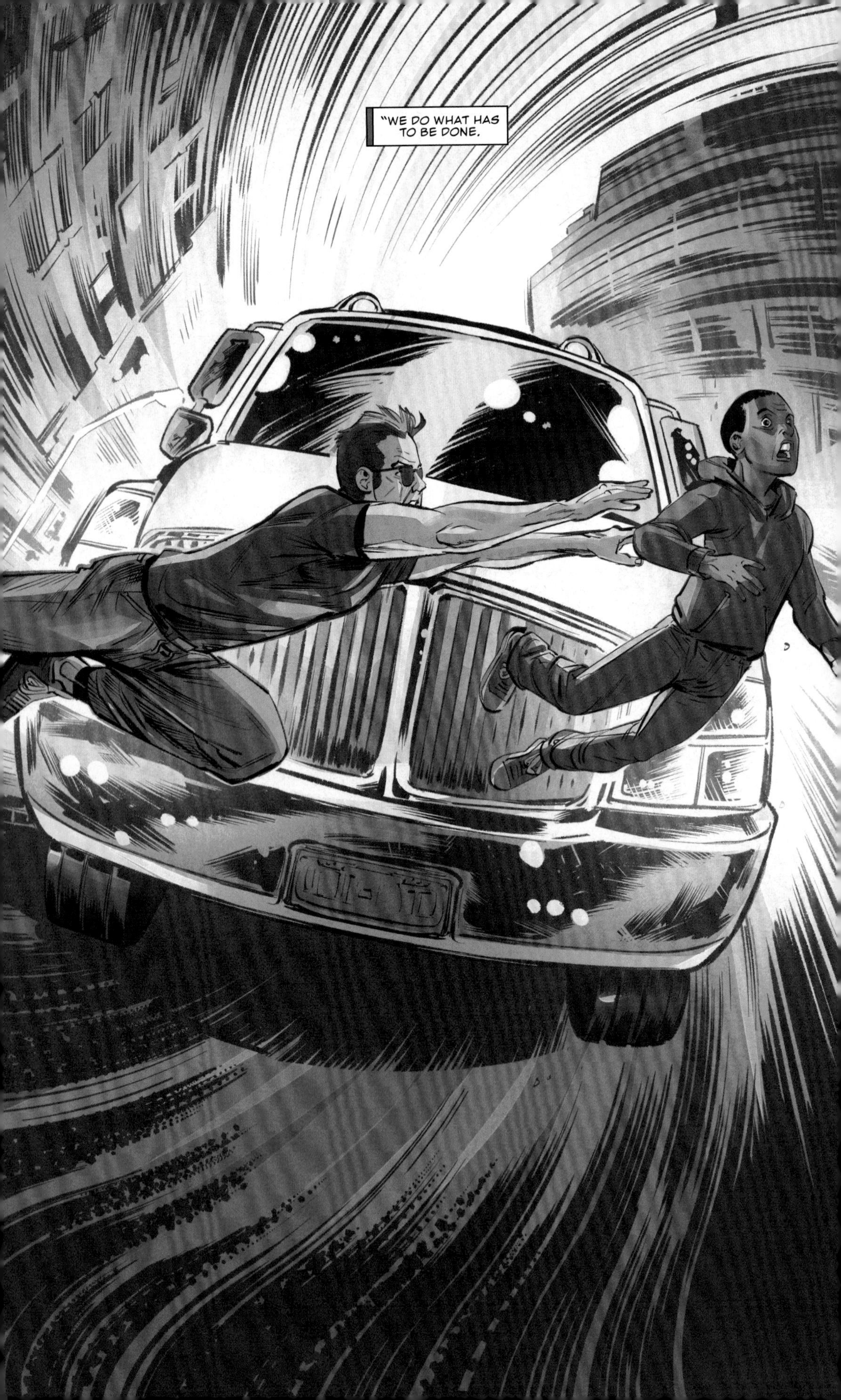
"WE DO WHAT HAS TO BE DONE.

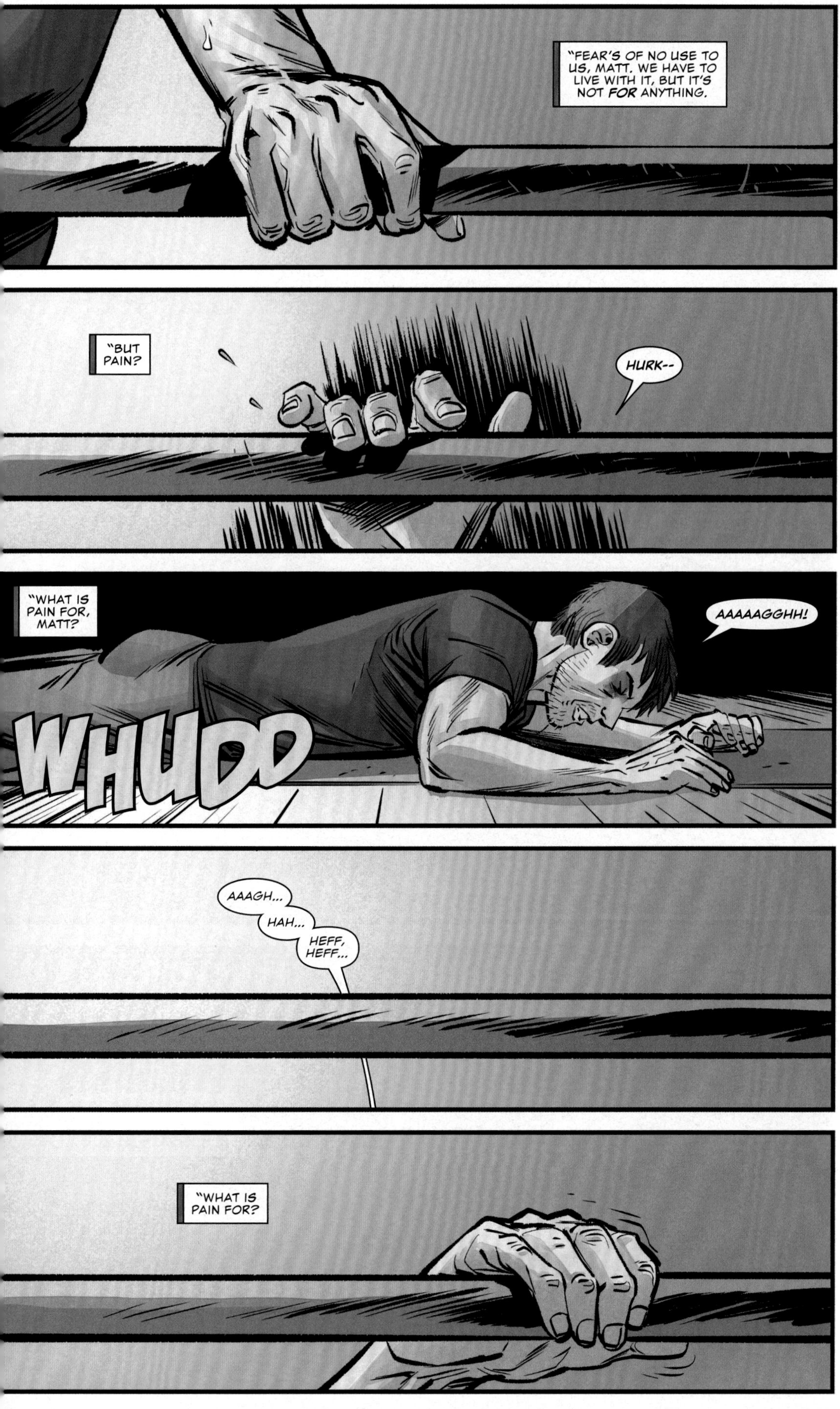
"FEAR'S OF NO USE TO US, MATT. WE HAVE TO LIVE WITH IT, BUT IT'S NOT FOR ANYTHING.
"BUT PAIN?
HURK--
"WHAT IS PAIN FOR, MATT?
AAAAAGGHH!
WHUDD
AAAGH...
HAH...
HEFF, HEFF...
"WHAT IS PAIN FOR?

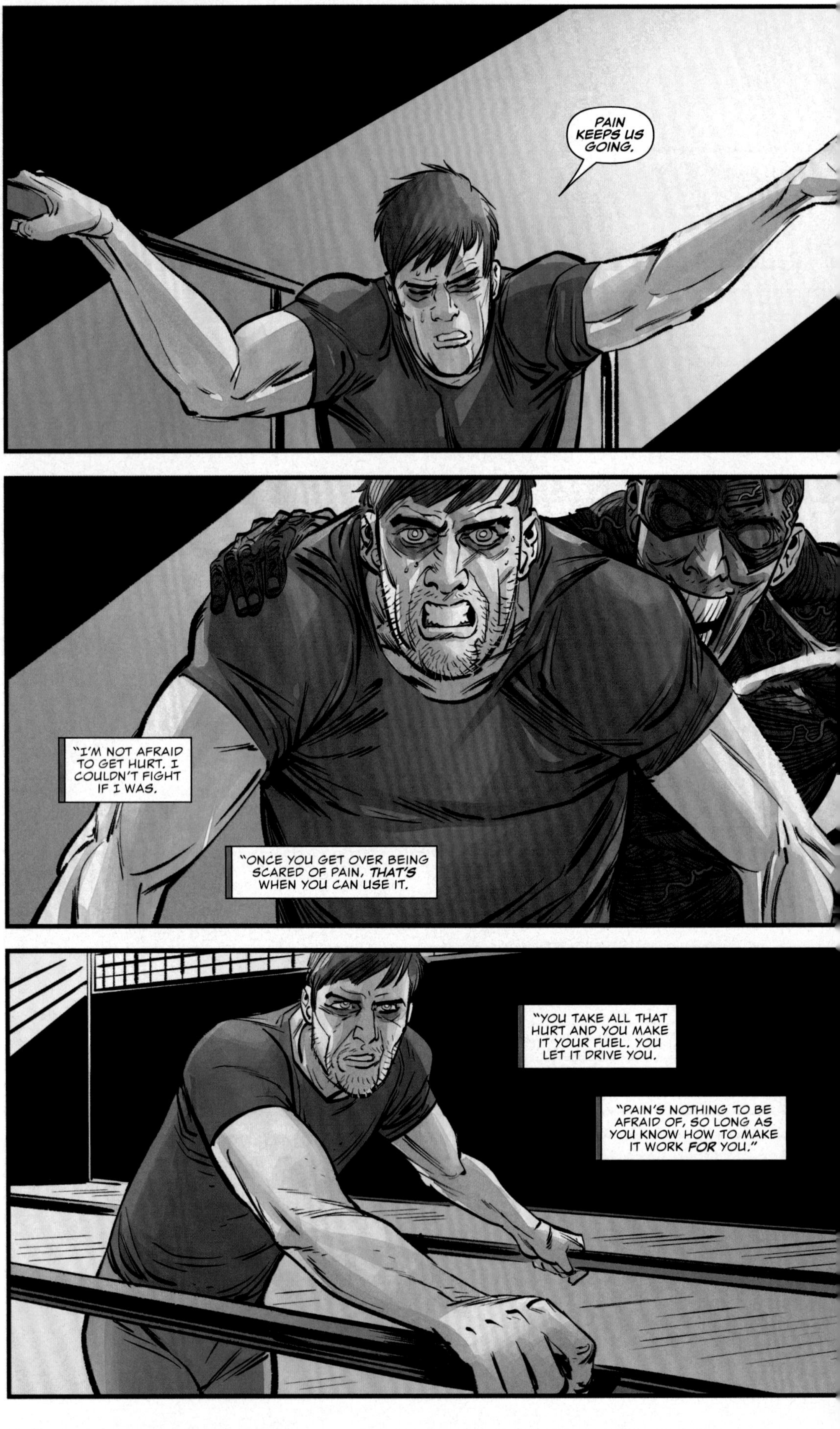
PAIN KEEPS US GOING.
"I'M NOT AFRAID TO GET HURT. I COULDN'T FIGHT IF I WAS.
"ONCE YOU GET OVER BEING SCARED OF PAIN, *THAT'S* WHEN YOU CAN USE IT.
"YOU TAKE ALL THAT HURT AND YOU MAKE IT YOUR FUEL. YOU LET IT DRIVE YOU.
"PAIN'S NOTHING TO BE AFRAID OF, SO LONG AS YOU KNOW HOW TO MAKE IT WORK *FOR* YOU."

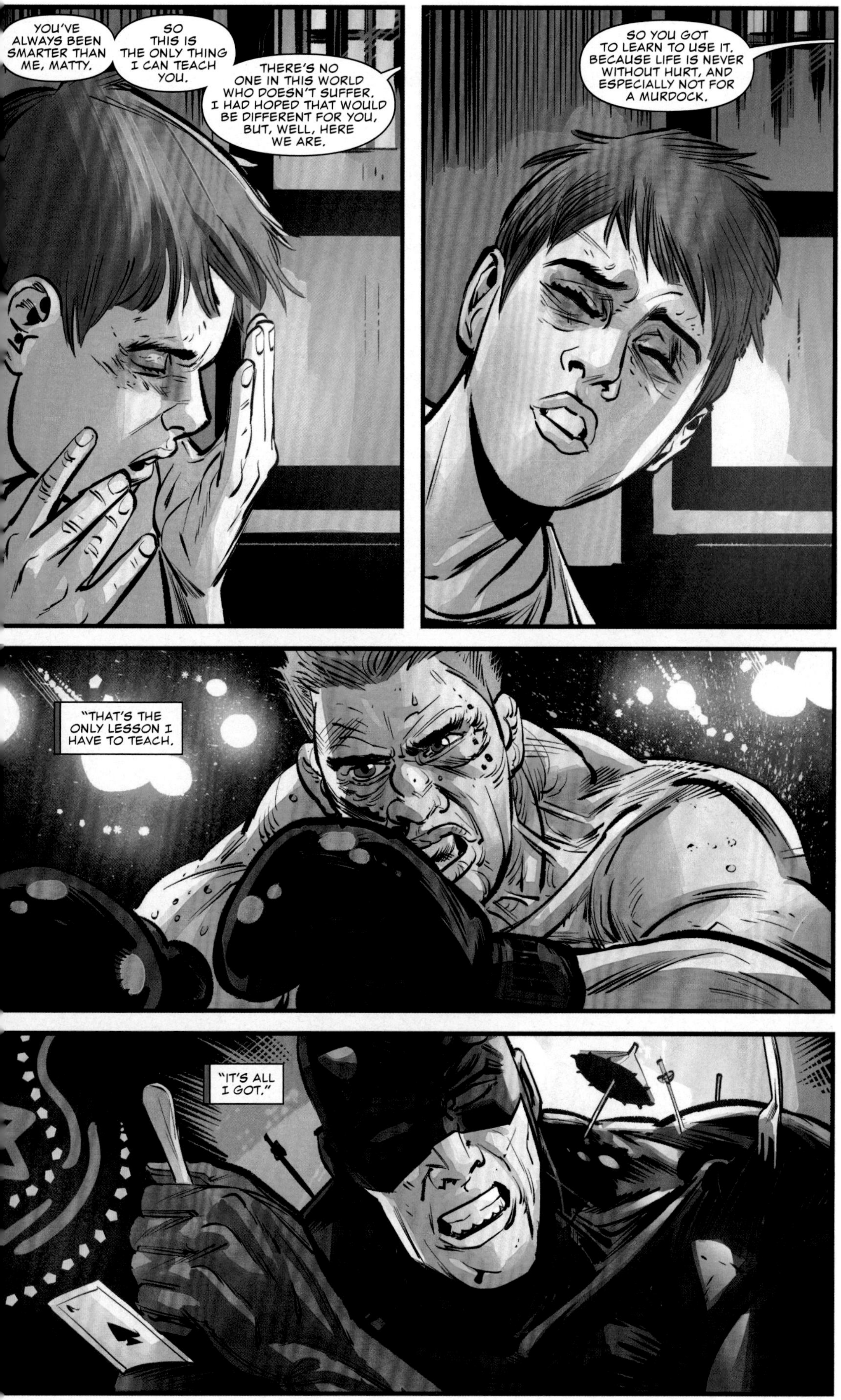
YOU'VE ALWAYS BEEN SMARTER THAN ME, MATTY.
SO THIS IS THE ONLY THING I CAN TEACH YOU.
THERE'S NO ONE IN THIS WORLD WHO DOESN'T SUFFER. I HAD HOPED THAT WOULD BE DIFFERENT FOR YOU, BUT, WELL, HERE WE ARE.
SO YOU GOT TO LEARN TO USE IT. BECAUSE LIFE IS NEVER WITHOUT HURT, AND ESPECIALLY NOT FOR A MURDOCK.
"THAT'S THE ONLY LESSON I HAVE TO TEACH.
"IT'S ALL I GOT."

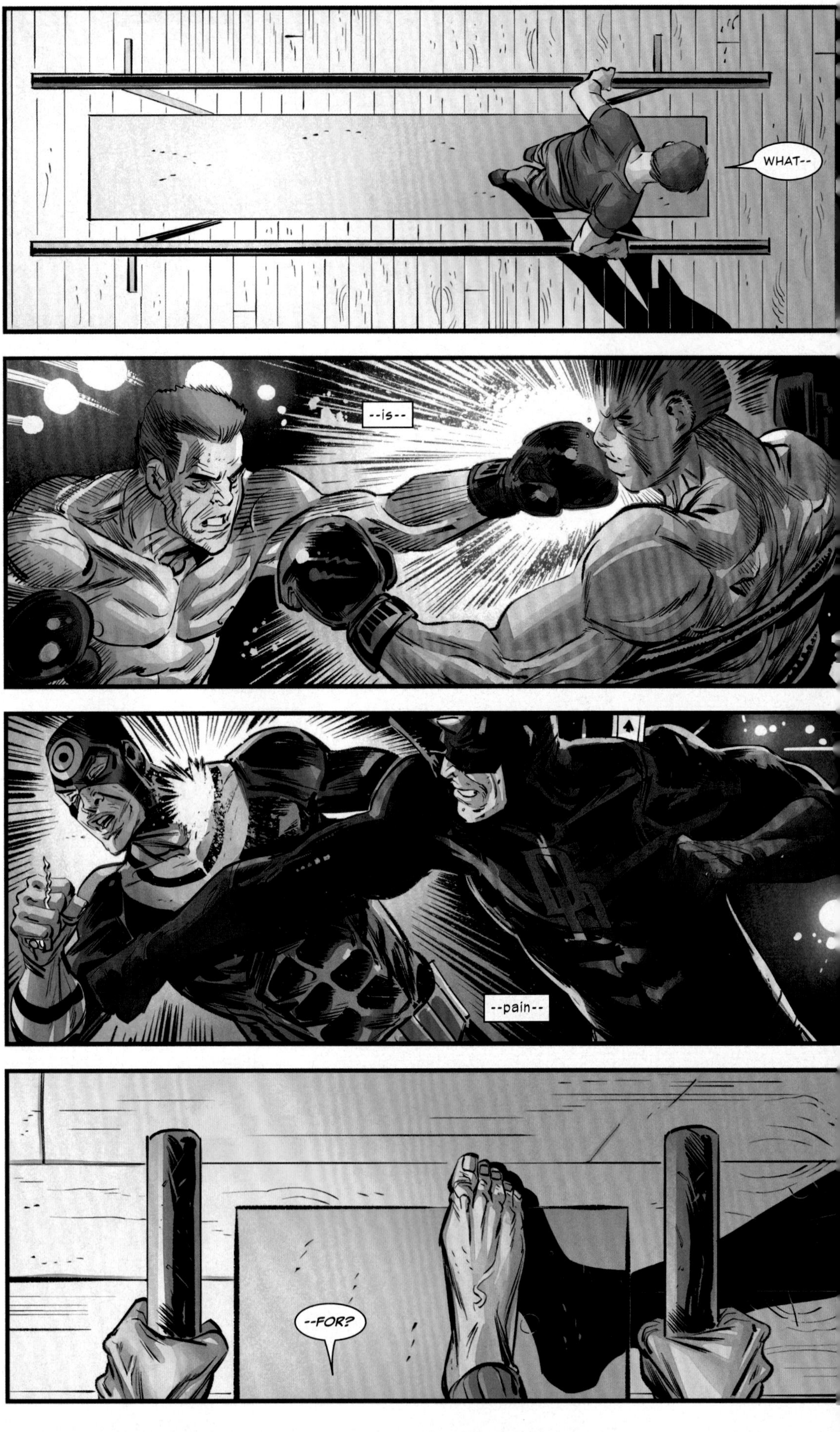

WHAT--
--is--
--pain--
--FOR?

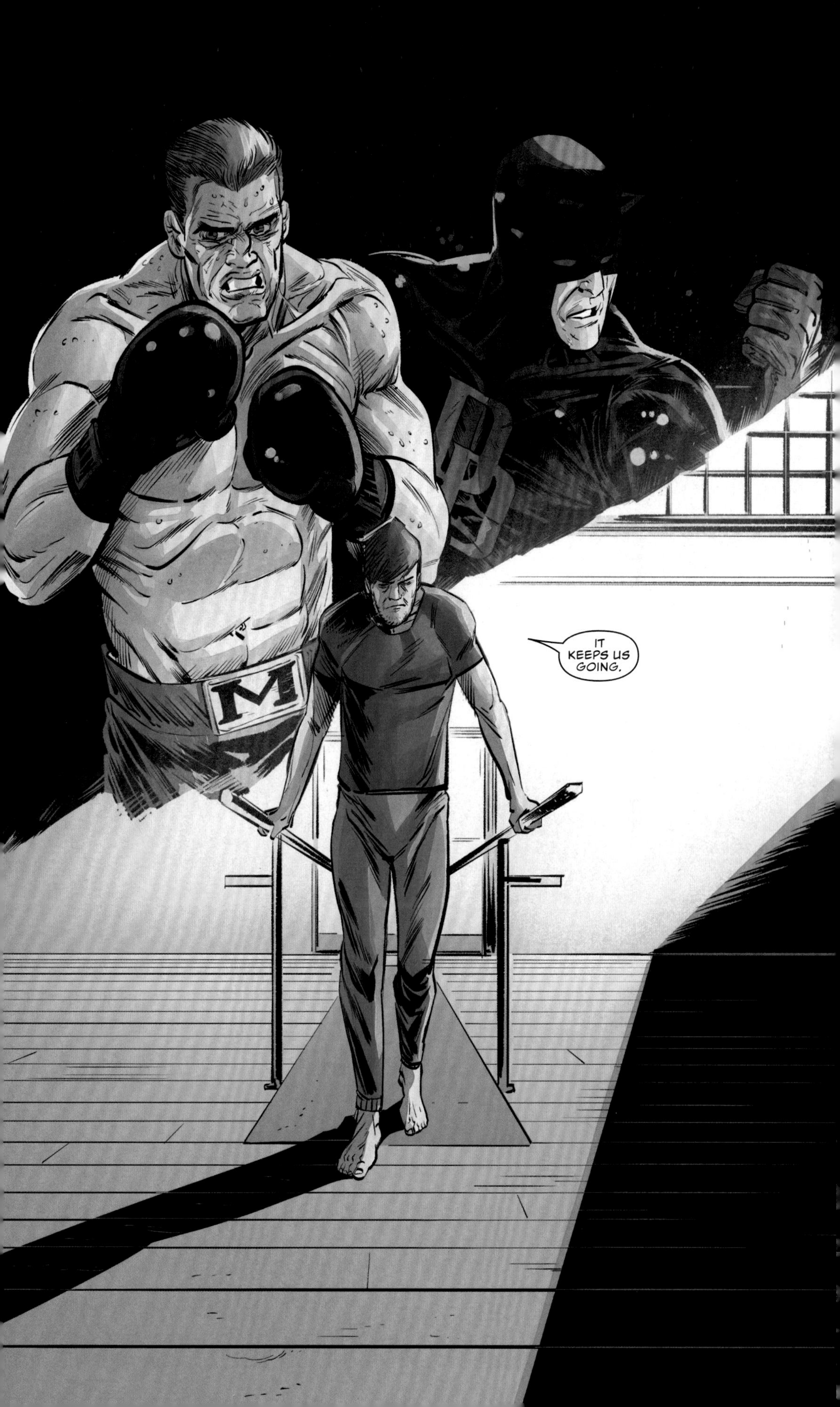
IT KEEPS US GOING.

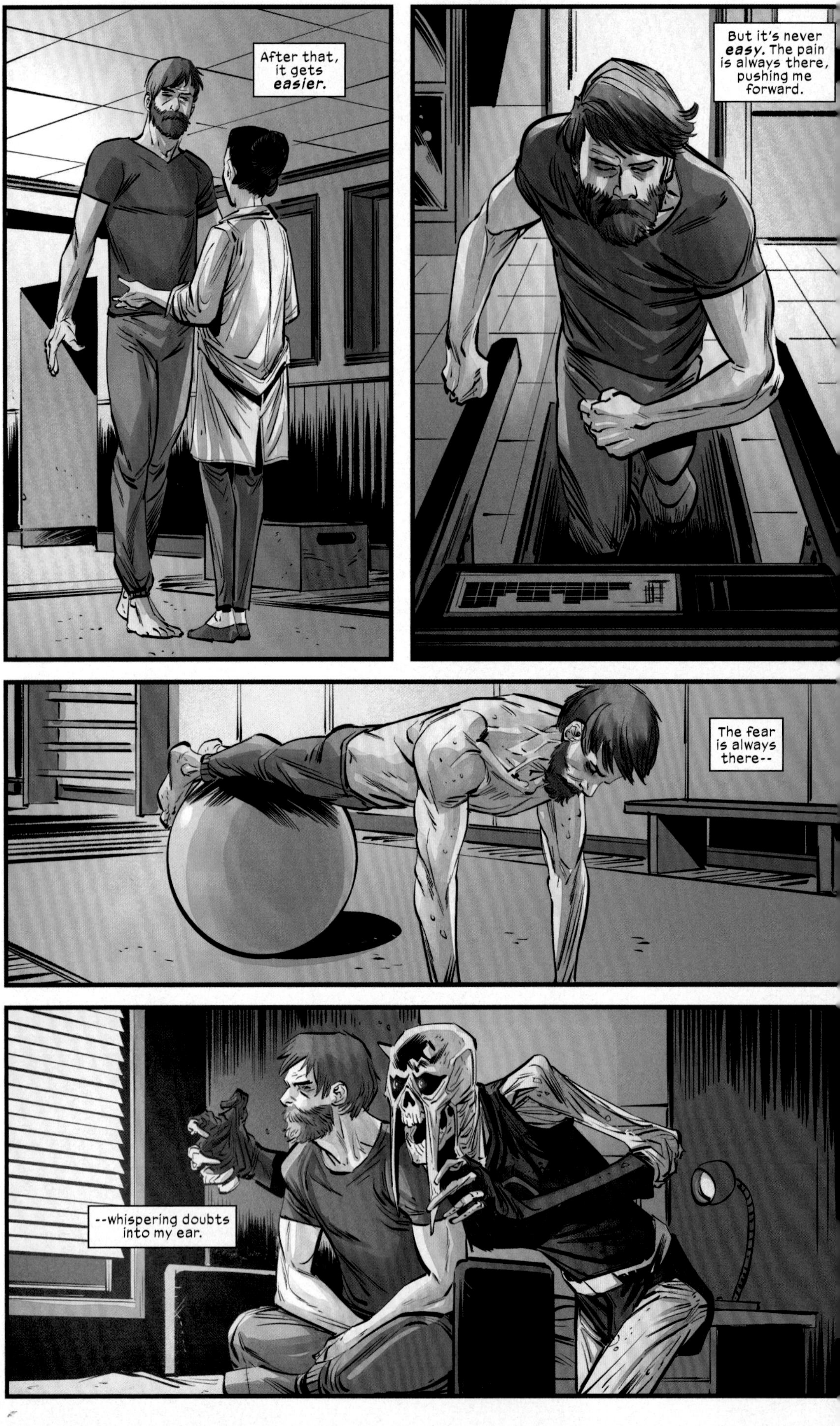
After that, it gets *easier*.
But it's never *easy*. The pain is always there, pushing me forward.
The fear is always there--
--whispering doubts into my ear.

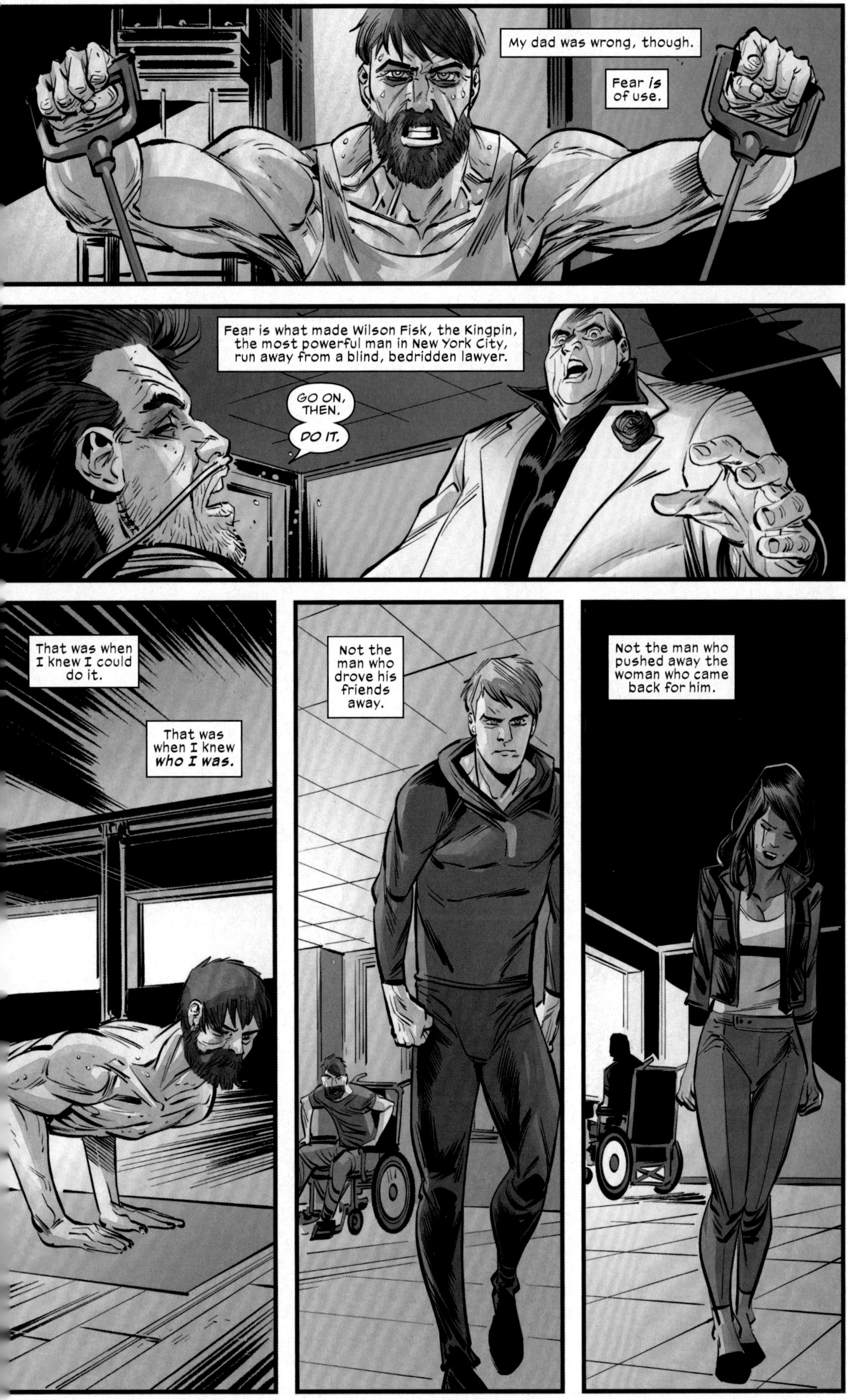
My dad was wrong, though.
Fear *is* of use.
Fear is what made Wilson Fisk, the Kingpin, the most powerful man in New York City, run away from a blind, bedridden lawyer.
GO ON, THEN.
DO IT.
That was when I knew I could do it.
That was when I knew *who I was.*
Not the man who drove his friends away.
Not the man who pushed away the woman who came back for him.

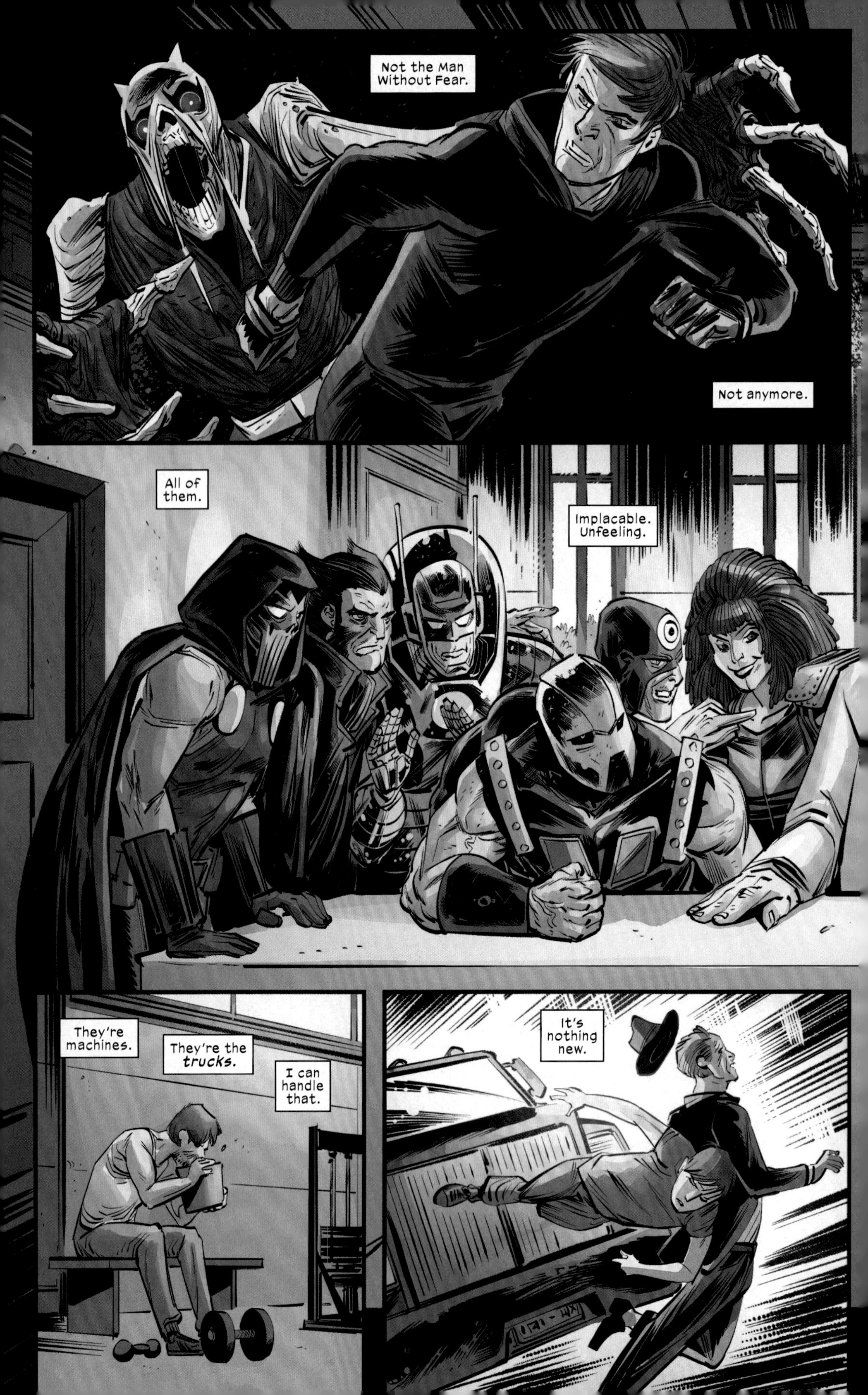
Not the Man Without Fear.
Not anymore.
All of them.
Implacable. Unfeeling.
They're machines.
They're the *trucks.*
I can handle that.
It's nothing new.

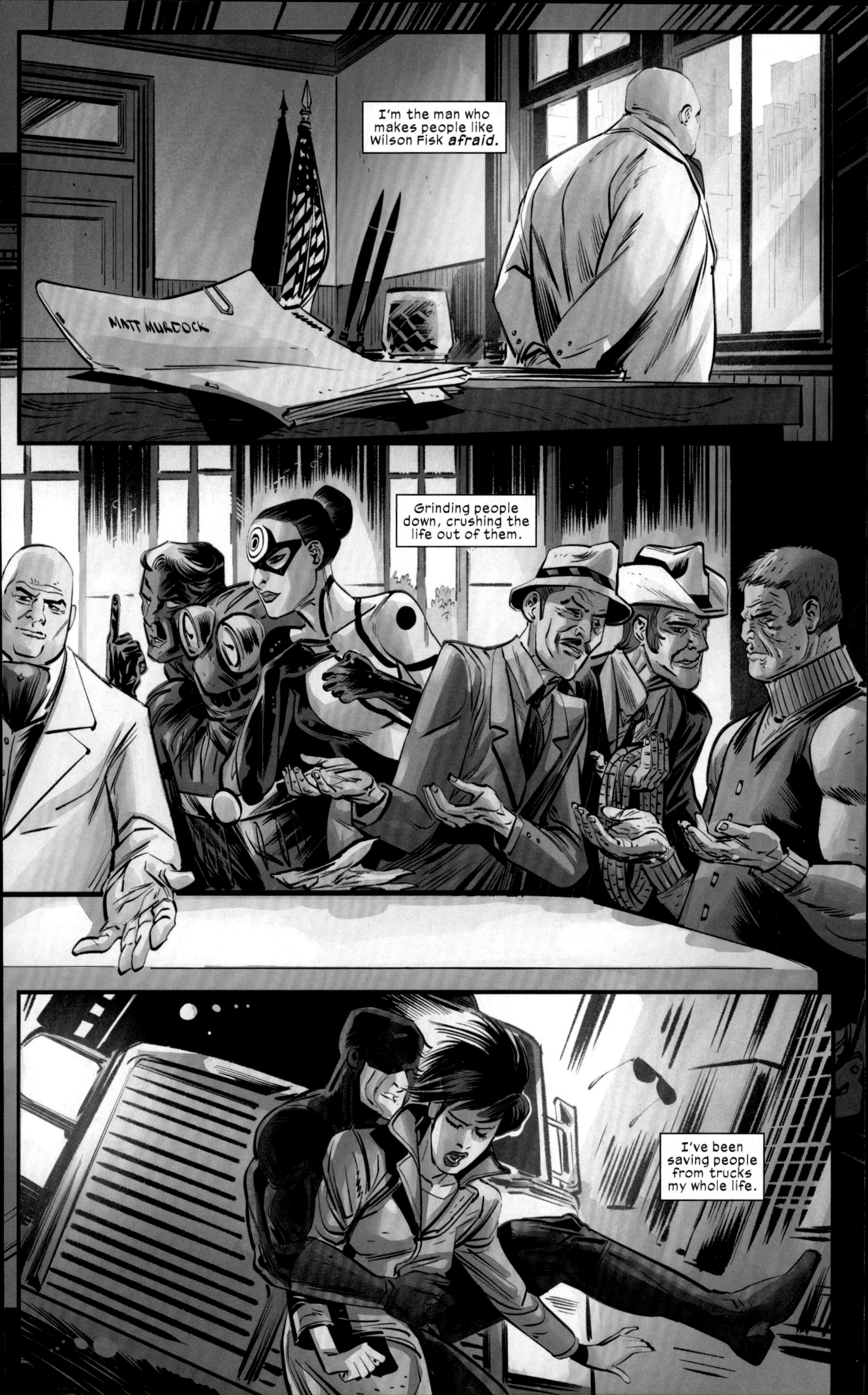

I'm the man who makes people like Wilson Fisk *afraid*.
MATT MURDOCK
Grinding people down, crushing the life out of them.
I've been saving people from trucks my whole life.

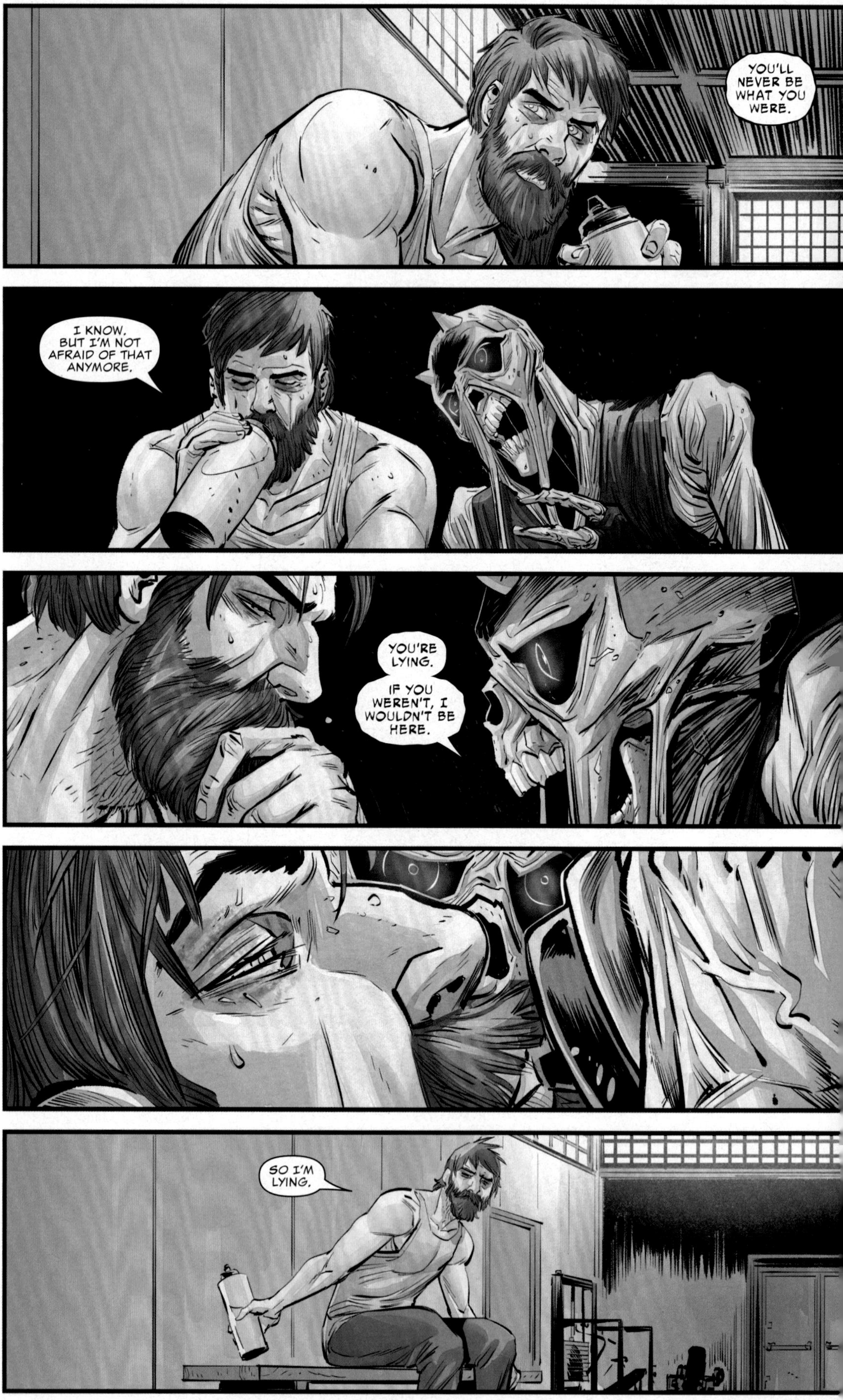
YOU'LL NEVER BE WHAT YOU WERE.
I KNOW. BUT I'M NOT AFRAID OF THAT ANYMORE.
YOU'RE LYING.
IF YOU WEREN'T, I WOULDN'T BE HERE.
SO I'M LYING.

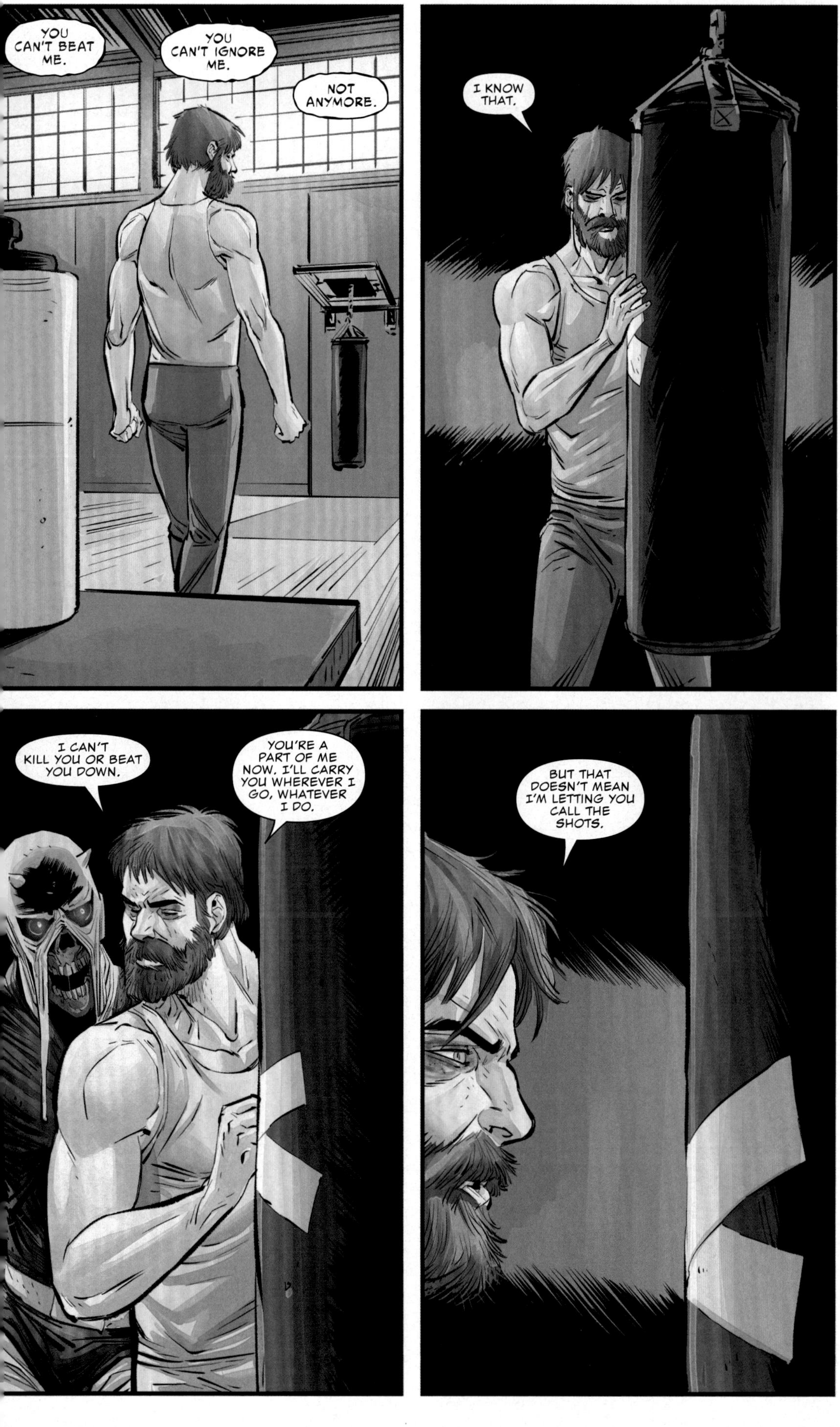
YOU CAN'T BEAT ME.
YOU CAN'T IGNORE ME.
NOT ANYMORE.
I KNOW THAT.
I CAN'T KILL YOU OR BEAT YOU DOWN.
YOU'RE A PART OF ME NOW. I'LL CARRY YOU WHEREVER I GO, WHATEVER I DO.
BUT THAT DOESN'T MEAN I'M LETTING YOU CALL THE SHOTS.

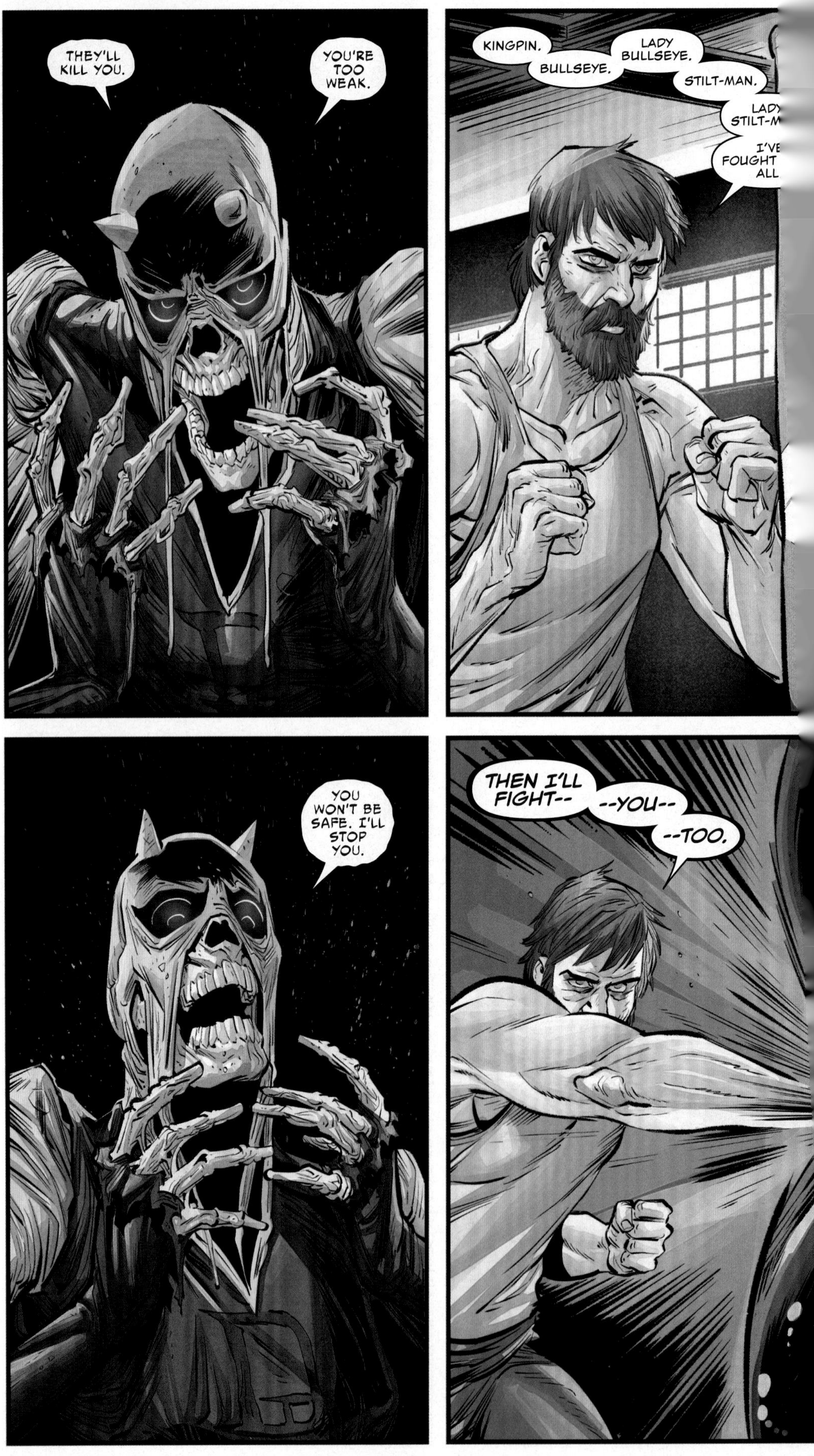
THEY'LL KILL YOU.
YOU'RE TOO WEAK.
KINGPIN.
BULLSEYE.
LADY BULLSEYE.
STILT-MAN.
LADY STILT-M
I'VE FOUGHT ALL
YOU WON'T BE SAFE. I'LL STOP YOU.
THEN I'LL FIGHT--
--YOU--
--TOO.

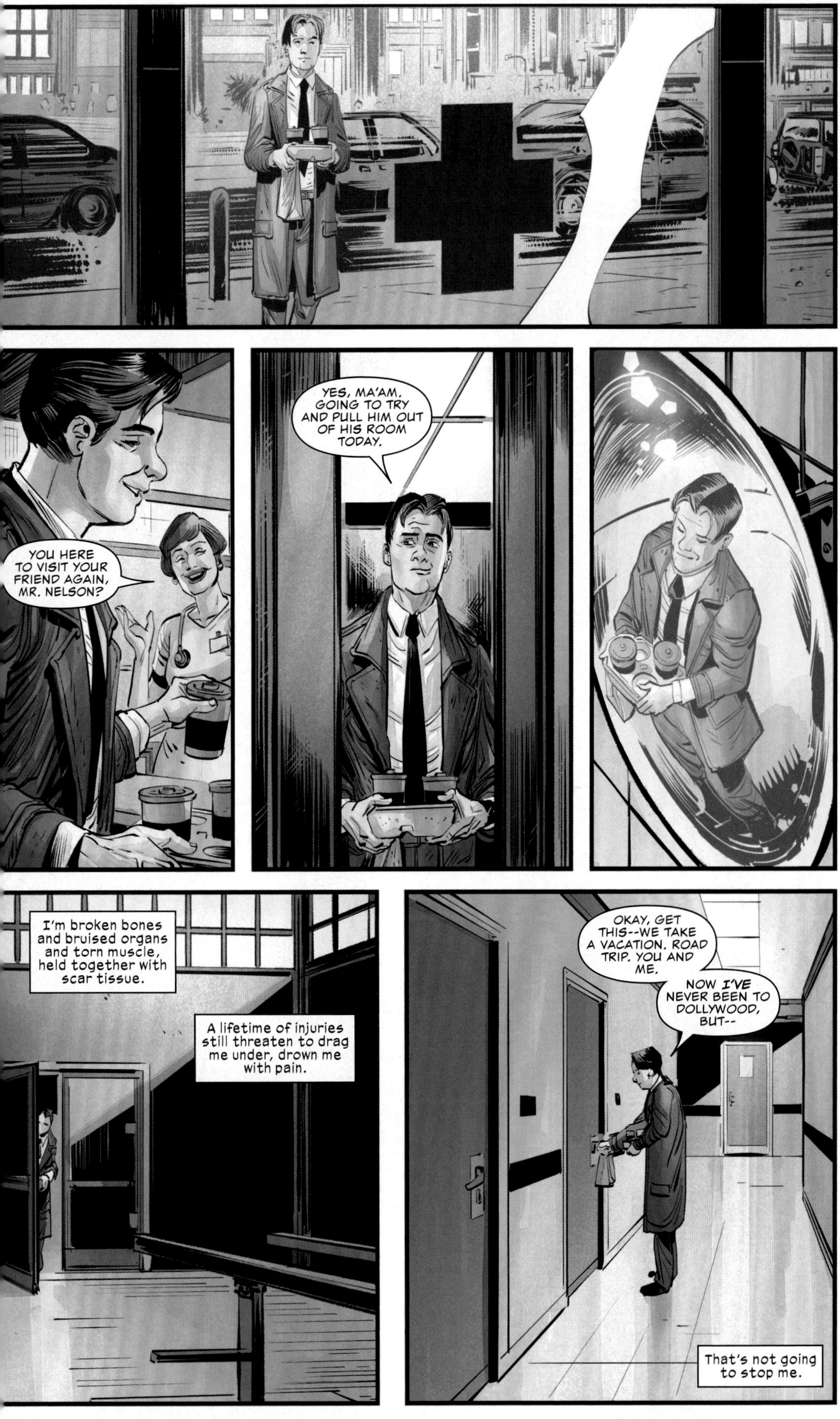
YOU HERE TO VISIT YOUR FRIEND AGAIN, MR. NELSON?
YES, MA'AM. GOING TO TRY AND PULL HIM OUT OF HIS ROOM TODAY.
I'm broken bones and bruised organs and torn muscle, held together with scar tissue.
A lifetime of injuries still threaten to drag me under, drown me with pain.
OKAY, GET THIS--WE TAKE A VACATION. ROAD TRIP. YOU AND ME.
NOW I'VE NEVER BEEN TO DOLLYWOOD, BUT--
That's not going to stop me.

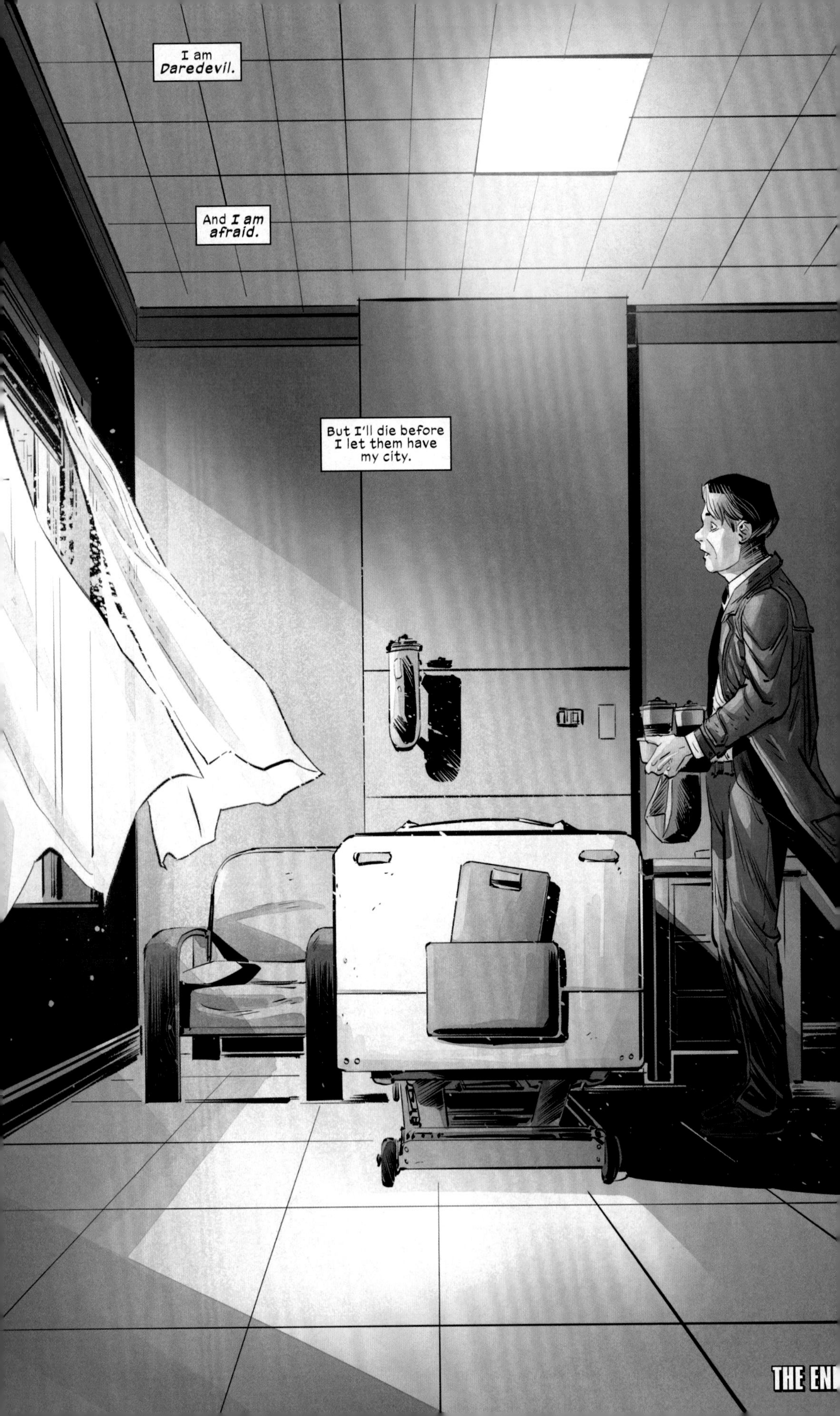

I am *Daredevil.*
And *I am afraid.*
But I'll die before I let them have my city.
THE END

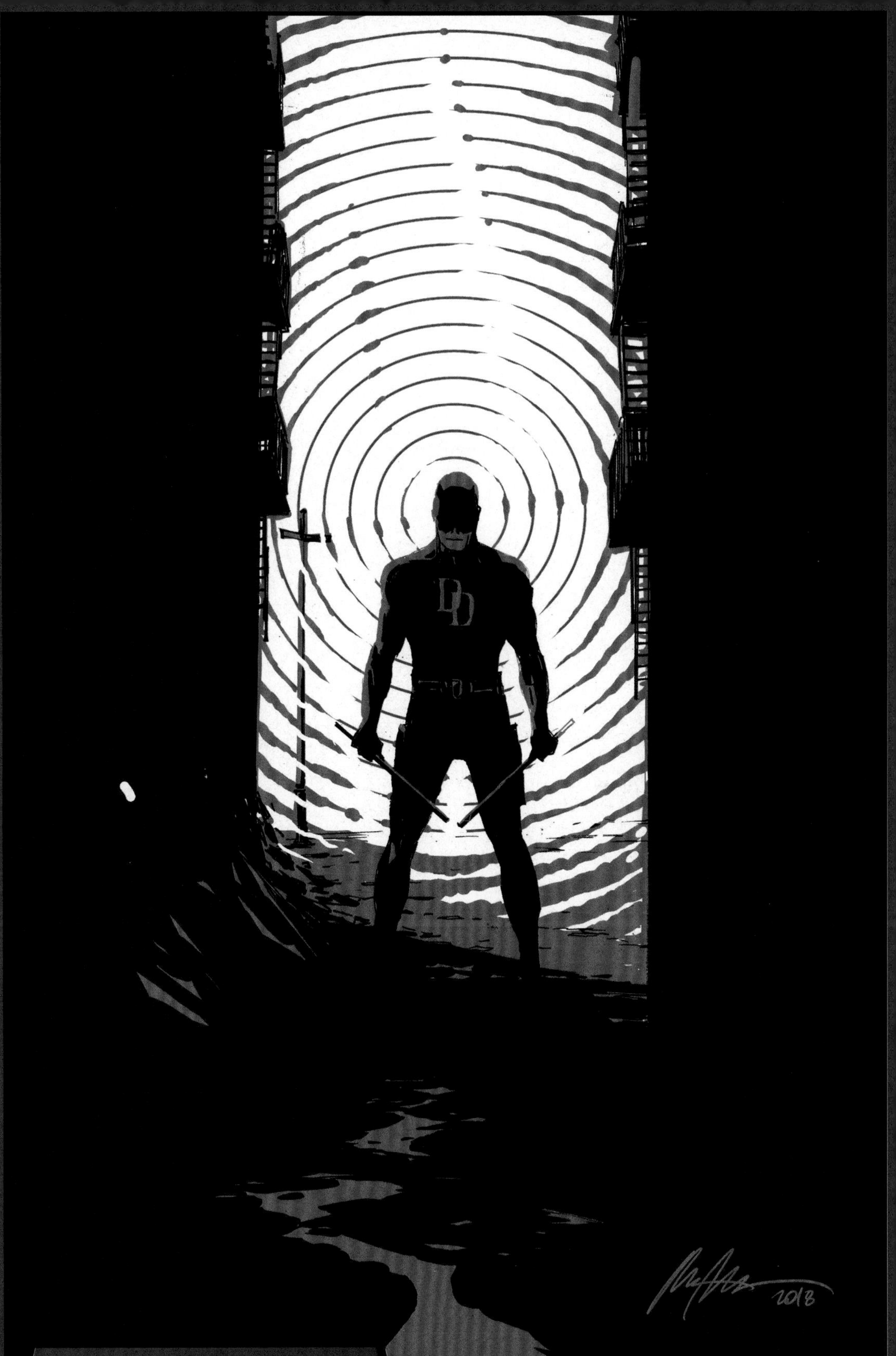
2018

#1 VARIANT BY RAFAEL ALBUQUERQUE

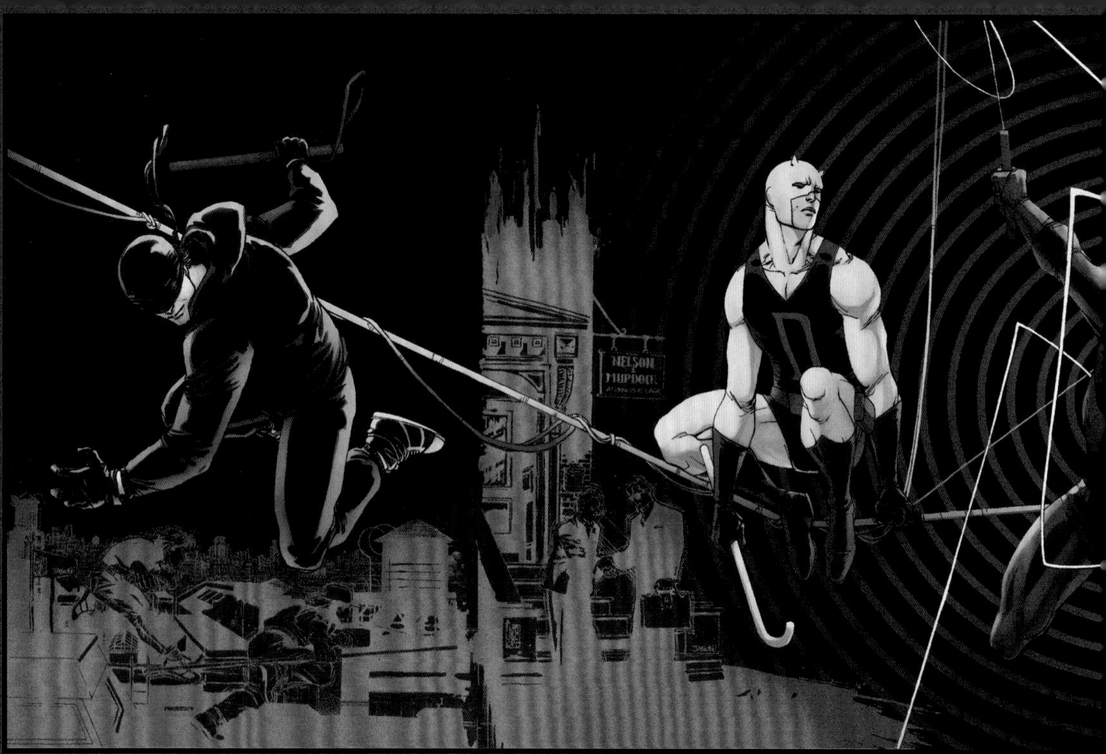
NELSON

#1–5 CONNECTING VARIANTS BY GIUSEPPE CAMUNCOLI & CHRIS SOTOMAYOR

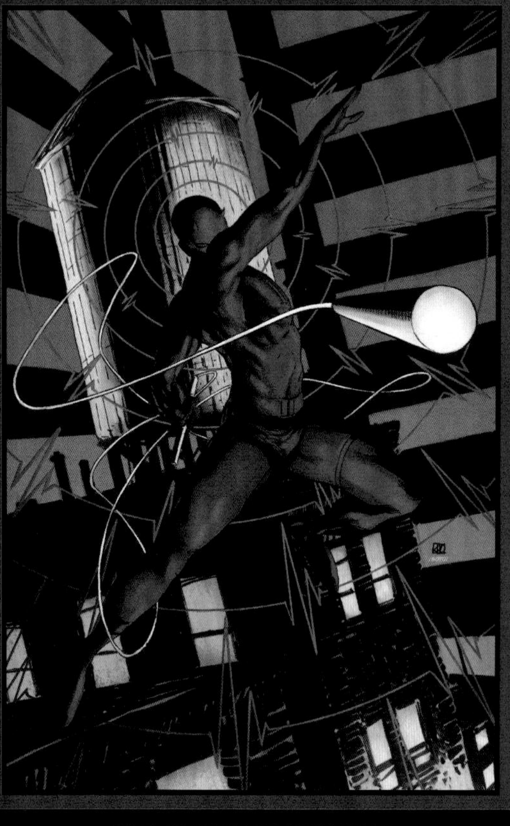

#1 VARIANT BY KHOI PHAM

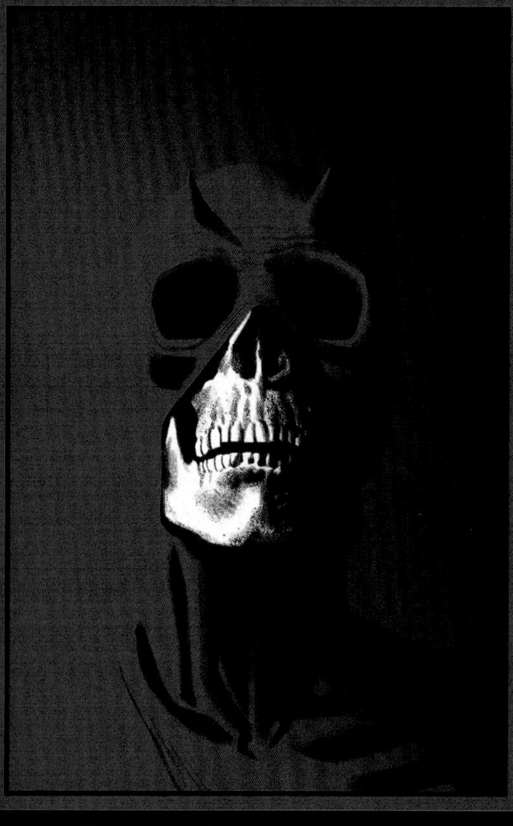

#2 VARIANT BY GREG SMALLWOOD

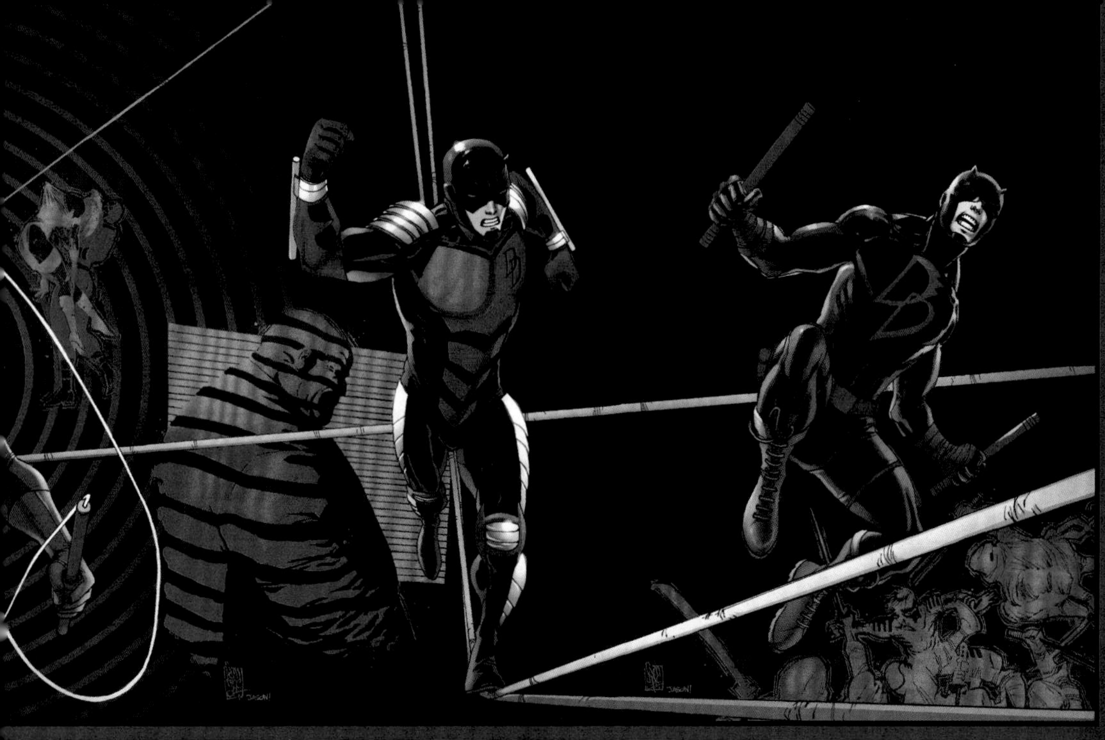

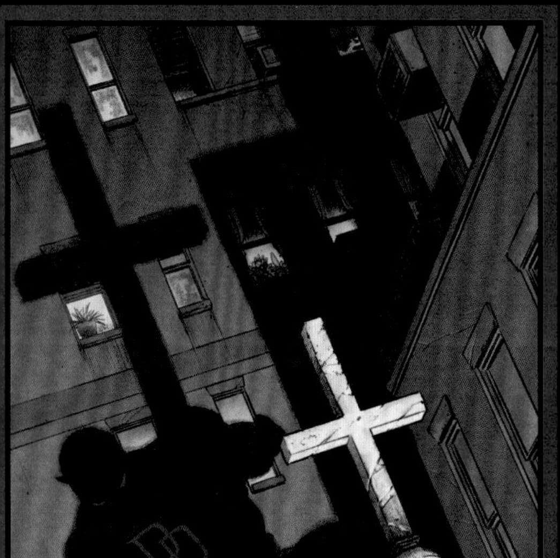

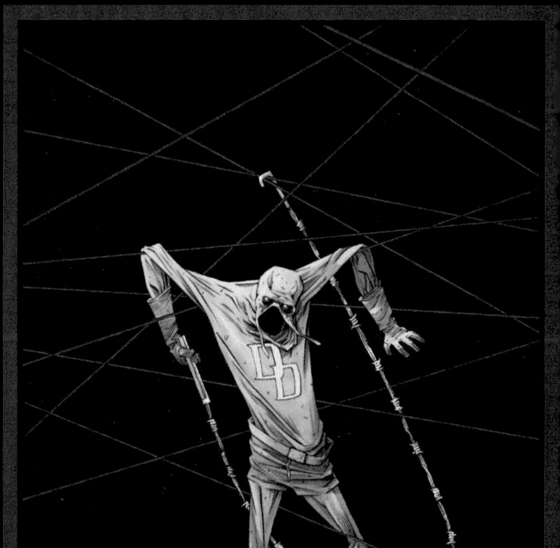

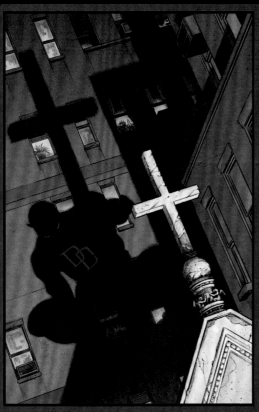

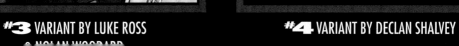

#3 VARIANT BY LUKE ROSS

#4 VARIANT BY DECLAN SHALVEY

& NOLAN WOODARD

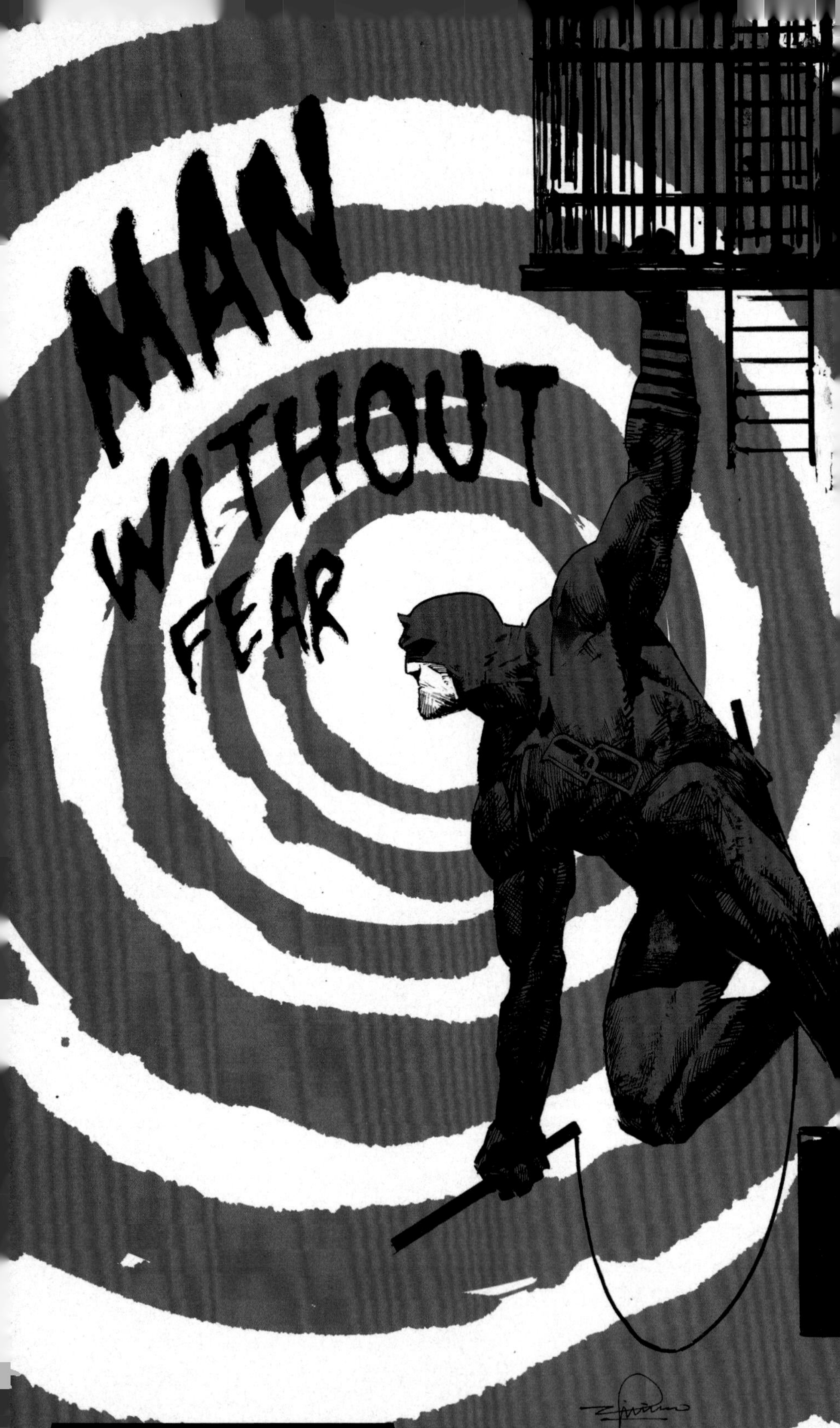
MAN
WITHOUT
FEAR